# STATISTICS
## *For the 21st Century*

**Proposals for improving statistics
for better decision making**

*By Joseph W. Duncan and Andrew C. Gross*

Published by

 The Dun & Bradstreet
Corporation

**Joseph W. Duncan** is Vice President, Corporate Economist and Chief Statistician of The Dun & Bradstreet Corporation. He is the corporation's chief economist and is responsible for interpreting global economic trends to assist management of the corporation and its divisions in developing business strategy. As Chief Statistician he oversees the quality of the databases maintained at all Dun & Bradstreet divisions. He works with the extensive information resources of the corporation to develop new products and services.

Dr. Duncan served as President of the National Association of Business Economists (1992-93). His presidential address in September 1993 featured material presented in this book. A longtime student of official statistics, he served as Deputy Associate Director in the Office of Management and Budget from 1974-1981, with responsibility for policy oversight of the federal government's statistical agencies. He was appointed by President Nixon to be the U.S. representative to the Statistical Commission of the United Nations, serving as Chairman of the Commission in 1981.

He writes a column on economic trends for *D&B Reports Magazine* and is the Executive Editor of *Dun & Bradstreet Looks at Business, Dun & Bradstreet Comments on the Economy*, both of which are bi-monthly newsletters on economic statistics. He is the author of "Statistics Corner" in *Business Economics*.

He is coauthor of *Revolution in U.S. Government Statistics, 1926-1976*, published by the U.S. Government Printing Office in 1977, and served as editor of two other books. He holds a Ph.D. in Economics from Ohio State University and an M.B.A. from Harvard University.

**Andrew C. Gross** is currently a professor of marketing and international business at Cleveland State University, where he has been a member of the faculty for the past 25 years.

He was a Fulbright Senior Scholar in Hungary in 1989 and 1992, and has served as a visiting professor at McGill University and McMaster University in Canada, and at the Budapest University of Economics in Hungary. In 1989, he was the first faculty lecturer at the newly established International Management Center in Hungary. He previously served on the faculties of Ohio State University and Lehigh University.

Dr. Gross also has worked in government and industry, beginning his career as an engineer with Ohio Edison and Standard Oil of Ohio. He worked for Statistics Canada, the Science Council of Canada and Battelle Memorial Institute. He was a founding partner of Predicasts, Inc., and served for many years on its board of directors.

Dr. Gross has published 15 monographs, over 50 articles and two books, *Business Marketing* and *Education and Jobs*. He is on the board of several marketing and international business journals.

He received a Ph.D. from Ohio State University in 1968, an M.B.A. from Western Reserve University in 1962, and a B.S. from Case Institute of Technology in 1957.

This book was produced using Adobe Garamond and Futura in QuarkXPress on an IBM PS/2 Model 90.

Design:
David Hake, Hake Associates, New York

Cover illustration:
Martin Haggland, MicroColor, New York

Electronic typesetting:
Herb Flores, DataConcepts, New York

Karen Sperling, The Write-Design Studio, New York

John Wu, Multimedia Creations, New City, NY

ISBN 1-56203-310-7

# Contents

# List of Figures

# Preface

Responsible decisions—whether they are made by businesses, governments, or individuals—have this central element in common:

> They are based on information that comprises the basic input required for the successful analysis of current conditions, the evaluation of proposed strategies, and the assessment of actions to be taken.

When it comes to the evaluation of economic and social decisions, there is a second area of often-overlooked commonality. Much of the common understanding flows from official statistics produced by the Federal government.

During the past two decades, the concepts and definitions used in federal data collections have become increasingly less adequate in measuring the pace of social and economic changes. This problem is not limited to the United States; it is also seen in the international organizations, such as the United Nations, World Bank, and International Monetary Fund, in the regional organizations such as the Organization for Economic Cooperation and Development and the European Economic Communities. Indeed, the problem exists in most countries around the globe as they seek to reduce the role of government, especially in the collection of data from people and institutions.

This study looks at the challenges posed by the need to bring the federal statistical activity up to speed with the changing realities. It is based upon over 25 years' experience of one of the two authors, Joseph W. Duncan—first, as a board member of the former Federal Statistics Users Conference; second, as a government official with responsibility for setting federal statistical policy; and, most recently, as a user of government statistics in business. This report is equally based on the experience by the second author, Andrew Gross, who has written a major text on using information in marketing, a text based on his work in several industries and his role in founding Predicasts, Inc., a market research and publishing firm. Dr. Duncan is Vice President, Corporate Economist, and Chief Statistician for The Dun & Bradstreet Corporation, and Dr. Gross is Professor of Marketing and International Business at Cleveland State University. Both authors have been assisted by many specialists, but they are solely responsible for the content of this report.

This is not a committee report but a particular perspective designed to initiate further discussion, debate, and action on an important and critical challenge. The design of a statistical system that will meet the needs of the 21st century is an enormous undertaking. Unfortunately, current developments lag in fully resolving the needs that are clearly evident. This report is intended to present one view of some important future needs, some current deficiencies, and some ongoing improvements that need to be accelerated. Thus, this document is not intended to be the expert's final word in summarizing a definitive solution, rather it is *a sentinel's early signal of a growing challenge.*

The objective is to focus attention on future needs and to challenge others to join the effort to bring about the changes that are clearly needed. The Dun & Bradstreet Corporation, as the world's leading marketer of information, software and services for business decision making, is pleased to sponsor this report in the interest of stimulating further research in the needs for improving official statistics as the foundation for decision making in the future.

Charles W. Moritz, Chairman
Robert E. Weissman, President

The Dun & Bradstreet Corporation
New York, New York, U.S.A.

September 1993

# STATISTICS
*For the 21st Century*

# Chapter 1

# Nature of Problem

It is an interesting and instructive intellectual exercise to try to imagine for a moment what a "perfect"—that is, perfectly complete, perfectly accurate—system of statistics might look like. Try to imagine, for example, a perfect system of world economic statistics. Such a system would, presumably, capture the economic significance, expressed in a constant and universal currency, of every transaction having economic implications anywhere in the world, as well as all stocks and holdings having economic value. Such a system would register not only the substance of each of those transactions, but also the effects in terms of augmenting or depleting the economic "stocks" of the participants and the larger communities of which they are a part.

There is a deceptive simplicity about such a description. It seems to suggest the clear core of what any system of economic statistics seeks to capture. This image suggests that the economic reality lies waiting to be measured, if only the physical means were at hand to do so. If only we had resources and time enough to register every transaction; if only we had a lens strong enough to see into every corner where economic activity takes place; if only we had computers powerful enough to register and analyze all the data from every such transaction. It is precisely such physical limitations, of course, which require us to take certain scientifically justified short cuts, like using sampling techniques rather than measuring every transaction in a full enumeration. This image suggests that despite physical limitations, there is a straightforward, fairly unambiguous economic reality—a network of transactions and stocks of value—waiting to be measured.

That image of statistical systems, while remarkably clear and straightforward, is deceptive because the economic—or demographic, or topical (environment, eco-systems, education, health care, etc.)—realities we seek to describe in statistical systems do not, as it were, simply lie there fully formed waiting for us to come up with instruments to measure them. That point emerges when we descend from the high level of abstraction in our description of the "perfect system" and start to define the constituent terms, particularly the term, "having economic significance."

Consider two real-life cases: In one case, a domestic worker cleans, cooks, tends children, and generally manages the house. In the second case, a spouse cleans, cooks, tends children, and generally manages the house. The first person is a domestic worker, who is paid wages, and who pays income and Social Security taxes. The second worker is the spouse of an employed worker, and receives no wages and pays no taxes. Should the work of both those "domestic workers" be recorded in our "perfect" system of economic statistics? Do they both engage in actions that have economic significance, or only the one who is paid wages and submits taxes?

A range of arguments could be—and have been—mustered on either side of the question whether the second person's work "has economic implications." The point, here, is not to decide that issue. It is instead to demonstrate that deciding that question—that is, defining the terms so that we know what to include and what to exclude—is not a matter of finding more time to describe the activity, nor is it a matter of finding a stronger lens through which to view it, nor a stronger computer with which to record and analyze it. *It is a matter of making very basic theoretical assumptions, assumptions that guide which data are to be collected and which excluded, assumptions which will also shape the way the data are analyzed.*

Those assumptions underlie any system of statistics in any field. (Just think of the definitional assumptions that must be done for a demographic study of ethnicity, for example.) Until those definitions on a variety of issues have been formulated, the object to be measured does not exist. And those assumptions usually follow in some way from the uses to which the system of statistics will be put.

Capturing economic reality with a statistical system can be compared to trying to capture, or represent, a physical landscape with a map. The map wanted by a geologist is very different from the map wanted by a taxi driver. Maps constructed for those two purposes will include and exclude very different items. The mapmaker who has no purpose in mind has no principle or set of principles on the basis of which to exclude any aspect of the terrain. Without such principles to exclude some aspects as irrelevant, such a map would have to be just the terrain itself. But, as the philosopher Wittgenstein once said, that would be like putting your hand on top of your head and saying, "I know how tall I am."

Systems of economic statistics, like maps, are devised to serve purposes, and those purposes—more or less explicit, more or less well understood—dictate the assumptions and the principles that govern which data are collected. They also shape how they are analyzed.

These reflections seem to suggest that we should simply decide on a set of purposes, and then build the system of statistics upon it. Of course, a moment's reflection shows that such a picture is far too simplified. The fact is that the very different, somewhat overlapping systems of statistics serve very different purposes. Those purposes are almost as varied as the different sets of users, and the purposes of any single user are likely to change and evolve over time.

Moreover, while it is certainly true that statistical systems have to be constructed with purposes in mind—otherwise there would be no decision procedure for ruling data "in" or "out"—most of the statistical systems most of us will use most of the time...we have inherited. While they were originally constructed to serve certain purposes, those purposes were likely not completely congruent with our own. They were constructed using means that are different from our own, and in circumstances different from the present.

Simply put, we are not—we cannot be—"present at the creation" of the system of statistics, whether in economics, demography, health care, or whatever. Most of it we inherit.

Even if we could, we would not want to create the system of economic statistics from the ground up. Much of the purpose of any system of statistics is to show trends over time, to compare the past with the present in order to try to assess the future. Without the statistics we inherit, that would be impossible. As we will discuss in greater detail shortly, that means that any changes in the systems of statistics should be mainly gradual, evolutionary, and conservative.

Starting from scratch is neither possible nor desirable. We start mid-stream, in a world seeming to overflow with information and data, but also too often suffering a shortage of useable knowledge and understanding. In part, that is precisely because of living in the midst of the so-called Information Age. Looking for useable knowledge these days has been compared to standing, thirsty, in front of Niagara Falls equipped only with a thimble.

The entire burden of this book is to encourage change and reform in our statistical systems in order to push them toward providing more useable knowledge. We live now in a world in which information has taken a larger role than ever before, a world in which the changes wrought by technological, demographic, and political revolutions have radically changed the situation we seek to assess with our statistical systems.

All our efforts to reform these systems must start with the recognition of our continued dependence on the inherited system. To borrow a metaphor, it is a boat within which we must stay afloat even as we repair it. We are not starting from "the ground up." Accordingly, this book will not have the elegance of, say, a proof in Euclidean geometry, starting with self-evident axioms and proceeding in logical lock-step to clear and certain conclusions. Instead, it starts from several points of departure simultaneously, and from a variety of different angles of attack. It is suggestive rather than definitive. It is empirical and intuitive, rather than deductive and categorical. And, quite unapologetically, it swings from sweeping suggestions for overhaul in some areas to suggestions for simply tinkering at the margins in others.

Before we look at a more detailed preview of the chapters to come, it is worth pausing to consider two over-arching realities that stand as the background for all of the discussion in this book: first, the nature of the so-called "Information Age," and, second, the changes in the global realities that call for new statistical systems.

## The Information Age

The concept of the "Information Age" suggests a number of propositions. It implies that there is more information now than ever before, which is indisputable. The concept also implies that more people spend more time producing and using more information than ever before, which is also indisputable. Beyond that, the concept of a new "Information Age" also suggests that the role of information is more important in the economy than ever before, and that information is replacing some earlier "fuel" of the American economy. These last two propositions are forcefully debated and disputed.

Here is a famous, and fairly typical, formulation from Peter Drucker: "Three hundred years of technology came to an end after World War II. During those three centuries, the model for technology was a mechanical one: the events that go on inside a star such as the sun...Since the end of World War II, however, the model of technology has been the biological process, the events inside an organism. And in an organism, processes are not organized around energy in the physicist's meaning of the term. They are organized around *information.*"[1]

The extended theory founded on this core belief divides U.S. economic

---

1. Peter Drucker, *Innovation and Entrepreneurship.* New York: Harper and Row, 1985, pp. 3-4.

history into different eras, depending on the primary economic activity during the period. From Colonial times until late in the 19th century, on this theory, the American economy was agrarian. Most Americans worked the land, and agriculture was the basis of the economy. Then, so goes this theory, roughly from the dawn of the 20th century through the end of the Second World War, the U.S. economy was pre-eminently a manufacturing economy. Industry—especially heavy industry—was the motor that drove the entire economic engine. After World War II, on this view, the American economy came increasingly to be dominated by its service sector: by the mid-1950s more than half of all U.S. employment was in providing services rather than in fabricating goods.

Then, more recently, as Peter Drucker and others have averred, a fourth stage can be distinguished: the American economy has come to be increasingly dominated by *information*—the gathering, analysis, distribution of data and knowledge. In one sense, of course, the information industry is a part of the services sector. Nevertheless, there are good reasons for distinguishing information services out from the rest of the services sector as a fourth separate component or stage of the economy.

For one thing, information is different from the non-information services in that the latter are generally *tangible* in a way that information is not. Think of such non-information services as transportation or public utilities. Yet, it is clear that the historical progression has been not only a movement through different economic eras, but also a movement from relative simplicity to daunting complexity. The transition from an agricultural to a manufacturing-based economy was essentially straightforward, unlike the subsequent transitions—first to a service-based, then to an information-based economy.

One source of confusion is the fact that the movements from manufacturing to services, and then to information, were of a different character from earlier transitions. In the first place, while the transition from an agricultural to a manufacturing-based economy was marked by a decline in the number of jobs in agriculture, there has been no such diminution in the number of manufacturing jobs after the shift to a service economy. Moreover, American manufacturing currently accounts for roughly the same percentage of U.S. Gross National Product as three decades ago.[2]

As a further complication, many argue that the services sector of the economy simply cannot be seen as a separate segment or an economic sub-

2. Stephen S. Cohen and John Zysman, *Manufacturing Matters: The Myth of the Post-Industrial Economy.* New York: Basic Books, Inc., 1987, p. 60.

system. Such observers instead insist that it "serves" precisely the manufacturing sector it is supposed to have replaced, remaining dependent—even parasitic—on manufacturing. Here is a succinct statement of that argument from the book, *Manufacturing Matters*:

"At the heart of our argument is a contention that tight linkages tie a broad range of service jobs to manufacturing... These services are complements to manufacturing, not potential substitutes or successors...Were America to lose mastery and control of manufacturing, vast numbers of service jobs would be relocated after a few short rounds of product and process innovation, largely to destinations outside the United States, and real wages in all service sectors would fall, impoverishing the nation."[3]

Moreover, coming up with clear definitions and boundaries for the information industry is, on reflection, a considerably complicated undertaking for a number of reasons:

- Most information products or services are provided free of charge or substantially below cost, with most of the cost borne by government, philanthropies, or corporate advertisers;[4]

- In one sense, virtually every corporation or business is at least partly in the business of providing information; at least insofar as they engage in advertising;

- Each of the two primary ways of defining and delimiting the information industry has weaknesses. The first definition includes all those firms that produce, gather, or disseminate information products. This definition would include many individuals—the paper delivery person, the custodian in a library—whose jobs are much more in the nature of physical labor than of "knowledge work." The second definition would define the industry in terms of individual occupations rather than companies, thereby excluding the library's custodian but including the consulting engineer for an automobile firm. But, of course, measuring the size of the industry becomes, on that definition, a virtually impossible task.

3. Ibid., p. 7.

4. Fritz Machlup, *The Production and Distribution of Knowledge in the United States*. Princeton, New Jersey: Princeton University Press, 1972, p. 28.

Another complicating factor is the fact that there is no very reliable way to assess the exact impact of any particular unit of information input on economic output. It is not certain, for example, that an increased investment in information as a percentage of GDP will result in more knowledge being provided. For example, if the U.S. expenditure for books increases, that could be because more books are being purchased and read (more knowledge consumed), or it could be because *fewer* but more expensive books are being purchased.

These complications in defining and measuring the information industry underscore some of the complexities in speaking of an Information Age. From one point of view, information has always been so much a part of the whole economy that it makes little sense to speak of a "new" information age. In fact, classical economic theory has always assumed the presence of information, and has given it a central role. As economist Fritz Machlup has pointed out, the mechanisms of the marketplace—supply, demand, competition—are all founded on the assumption that sellers know the highest price at which they can sell their products while buyers know the lowest price at which they can purchase them.

Moreover, the classical theory always assumed that producers know the available technology of their era and, thus, the lowest cost of producing those goods; such close observers of capitalist economic arrangements as Karl Marx and Joseph Schumpeter both remarked on the central role that statistical information plays in free market economies.[5]

The pace of change has been accelerating for many years. In fact, the 20th century has been characterized by dramatic changes in technology, communications, social, and political change, with the 1990s reaching a pace of unprecedented speed and range, such that the impact of change is far-reaching. Major events in just the past five years would be considered major revolutions in earlier periods. A listing of some of the major events of the past five years is provided in Figure 1.

This list is merely suggestive. It is neither comprehensive nor representative. The list is intended merely to illustrate the fact that an observer five years ago would not have anticipated more than a few items on this short list of twenty-six developments. Furthermore, most readers of the list would conclude that, in sum, a true revolution in economic and social conditions is underway. The framework for designing social policy, for stimulating

---

5. Ibid., pp. 3 and 4.

Figure 1

# Major Events 1989—1993

**1989**
- The collapse of the Berlin Wall - a symbol of the end of the Cold War
- Tiananmen Square riot in China - an emergence of popular power in a dictatorial society
- Growth in Europe based upon the 1992 program
- Japan announcement of first commercially available HDTV
- Congress passes legislation to rescue the savings and loan industry (August 9 signed into law)

**1990**
- Western Germany begins effort to absorb Eastern Germany and it opens its borders to immigrants from Central Europe
- Start of shock treatment in Poland
- In August Iraq overruns Kuwait
- President Bush signs bill designed to reduce budget deficits by nearly $500 billion over 5 years (November 15)

**1991**
- The coup in Russia - the Fall of Gorbachev
- War with unprecedented United Nations joint action
- The Conservative government of UK overthrows Margaret Thatcher after 11 1/2 years
- Bank mergers (Chemical and Manufacturers Hanover) and (Bank America and Security Pacific)
- Charges dropped against Oliver North
- Charles Keating convicted of securities fraud

**1992**
- Election of Clinton - end of Republican Administration after 12 years
- Near collapse of the ERM
- Environmental summit in Brazil signals worldwide sensitivity to emerging conflicts between development and the environment

**1993**
- Collapse of IBM becomes recognized with selection of new chairman and drop in street value from $80 billion in early 1991 to under $30 billion today
- War in Bosnia as signal of inability of UN and European community to deal with internal problems in a sovereign state with historic tensions
- Fall of the LDP in Japan and growing sense that Japan has lost direction in internal consensus and in economic policy
- Agreement in the U.S. among competing designs for HDTV yielding a new dimension to the redesign of that industry
- Corporate downsizing expands to include healthy companies
- U.S. stock market hits all time record high
- Europe struggles with growing unemployment
- Clinton signs bill to cut deficit by nearly $500 billion over 5 years (see 1990!)
- Israel and PLO agree to mutual recognition

economic growth, and for planning business and personal decisions has been upset by the emergence of totally new conditions in the United States, Japan, Europe—indeed in the world.

Throughout this period, world trade has increased significantly, even as economic conditions have weakened. This underscores the economic interdependence of nations around the globe. As shown in Figures 2 and 3, trade measured as the sum of global imports and exports has increased at a rapid rate in recent years. The result is a growing recognition today of the interactions among countries.

The so-called "jobless recovery" is a problem that transcends national borders. Unemployment in Europe has been at a high level, even during the 1980s when employment in the U.S. increased by 20 million jobs following the 1982 recession. Technological development, global outsourcing, excess world capacity, and intense international competition are all converging in international debates about trade policy, national fiscal policy, and industrial organization—including the role of the global corporation. Economic policy makers and corporate decision makers are struggling to make sound decisions in this environment of far-reaching change.

In the midst of these dramatic changes in just the past five years, the basic data we collect to measure economic and social progress have been essentially unchanged. As will be discussed in this report, there have been some important improvements, such as:

- International agreement on an improved United Nations System of National Accounts (SNA) for measuring national economic output;

- Implementation of a common system of commodity classification —The Harmonized Commodity Description and Coding System, known as the Harmonized System (HS) concepts; and

- An international program to help redesign the statistical systems of the formerly planned economies.

These changes take a long time. The SNA revision began in 1983 and was finally adopted by the United Nations in July 1993. As will be discussed later in this report[6] the U.S. is now in the process of planning to move the U.S. national accounts towards that system. Work on developing the Harmonized

---

6. See chapter 5.

## Figure 2

## Growth in Trade and GDP

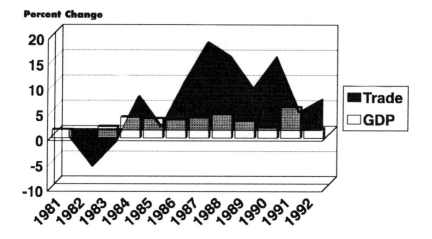

Percent Change

## Figure 3

## Trade and GDP

|      | World: GDP at Constant Prices (%) | World Trade* at Constant Prices (%) |
| ---- | --------------------------------- | ----------------------------------- |
| 1981 | 1.6%                              | -1.2%                               |
| 1982 | 0.0%                              | -7.2%                               |
| 1983 | 2.2%                              | -2.5%                               |
| 1984 | 4.1%                              | 6.6%                                |
| 1985 | 3.8%                              | 0.6%                                |
| 1986 | 3.6%                              | 9.5%                                |
| 1987 | 3.9%                              | 17.5%                               |
| 1988 | 4.6%                              | 14.3%                               |
| 1989 | 3.3%                              | 8.1%                                |
| 1990 | 2.0%                              | 14.3%                               |
| 1991 | 6.0%                              | 3.5%                                |
| 1992 | 1.8%                              | 6.0%                                |

Source: International Monetary Fund

* = Volume of Exports + Imports

10   Statistics in the 21st Century

System began in 1970 by the Customs Cooperation Council. It was finally implemented in 1988. Implementing statistical program changes in the former command economies will take many years, but the new and improved frameworks, such as the SNA, should be the basis for fundamental improvement in those countries.

## The Pace of Change in Statistics

The loosely interlocking system of statistics can be seen as a sort of "conceptual net" thrown over rapidly changing economic, social, demographic, and other realities in an effort to bring them into closer focus, to assess their size and meaning, and to try to determine their future direction. *As the 21st century approaches, it is increasingly clear that our current conceptual net, designed for earlier realities, fits our current situation only very imperfectly.*

However, the task of reforming the statistical network is immeasurably more complicated than simply redesigning it to bring it up to date. The reality is that there are very good reasons—beyond just, say, institutional inertia—for taking a very conservative approach to changing statistics. Whereas there are several sound reasons for this slow evolution, sluggish change also creates certain problems, as will be discussed later.

Before this report approaches the question of needed changes, it is useful to consider the positive aspects of keeping the pace of change in statistics moderate. First and foremost, official statistics are most valuable as a reference point for measuring progress or lack of progress. Thus, an important characteristic of official statistics is the development of a time series of consistent measures over an extended period of time so that comparisons can be made. For example, in economic terms, it is especially important to compare developments at different points in the business cycle. In an industrial sense, many businesses want to have a consistent history of their marketplace, so they can gauge their relative progress and evaluate the changes in their marketplace in relation to other parts of the economic system.

Therefore, there is a strong bias among both producers and users of statistics to keep the definitions, concepts, and classifications consistent over time. This is well illustrated by the Standard Industrial Classification system, developed in the 1940s when the U.S. economy was essentially focused on manufacturing activities. Despite revisions over the last four decades, the Standard Industrial Classification system is still focused on industrial concepts, with particular detail on specific manufacturing activities.

A second factor restricting change in statistical series is the recognition that current developments are often short-term in character. Thus, a revision of statistical concepts to reflect a new tendency, or perhaps a fad, risks being labeled as "capricious" in the sense that such short-term developments are transient changes in the structure. An attempt to focus on transient factors can ultimately distort analysis of fundamental conditions.

A third important reason for sticking with old definitions is that such stability avoids the dangers of changing the measurement system in response to shifting political objectives. The resistance to change in the definition of poverty, for example, reflects a natural political resistance to avoid creating additional demands on the budget even though the older measures may be outdated in terms of current social and economic conditions as discussed below.

Thus, we see there are some good reasons for the official statistical system to evolve slowly and to resist short-term changes. Nevertheless, we must recognize that failure to change the statistical system over a long period of time results in distortions of our measurements and our ability to understand current economic and social conditions. In effect, the statistics lose touch with reality.

The difficulties of lack of change are illustrated in the two cases presented above. Currently, the U.S. economic system is characterized by a lack of emphasis on service activities. In the Standard Industrial Classification coding system, employment data exist for 192 4-digit subclassifications in the manufacturing sector, which had 17.9 million employees as of June 1993. In contrast, data exist for only 36 SIC codes in the nonfinancial services areas, which covers 30.4 million employees. This illustrates the fact that we have much less detail and therefore much weaker understanding of the services sector.

The definition of poverty also illustrates this point. The current poverty level definition originated in the 1960s when Molly Orshansky analyzed food consumption and determined that one-third of the typical family budget was devoted to food expenditures. Then, using a minimum nutrition standard to determine the market basket needs for a family, the food component was defined for the poverty level as a minimum sustained budget. This number was multiplied by 3, since food accounted at that time for one-third of total household expenditures. Today, however, compelling arguments have been made that food accounts for only one-fifth, rather than one-third, of family expenditures. This would argue for multiplying the food component by 5 rather than 3, resulting in the difficult political choice that budgets for maintaining poverty level income would be forced to accelerate further. On the other hand, governmental programs to deal with poverty now include many payments in kind, which are not reported in received income. These include the earned income tax credits, food stamps, and housing allowances.

Thus, the definition of poverty in the 1990s is a much more complex concept than was characteristic in the 1960s. The countervailing political powers, however, make it virtually impossible to undertake at this time an objective analysis of how to redefine the statistical dimensions of poverty.

Another problem resulting from the failure to change is that, by the time the change is proposed, it takes additional time to develop a sufficient time series. For example, in the revision of the Consumer Price Index (CPI) in 1978, there was initially a six-month period of overlap between the unrevised CPI and the new CPI. Thus, while we can point out anomalies in the official statistical system that do not reflect existing conditions, it is important to recognize the built-in control systems that avoid unnecessary change and dampen the risk of political manipulation.

## Environment for Statistics

In a book published in 1978,[7] Sir Claus Moser, then the Director, Central Statistical Office of the United Kingdom, offered the following comment on the role of official statistics. His observations hold true more than fifteen years later. He commented:

> "The enormous increase in the demands of governments for more and better statistics has reflected the increase in government itself. Wherever one looks, governments have tended to govern more, and it is a basic question whether this trend is likely to continue. There are two contradictory streams of demand. People and organizations call for more intervention and services from government and they also express growing concern about the extent of government intervention in their lives; many take the view that governments should govern less. It is anyone's guess to what extent the cries for less government and less interference will carry the day against the opposite view. The

---

7. Joseph W. Duncan, Ed. *Statistical Services in Ten Years' Time.* New York: Pergamon Press, 1978, 189 pp.

chances are that the pressure for less central governments will have some success though perhaps not enough to affect the central government appetite for official statistics; but there is no doubt it will make the climate in which we work tougher, with more public resistance to requests for data, and thus threats to reliability. At the same time, the activities and importance of regional and local government are likely to increase, and with it the demand for small area statistics.

"But even if one assumes that the central government environment ten years hence will be such as to require at least as much statistical support as today, this is not to imply an unchanged official environment for statisticians. Far from it: I believe that the continued government demand for statistics will be set in a *very* changed context.

"First, *resources* will not grow in parallel with demands. Public expenditure will come under increasing scrutiny and the size and growth of civil services in particular will be kept more in check, including the statistical activities. Yet the demands are certain to increase, and partly because governments themselves will need good data for setting their own priorities. An increasing conflict between demands and resources is likely, and this will mean:

"a. A greater emphasis on *efficiency* in statistical organization and production and on cost reduction generally, and a greater reliance on cheaper (e.g., administrative) sources.

"b. A much greater need for rational setting of statistical *priorities,* with strictly structured medium-term statistical programmes becoming the norm—related to policy needs, and with the more sophisticated use of cost-benefit techniques applied to statistics...

"Second, the *nature of government demands* for statistics is likely to change. This is meant in several senses:

"a. Governments attempt to steer economies—and, up to a point, social developments—with the aid of statistics...

"b. Government users of statistics will look for greater simplicity...

"c. Policy-makers will increasingly want to supplement general background statistical information with data bearing on specific problems—to help them in making particular decisions and in monitoring their consequences...

"d. Above all, policy-makers in government will expect from their statistical offices not so much the production of more data as, increasingly, their analysis and interpretation...

"In sum, the government environment ten years hence will be tougher as regards resources and more critical about what official statisticians produce. The magic of numbers may be less seductive than now. Ministers and top administrators will be sophisticated enough about statistics to want guidance about the accuracy of the figures, as well as greater timeliness and relevance in the figures themselves; they will want more help in analysis and interpretation. Priorities and statistical programmes will have to be explicit, with *user*-orientation (for users outside and inside  government) dominating their choice. Regular routine statistics may become less  important, 'one-off' surveys and analyses more so."[8]

This similarity in the environment for statistical programs today, compared with 1978 has been used by some to suggest that change is not possible. We believe it is possible. What is needed is aggressive leadership and the development of a better understanding of both the needs for change and the benefits to society of having statistics that do an improved job of measuring economic and social conditions. That is the reason for our discussion in the next few chapters and for the recommendations made later.

## The Long-term Elements of Government Decision Making About Statistics

The nature of government decisions concerning  the budget for statistical activities results in a long time frame for implementation of new programs. In order to develop a new statistical program it is necessary to undertake research to define appropriate concepts, classifications, and standards, and to determine feasible data collection methodologies.

Too often, there is a lack of research funds for undertaking these preliminary investigations. New concepts may originate in universities or in special contract projects related to specific governmental programs. Rarely are these concepts initiated in statistical agencies studying long-term issues related to social and economic measurement. *Lack of funding for fundamental conceptual research at the National Science Foundation and other agencies also restricts the amount of attention given to these questions.*

Once a proposal is developed for improving statistical measurement,

---

8. Ibid., pp. 6-8.

other difficulties arise in trying to implement them. First, in the normal budgeting process, it is important to get support in the agency that is the home for the statistical activity. In the executive process, the home agency is required to submit the budget request and inevitably there are many competing demands with all major cabinet departments. Thus, during budget-setting time, the proposals to improve statistical programs compete with other major activities within the host departments. This makes it difficult to gain departmental support to even begin the process of seeking support within any given administration.

After the departmental hurdle is overcome, it is also difficult to gain approval at the Office of Management and Budget, where competing demands among all aspects of governmental activities make it difficult for long-range statistical improvement to gain attention. It is a natural tendency for every administration to seek programs that will have immediate political benefit. Thus, long-term programs that may not yield results for several years (often well beyond the tenure of the decision makers) are not often undertaken. In fact, it is remarkable that any proposals emerge from the executive branch to deal with improved statistical activities.[9]

The next barrier in initiating a new statistical program is the Congressional appropriations process. As is well known, the interests of Congressmen and Senators are relatively short-term and they are often driven by the interests of key constituents. Thus, it is difficult to gain support for proposals that originate in the executive branch and which will have little direct benefit to the congressional leadership. The record is full of congressional rejection of statistical initiatives for that reason.

Once the proposal for improvement has cleared the hurdles of departmental, administration, and budget analysis, executive branch approval, and congressional review, we are only at step one. The next part of the process is also lengthy.

The implementation of authorized improvements in official statistics also requires a long time period. First, there is a requirement to test and implement the design that was envisioned. Second, there is the need to refine the data collection process as difficulties arise from conflicts with recordkeeping requirements, ability to provide accurate reporting, etc. And then, of course,

---

9. A notable exception is the program that was initiated by Michael Boskin, Chairman of the Council of Economic Advisors, during the last three years of the Bush administration. While all funding requests were not approved, this effort serves as an illustration of how executive branch leadership has resulted in building a concrete program for long-term improvements. See Appendix 4 for program increases associated with this initiative.

we come back to our initial focus, the development of a time series. That in itself takes several years. Under the most optimum of circumstances, it is clear that there is at least a five-year gap between identifying a need for statistical programming innovation and useful output. In reality, the change is more likely to be more than a decade. This overall process is outlined in Figure 4 which generalizes the time line for statistical program improvement.

These delays can be illustrated by one program: the Survey of Income and Program Participation (SIPP). Initial proposals to measure "income-in-kind" with other income measures was officially addressed in the early 1970s. After major efforts to secure modest funds for research on SIPP, the survey was finally approved by the Congress and data collection began in 1983. Today, the evolution of the program continues, though the time series data are relatively weak.

## The Ultimate Trade-offs

Another characteristic of statistical programs is that as the statistics become available, they generate a set of users. That is part of the justification for the program, but the users then bring their own demands. It is nearly universal that users of statistics quickly identify deficiencies. They push for improvements in the timeliness of the series, seeking efforts to speed up data processing and reporting so that early results are available. Sometimes this conflicts with their second concern, which is accuracy. The conflict between accuracy and timeliness is most evident in the National Income and Product Accounts, but it is also characteristic of virtually every series where people seek early estimates so they can make current decisions. Finally, as time passes, the users discover more and more applications for the statistics, and there is a call for more comprehensive measures. Comprehensiveness, of course, brings with it additional costs and additional reporting burdens.

Government statisticians have long been concerned about minimizing the burden of providing information required by statistical inquiries.[10] In the 1930s the Central Statistical Board studied statistical reporting burdens at the request of President Franklin D. Roosevelt. Other studies of the paperwork burden include the Mills-Long Report (1948), the Federal

---

10. A detailed discussion of this topic is found in Office of Federal Statistical Policy and Standards, *A Framework for Planning United States Federal Statistics for the 1980s.* Washington, DC: U.S. Government Printing Office, 1977, pp 337-347.

## A Decade of Decisions
**Time Line for Statistical Program Improvement**

Figure 4

|                                        | Year 1 | Year 2 | Year 3 | Year 4 | Year 5 | Year 6 | Year 7 | Year 8 | Year 9 | Year 10 |
|----------------------------------------|--------|--------|--------|--------|--------|--------|--------|--------|--------|---------|
| Develop basic concept (1-10 years)     |        |        |        |        |        |        |        |        |        |         |
| Develop budget proposal                |        |        |        |        |        |        |        |        |        |         |
| approval by department                 | ▬      |        |        |        |        |        |        |        |        |         |
| approval by OMB                        |        |        | ▬      |        |        |        |        |        |        |         |
| approval by Congress                   |        |        | ▬      |        |        |        |        |        |        |         |
| Funding                                |        |        |        |        |        |        |        |        |        |         |
| design and test program                |        |        |        |        | ▬      |        |        |        |        |         |
| start data collection                  |        |        |        |        |        | ▬      |        |        |        |         |
| first results                          |        |        |        |        |        |        |        | ▬      |        |         |
| time series available                  |        |        |        |        |        |        |        |        |        | ▬       |

Paperwork Jungle Hearings of the Subcommittee on Census and Population (1965-66), the Kaysan Committee (1966), and the President's Commission on Federal Statistics (1971). However, the most thorough study was undertaken by the congressionally established Commission on Federal Paperwork, which undertook its study during the period 1975 to 1977. During this time it issued 36 separate reports on many topics such as statistics and reporting burden. Its final report was issued on October 3, 1977. The Commission's findings led to the Paperwork Reduction Act of 1980, which is the current legislative basis for statistical policy coordination and reporting burden control in government.

The preceding section has outlined a number of positive and negative reasons why evolution of the statistical system is slow. These range from the nature of statistical activities themselves to the difficult process of achieving budget authority and program implementation. This report is written with specific recognition of these inhibiting factors. However, in the judgment of the authors, it is indeed time for a full-scale approach to the redesign of statistical systems. As noted earlier, the pace of change in social and economic institutions is dramatic at this time in history. The need for better information in the Information Age is increasingly recognized. Therefore, this report is developed to build a case for more attention to the issues of defining the information required for decision making in the years ahead. The 21st century is only seven years away. The time frame presented earlier suggests that it is unlikely that, even if action is taken today, significant changes will be available as we enter the new millennium. If we do not begin to address these questions, we will never get to the point of having adequate information to handle the difficult questions posed by our rapidly changing social and economic conditions.

## Description of Chapters

Immediately following this chapter, in Chapter 2, we take up a careful analysis of the strengths, weaknesses, and opportunities (what we call a 'SWOT' analysis) presented by the statistical information emanating from four separate sources. After that, in Chapter 3, we consider the three primary dimensions of statistical information: uses and users; products and producers; and dissemination and presentation.

It was the philosopher Plotinus who once said, "Knowledge, if it does not determine action, is dead to us." And that's perhaps especially true of statistical knowledge: its purpose is to shape policies and determine action. For that reason, the next three chapters of this book are quite specific, seeking to seize concretely how current statistical systems either are or are not adequately determining action: Chapter 4 looks at how information is used in a specific policy area (Health Care).[11] Chapter 5 looks at the ways statistical systems are being revamped toward greater adequacy (the System of National Accounts). Chapter 6 examines an area which today particularly calls out for more attention and better statistics (Global Interaction).

Chapters 7 and 8 consist of recommendations[12] for improvements in, respectively, the System of National Accounts and the international economy. Chapter 9 contains our concluding remarks.

We have included six rather hefty appendices, including discussions of the role of the GAO, errors in GDP estimates, budgets for statistics, some detailed problems with data on international services, and quite voluminous bibliographical material. We have included these appendices in order to make this volume more useable to the reader. We recognize that what Plotinus said about knowledge in general applies equally to the contents of this book.

---

11. At the present time the National Center for Health Statistics is preparing a major review called Health 2000. Some materials from the present review were used in Chapter 5.

12. There have been a number of reviews of the U.S. Statistical System in recent decades. All statistical agencies have encouraged outside review panels. Often, detailed studies of individual data series have led to important improvements. The present report takes a more global perspective. Similar studies in the past include The National Commission on Federal Statistics, 1970; The Bonnen Committee report for President Carter's Statistical Reorganization Project, 1977; and the recent report from the Committee on National Statistics entitled "Principles for Statistical Agencies." Also see U.S. Department of Commerce, Office of Federal Statistical Policy and Standards, *Gross National Product Data Improvement Project Report.* U.S. Government Printing Office, October 1977, 204 pp.

---

# Chapter 2

# "SWOT" Analysis for Statistics

The acronym "SWOT" refers to Strength, Weakness, Opportunity, and Threat. SWOT is a standard tool, a method of case analysis, used by business analysts to size up a company's situation in the marketplace. Strength and weakness refer to internal factors within the organization; opportunity and threat are external factors. SWOT in short is a way of sizing up what is happening. It thus serves as a basis for analysis and the development of recommendations for action.

SWOT can be applied to the realm of statistics, whether public or private, local or international, longitudinal or cross-sectional. We are going to discuss briefly the strengths and weaknesses of existing data in four different types of organizations: international agencies, national governments, business firms, and a category we call statistical/information industry firms including nonprofit agencies. The discussion of these categories illustrates the type of analysis that can be done. We will highlight opportunities and threats. We will focus on how the statistical output from various sources are utilized by the customers. We do not present this as a final conclusion; rather it is intended to illustrate the type of review that is needed to plan for the future.

The U.S. is a "statistical society." Statistics are news. Statistics make the news. Consider the July 10, 1993, edition of the *New York Times,* specifically, the front page of the business section. The statistically related stories are shown in Figure 5 (Statistics in the News) on the next page.

Consider another widely read daily newspaper, the *Wall Street Journal,* specifically, the "Outlook" column on July 26, 1993. The headline reads: "Likeliest Forecast: More Weak Growth." The writer, A.L. Malabre, Jr., concluded that the economy will continue to expand, but at a subdued pace. What did he base his evidence on? Consider his sources:

- *Blue Chip Economic Indicators,* a private newsletter that summarizes the views of economists who fearlessly forecast up to eighteen months ahead (it may be noted that the consensus of their forecasts is generally superior to any individual's record).

**Figure 5**

## Statistics in the News

| Headline/Topic | Underlying Concepts/ Statistics | Sources (actual and/or implied) |
|---|---|---|
| 1. Global joblessness, jobless recovery, job creation, etc. | Unemployed, under-employed, underutilized workers, payrolls, new entrants, etc. | Governments, espccially Western, especially USDL/BLS |
| 2. Early retirees | Retirement age benefits | Foster Higgin |
| 3. Asian airlines fear U.S. airlines (sabotage) | % boarding each type, landing rights, transfers, discounting, frequent flyers | ICAO, IATA, AIA, governments, individual airlines |
| 4. Federal Reserve Board policy on interest rates, etc. | Interest rates, past and present, other economic data policy implications | FRB, individual banks, nonbank financial institutions |
| 5. Jack in the Box food poisoning incident | Fast food service, customer loyalty, nutrition, competitors' market share | Fuddruckers, NYSE, news agencies, etc. |

- "The U.S. Department of Commerce's index of leading indicators, recently has been wobbly...but that does not mean a recession is imminent...(but) it does behave in an erratic fashion after the economy has been expanding for a considerable time."

- Columbia University's Center for International Business Cycle Research publishes a "long-leading index," which provides an appreciably longer lead time than the Commerce Department's. "This index has been climbing steadily, with little interruption, since the 1990-91 recession."

We could pick similar examples from the *Financial Times* and *The Economist,* from Japanese journals, or bank newsletters, all of which tend to rely on a vast mix of sources (government, private and nonprofit sectors) for their own analysis.

What do the above examples reveal about the underlying data, specifically about the SWOT aspects of the statistics? Simply stated, the strength of statistics is their wide availability. There are thousands of sources, producing millions of data bits.

But this is also their weakness. Simply put, there are too many numbers to absorb, too much data to interpret. And there are questions about every source:

*Can we be sure the producers of data used the same definitions and classification?*

*What methods were employed to collect the data?*

*What is the likelihood of revisions in the numbers, and whom should we believe?*

Businesses of all sizes and individuals of every description are hungry for good data and are willing to support organizations and programs that provide them. With the advent of on-line computer data bases and CD-ROM type delivery, statistics can be put into users' hands easily and quickly. With sophisticated software packages and other "interfaces," we can compare and analyze the mass of available data. The threat is also real, however: With too many revisions, too many sources, contradictory information, and lack of analysis, the users may become less confident and the data less useful. We now present a brief SWOT analysis of four different categories of data-producing organizations.

## Data from International Agencies

Many international agencies issue statistics on a regular basis. Others gather data for internal use and publish only an occasional report. Our emphasis will be on the former. In this category are the United Nations (U.N.), the Organization for Economic Cooperation and Development (OECD), the International Monetary Fund (IMF), and its sister institution, the World Bank (WB), the Statistical Office of the European Communities (EURO-STAT), the various regional banks, e.g., the Inter-American Development Bank (IADB) and the Asian Development Bank (ADB). Other agencies encompass a wide variety of fields, ranging from air transport (the International Civil Aviation Organization, or ICAO, in Montreal, Canada) to atomic energy (the International Atomic Energy Agency, or IAEA, in Vienna, Austria). While the larger organizations focus on broad economic/business data gathering, others emphasize more narrow areas. We can expect an expansion in selected regional categories. For example, as Eastern Europe rebuilds, it will likely develop better data bases focused on regional issues.

### Strengths

The U.N. is almost fifty years old and has developed an impressive set of statistics and publications encompassing all member nations. In general, there is good continuity in its various statistical yearbooks. The economic data of even small nations are treated in depth. The OECD is the prime statistical agency for data on the developed Western nations. As such, it has done good work in both gathering and publicizing its data bank. Some of the OECD information is available in computer-readable format; other data are subjected to analysis and interpretation. The World Bank has developed an impressive set of world indicators that are published in over thirty tables as an appendix to its *World Development Report*.[13] Statistics in this volume go beyond economic/business data, encompassing a wide variety of social and cultural indicators. The regional and industrial agencies have become experts in their fields. The ADB knows its Asian membership and the ICAO has kept a good time series on air transport and even on airport size.

The statistical data bases of these international agencies can be considered the starting point for any global or regional research undertaking. Any major departure from them would require justification. They have collected

---

13. The World Bank, *World Development Report* (1993) and *World Tables 1993*. Published for the World Bank by The Johns Hopkins University Press, Baltimore.

long time series and on occasion they can marshal good cross-sectional data. They have well-defined categories and have established meaningful classifications. In short, comparison is possible both over time and across countries—up to a point. The narrower the scope of the agency's work, the more likely it is to be an expert on that topic (see ICAO and IAEA). While some agencies guard their data bank holdings zealously, others have learned to profit handsomely from the sale and distribution of their data.

### Weaknesses

International organizations ultimately depend on the cooperation of member nations, special interest groups, and individuals. No matter how good the definition and classification systems are, they may be and are interpreted differently by their member constituencies. Few organizations have the means of a large independent staff dedicated to primary worldwide surveys. Furthermore, these agencies are not quick to adjust to new conditions and to start new categories and new time series. For example, like national governments, they have been slow to recognize the need for gathering data on the services sector.

O. Morgenstern[14] wrote about the accuracy of economic observations three decades ago. Using his own research as well as that of S. Kuznets and E.J. Russell, he estimated that worldwide economic data had a range of error of 5% to 20%, depending on country and product category involved. To put it bluntly, he said, "Economics is a one-digit science."

More important than the question of definition, revised figures, and subsequent disagreement (which is often labeled "range of error") is the matter of continuity and of reporting. Here, the situation seems better, but is certainly not always encouraging. As one key example: The U.N.'s publication, *National Accounts Statistics: Main Aggregates and Detailed Tables* was last issued in 1992, but the reference period for the data was 1990. Certain capital-spending time series available earlier from the U.N. also have not come to light in recent years. The IMF and WB have finally realized that the gross national product per capita is not meaningful in terms of exchange rates and began publishing GNP per capita on a purchasing power parity basis. For developing nations, the latter shows a two- to five-fold increase in this key number. To some readers, this will be useful; to others, it will certainly seem rather confusing.

---

14. Oskar Morgenstern, *On the Accuracy of Economic Observation.* 2nd Ed. Princeton, NJ: Princeton University Press, 1963, pp. 279, 286.

As for the disagreements among the data issued by the various international agencies, these have not been resolved as each one clings to its own established routine. Finally, some nations are unwilling to provide figures to international agencies even on their most basic statistics (e.g., Saudi Arabia), while others are unable to do so due to internal turmoil (e.g., Eastern Europe).

## Opportunities

The major international data-gathering bodies are good at ensuring their own survival. They have succeeded in obtaining funding through much of their existence and have published statistics that provided a certain degree of continuity. But there is fraying at the edges and even in the center. *The world has changed rapidly and they have been slow to adjust. The opportunities lie in recognizing which portion of their output is valued highly and in marketing those statistics.*

A good example along these lines is the OECD, which is now aggressively selling its data base in various formats. Some of the specific agencies are responsive to requests, but others are not willing to share the information with commercial or academic audiences. *The "parent" organization or the policy-making board must see to it that these agencies begin the most elementary market research: Who uses data? How and why? How can we cater better to their needs and wants?*

Creating and then delivering millions of data bits in print or electronic format is by no means easy. The international agencies, however, have a definite opportunity in this regard as the prices of small computers and workstations drop. Providing appropriate hardware and software to both those who provide the data (member nations and organizations, but ultimately individuals) and users who "massage" the numbers, will result in a more efficient collection. At the dissemination end, in a similar fashion, the data should be available in not just print form and on-line, but also in a CD-ROM format, as is the case now for the National Trade Data Bank of the U.S. and the global trade data of Statistics Canada.

While new time series and new formats can be encouraged, it is crucial for these organizations to maintain continuity. Justification must be provided for sudden departures in definitions, and new series should be linked with old ones. It seems also wise to provide a band or range rather than point estimates. Early figures should be so defined and be visible as such, and not just marked with a footnote or a small "e" (for "estimate") after the number. Instead bold letters, "estim," should be put in front of the preliminary numbers.

Revisions should have explanations and should state the percentage difference from the previous values. Readers can be directed to alternative sources for comparison. The marketing of the data ideally should be entrepreneurial. Institutions can choose a range of options from being a manufacturer or wholesaler of statistics, to working out a system of incentives, quantity discounts, multiyear subscriptions, and the like. Customer responsiveness and customization have not been the hallmarks of delivering data in the case of international agencies. But the opportunity exists for reform in this regard.

### Threats

The biggest threat to the international statistical bodies is the sharp cutbacks in their budget allocations (from member nations and/or other supporting bodies). We have noted that some agencies, including the U.N., have discontinued gathering and/or publishing certain statistics. But this can be overcome in two ways:

1. by emphasis on publishing data that are relevant to users, and

2. by aggressive marketing to actual and potential clients.

These steps also imply an "in-touch" policy with users of the data.

There are other threats as well. Some nations object to transborder data flow; others complain about issues of workload, secrecy, privacy, security, data exchange, access, and so forth. Any international agency must reassure those who provide it information that it will not cause them undue burdens. It must also stress its objectivity and equal treatment in its data-gathering and disseminating activities. If its sale of the data results in much income, part of the gains can be distributed back to the membership who supplied them. Ultimately, as is the case for national government bureaus, the international agencies must think and act in an entrepreneurial fashion.

## Statistics from Government Bureaus

In 1989, Henry Kelly and Andrew Wyckoff of the U.S. Office of Technology Assessment wrote an article entitled "Distorted Image" in MIT's *Technology Review*,[15] in which they argued that:

1. The ability of government statistics to tell us what we most need to know has become more questionable than ever;

2. It takes so long to create some statistics that by the time they are published, they no longer accurately reflect reality;

3. Modernization of government statistics must begin with managerial reform; and

4. New technologies could increase the timeliness of government statistics and reduce the burden on firms.

Criticisms along these lines are not unique to the U.S. government, nor to the present time. Consider the following excerpt from a book review by N. Virts of A. Friedberg's *The Weary Titan*.[16]

"When faced with the task of measuring such complex phenomena as economic and military power ...officials relied extensively on easily computed measures, trade statistics for economic power and number of battleships and infantry reinforcements for military strength. Unfortunately, such statistics often hid more than they revealed."

The place and time? Britain from 1895 to 1905.

Overall, the points of the 1989 article by Kelly and Wyckoff have been echoed in many places, ranging from I. Kaminow's article on "Statistical Stagnation"[17] to M. Hillman's review, "Uses and Abuses of Transportation and Road Safety Statistics."[18] Writing in the same year as Kelly and Wyckoff,

---

15. Henry Kelly and Andrew Wyckoff, "Distorted Image," *Technology Review*, February/March 1989, pp. 53-60.

16. *Wall Street Journal Europe*, May 30, 1989, p. 6.

17. *Government Executive*, July 1, 1992, p. 48.

18. *Policy Studies*, July 1, 1992.

---

H. Stout focused on the constant revision process of government data.[19]

More recently, in a one-page "Call-to-arms," an article by Walter Wriston in the June 21, 1993, issue of *Forbes,* argues that "economists cannot measure economies and if you cannot measure how can you manage?" He cites the IMF's drastic revision of China's output (fourfold upward), then went on to castigate the U.S. Department of Commerce for its constant revision of economic growth, and referred to four differing definitions of the deficit. Finally, Wriston echoes the two often stated points: that the U.S. Federal government is not using an accrual basis (that is, counting infrastructure monies as an expense rather than as an investment); and that there is a lack of emphasis on services sector industries.

We agree with the general thrust of all the articles cited above, although the tone is somewhat overstated. We especially applaud the call for more timely data, reform, and upgrading. We also hold that integrity, accuracy, timeliness, and interpretability of data are crucial, and we believe that the current situation reflects the high level of professionalism among governmental statisticians.

However, we are not certain that a new independent statistical agency is needed to regulate government data collection, agency coordination, and dissemination as advocated by Kelly and Wyckoff.[20] There is much strength in the existing agencies. It is quite possible that streamlining policies and mandating public-private sector cooperation may accomplish the same thing as centralization. *There is little doubt, however, that major changes are needed and, when instituted, will result in both better government policies and better private sector decisions.*

### Strengths

Possibly the greatest strength of U.S. and other national government statistics is their uniqueness. There is only one sovereign government in each nation and it has a monopoly on government data. Governments are in the unique position to provide continuity and stability in statistical services. Policies and regulations can be established to ensure compliance and cooperation. In short, a leadership role can be asserted, and with gentle or firm arm-twisting, collaboration can be assured.

---

19. "Shaky Numbers/U.S. Statistics Mills Grind Out More Data That Are Then Revised/Fed, Companies and Markets Can Be Seriously Misled; One Cause: Budget Cuts/Alan Greenspan Prefers Speed," *Wall Street Journal,* August 31, 1989, p. 1.

20. See Chapter 9, Concluding Remarks.

The second major positive feature stems from the first. With continuity and stability, government bureaus are able to provide a long-run perspective of the economy. Thus, for example, historical time series in the U.S., the U.K., and Canada provide an excellent overview of trends during decades and even centuries. These permit meaningful analysis under a variety of economic conditions. Many nations are envious of *Historical Statistics of the United States, Colonial Times to 1970* and *Historical Statistics of Canada*. Economic and business historians have made wide use of these two volumes in their research.

A third strength (which some observers view as weakness) is the duplication of data collection by various agencies. In our view, it is an advantage that in the U.S. the two Department of Commerce agencies (Bureau of Economic Analysis and Bureau of the Census), and the agency in the Department of Labor (Bureau of Labor Statistics) all get involved in gathering price, productivity, and other measures of economic activity. *In effect, this provides a system of "checks and balances," though it takes a skilled analyst to "make sense" of what may seem at first contradictory information.* The Bureau of Economic Analysis has done good work in developing detailed input-output tables. No one else would have been able to perform this pioneering work on the structure of the U.S. economy. Dozens of other government bureaus are hard at work collecting administrative data, supplementing the work of the key statistical agencies.

Another strength is the willingness of government bureaus to listen to their audiences and to make changes as warranted. For example, as the U.S. economy became more and more integrated in the global economy, the Department of Commerce made numerous adjustments and has developed various ways of accessing data. An example of this is the downloading of consultant reports onto CD-ROM diskettes in the case of trade data. Known now as the NTDB, the National Trade Data Bank is an easy way of looking at market opportunities abroad for U.S. goods and services. (We shall refer to a major shortcoming of NTDB in the next section.)

Moreover, there is a gratifying ability and willingness of U.S. government statisticians to discuss the data with outsiders over the phone, via mail, or even in person. Our experience over three decades indicates that statisticians are approachable. A concrete example of this is the listing of specialists' phone numbers in the annual *U.S. Industrial Outlook,* a key tool used by almost all business researchers.[21] In a similar fashion, our interaction with chief statisti-

---

21. Such directories are available from all major statistical agencies. Contact the public affairs offices for further detail.

cians and members of their staff in many other nations provides further strong evidence that the "keepers of the data" are willing to discuss problems that arise from assumptions, definitions, and matters of classification.

Last, but certainly not least, one of the major strengths of U.S. Federal statistics (true for many other Western nations' data) is their integrity. Indeed, the July 1993 issue of *Business Economics*[22] is devoted largely to this topic. These articles, by members of the General Accounting Office, the Bureau of Economic Analysis, and the Bureau of Labor Statistics marshal impressive evidence that such vital integrity has been safeguarded and will continue to be observed. This means that the task of gathering, processing, and disseminating data remains free of political interference. *The credibility of official economic and social statistics is truly crucial for the proper functioning of a democratic, diverse society. Without it, trust and usage would be quickly lost!*

In this volume, we cannot explore in detail the strengths and weaknesses of the output of other nations' central statistical bureaus. But according to a panel of statisticians,[23] Canada had the most accurate and Italy had the worst set of statistics among ten OECD nations. Canada had the smallest number of revisions between the first and final set of published figures. The panel judged the agencies on three criteria:

1. coverage and reliability;

2. methodology used; and

3. integrity and objectivity of the statistical agency.

Centralized systems, such as those in Australia and Canada, avoid duplication, display more integrity, and show better response to the shift toward services. Since only a single entity collects the data, this minimizes interference from the political process. The panel was concerned that in decentralized systems, including that in the U.S., the numbers are more exposed to politicians. While we have referred to the integrity of U.S. statistics above, this does remain a danger. As noted below, duplication also occurs in a decentralized system, but this can be a point of strength (see above) or one of weakness (see below).

---

22. *Business Economics*, Vol. XXVIII, No. 3, July 1993: Joseph W. Duncan, "Integrity in Official Statistics;" Bruce Johnson and Lori Rectanus, "The Integrity of Federal Statistics: A Case Study From the GAO Perspective;" Carol S. Carson, "Assuring Integrity for Federal Statistics: Focus on GDP;" Janet L. Norwood, "Perception of Reality: Can We Trust Federal Statistics?"

23. "The Good Statistics Guide," *The Economist*, Sept. 7, 1991, p. 88. See also "The Good Statistics Guide," *The Economist*, Sept. 11, 1993, p. 63.

## Weaknesses

There is no shortage of criticism aimed at federal (as well as state or provincial and local) statistics. The charges leveled include faulty assumptions, along with old-fashioned definitions and classification; long-time delays in publication, especially in regard to censuses, coupled with revisions; outright errors, discrepancies, and data gaps; overflow of information along with duplication; and, finally, competition with the private sector, including charges of too much and too little rivalry. The list could easily be expanded and could include "the flip side" (e.g., some charge there is too little information and interpretation). Let us briefly examine each of these, with special reference to U.S. federal statistics.

Government statistics trace their ancestry back many decades, even centuries. The data-gathering bureaus, by definition, bring stability and continuity to their tasks. Yet, it is not surprising that early assumptions, classic definitions, and initial classification schemes that worked well in the past are no longer valid. Critics often point to the way government treats expenditures on highways and other structures (as well as research, education, etc.). Such spending is counted as an expense; there is a lack of accrual accounting. In short, public investment is not recognized as such; this makes for poor policy decisions. The General Accounting Office and others recommend changing the situation, but old ways prevail. Similar criticism is aimed against the Standard Industrial Classification system whose categories focus far too much on old-line manufacturing, far too little on high-tech products and service industries. The various branches of the U.S. government need to settle a host of similar problems, e.g., defining the budget and trade deficits in a more precise manner.

Delays in the release of government data adversely affect decisions in both the public and private sectors. Many observers commented on delays that range from months to years; a newly formed input-output benchmark, based on 1982 census data, was released in 1989. Portions of censuses of population, manufacturing, services, agriculture, etc., "dribble out" in bits and pieces, with full volumes available only after excruciating waits of several years. What infuriates users of the data even more are the constant revisions that occur not just for the gross national product, but for other series as well. Changes in housing statistics (new starts, etc.) are especially frequent and leave users wondering when final/correct figures will arrive. Needed revisions in industrial production and capacity utilization indices are just now getting done by the Federal Reserve.

Errors, discrepancies, and data gaps in government statistics do occur despite the best efforts of the staff. Notable in this regard is the 1990 Census of Population, which undercounted by about 5.3 million people. But, according to an authoritative GAO report, there was a far bigger dual problem: the Census missed between 9.7 million and 15.5 million people and double-counted between 4.4 million and 10.2 million people. On the estimation front, the Central Intelligence Agency has vastly overestimated the economic and military strength of the old Soviet Union and underestimated China's.

Because each government bureau has its mandate, it is not surprising to find a certain amount of duplication and information overflow. Up to a point, this may even be desirable, but recent evidence indicates that the current arrangement also results in waste and confusion. For example, Kelly and Wyckoff,[24] as well as others, note that food consumption data are available from both the Agriculture Department and Bureau of Economic Analysis. While both track money spent on food eaten outside the home, each agency defines it differently. Enterprise and labor statistics also originate from various sources, with the result again being duplication and information overload. Though each bureau has good reasons for its methodology, to outsiders—even those experts at interpreting data—the results can be confusing.

The U.S. government, as well as state and local bodies, have been criticized for being in the information-gathering and dissemination business. However, the U.S. Constitution mandates the population census. The track record and integrity of the bureaus also argue in favor of continuing the collection of information by governmental agencies. Thus, it is more at the dissemination end that we find criticism and strong recommendations for commercialization. The pros and cons of this have been explored in *The Politics of Numbers*.[25] Good arguments are marshaled on both sides of the issue, which has not been resolved to date.

An example is the 1993 debate over the way in which the Securities and Exchange Commission shares data with the public.[26] The SEC plans to allow Mead Data Central to offer the SEC electronic data base of 15,000 publicly traded corporations on-line at about $160,000 per year. Librarians and individuals object to this commercial involvement in the electronic dis-

24. Henry Kelly and Andrew Wyckoff. "Distorted Image," *Technology Review*, February/Mark 1989, pp. 53-60.

25. William Alonso and Paul Starr, Eds. *The Politics of Numbers*. New York: Russell Sage Foundation, 1987.

26. "Trove of SEC Data Available by Computer—for a Price," *Washington Post*, July 26, 1993.

tribution of public records. In contrast, Mead and others defend the practice by saying, "You need to be careful not to pre-empt the market vision," and arguing that competition among on-line firms will hold down the price to final users.

A possible resolution of the above debate can be seen in the deal that the SEC has struck with another contractor, Disclosure, Inc. This firm is in charge of releasing corporate reports (annual, 10K, and other filings) to the public at a charge; e.g., it charges $25 for an annual report. It also resells the information in CD-ROM format and via on-line electronic data bases. But it maintains public reference rooms in Washington, New York, and Chicago, where the same information is free (but more cumbersome to assemble).

## Opportunities

The following avenues are open to government statistical bureaus to enhance their relationship with individual users and user groups:

1. improve the existing statistics (fewer errors, minimal revisions, less delay, etc.);

2. create new series, sharpen sampling, possibly at the expense of censuses;

3. coordinate with other sources, eliminate duplication; and

4. become user-friendly in terms of getting the data in and out; that is, soliciting advice, speeding delivery, reducing pricing, and streamlining operations overall.

It would be foolhardy to enumerate at this point all the existing series of federal and other government statistics that are in need of improvement and/or to cite all the new time series and cross-sectional data that should be created. Instead, we marshal summary statements in this regard, using three exhibits, Figures 6 to 8. The first of these is an abstract of "Reviving the Federal Statistical System: The View from Academia"[27] by J. Miron and C. Romer, which, while three years old, is still valid. The second is an abstract from a sequence of articles by co-author Joseph W. Duncan,[28] which again

---

27. J. Miron and C. Rome, "Reviving the Federal Statistical System: The View from Academia," *American Economic Review*, May 1990.

28. Joseph W. Duncan, "The Statistics Corner," *Business Economics*, January 1989

---

# Reviving the Federal Statistical System

Title: *Reviving the Federal Statistical System: The View from Academia*

Authors: Jeffery A. Miron and Christina D. Romer

Journal: American Economic Review (AER) ISSN: 0002-8282
Vol: 80 Iss: 2 Date: May 1990 p:329-332
Illus: References

Companies: Federal Reserve Board

Subjects: Economics; Statistics: Statistical methods;
Consistency; Consumer spending; Revisions; Recommendations

Codes: 9190 (United States); 1110 (Economic conditions & forecasts); 9550 (Public sector)

Abstract: Academic researchers are concerned about assumptions and consistency over time of official government statistics. To address the first concern, the government might: 1. try to derive series based on more actual data and fewer assumptions, 2. provide both the final series and the actual base data to researchers, 3. state assumptions more clearly, and 4. present data without seasonal adjustments. Government statisticians might mitigate the inconsistencies resulting from the very different ways long time-series are constructed in the prewar and postwar eras by: 1. using additional resources and effort to improve existing prewar estimates of many economic aggregates, 2. documenting the existing prewar series more thoroughly, and 3. flagging inconsistencies more diligently. Inconsistencies within the postwar era might be minimized by not undertaking date revisions lightly, by taking revisions as far back as possible, and by providing a period of overlap between old and new procedures when revisions cannot be taken back in time.

See also the following in the same issue of AER:
•"Reviving the Federal Statistical System: A View from Industry," by R. Cole            333-336
•"Reviving the Federal Statistical System: International Aspects," by R.E. Lipsey        337-340
•"Reviving the Federal Statistical System: A View from Within," by J.E. Triplett        341-344

**Figure 7**

# The Statistics Corner

Title:   *The Statistics Corner*

Authors:  Joseph W. Duncan

Journal:  Business Economics (BEC) ISSN: 0007-666x
     Vol: 24 Iss: 1 Date: Jan 1989 p:48-50

Subjects:  Economics; Statistics; Reliability; Poverty; Merchandise;
     International trade; Data; Errors

Codes:   1110 (Economic conditions & forecasts)

Abstract:  Substantial evidence indicates that government statistics are subject to large revisions and are not reliable enough for business and government to use in making informed decisions about what is happening with the economy. Much of the data can even result in making wrong decisions. Five main problem areas need to be addressed. First, the goverment must use more timely methods for sampling and measurement. Such methods are widely available and are used daily by the private sector. Second, new sectors of the economy must be measured. The process of change in the economy has not been matched with change in the statistical base and statistical methods. Third, new directions in statistics are needed instead of relying on concepts. Fourth, the statistics must be made more reliable. Finally, the apparent antagonism between the business community and the data gatherers must be eliminated.

**Figure 8**

## How to Lie with Statistics

Title:        *How to Lie with Statistics*

Authors:      J. Lisle Bozeman and Barry Bozeman

Journal:      Public Productivity & Management Review (POP) ISSN: 1044-8039
              Vol: 13 Iss: 1 Date: Fall 1989 p: 13-26

Companies:    Bureau of the Census

Subjects:     Local government; Statistics; Statistical methods;
              Factors; Improvements; State government

Codes:        9190 (United States); 9550 (Public sector)

Abstract:     A local government view of statistical policy is provided and some steps local government officials can take to enhance the utility of federal statistics are suggested. Problems cited include: 1. the incompatibility of data obtained from multiple sources, 2. the dissimilarity of data collection methods between local, state, and federal agencies, and 3. a reduction in funds and an increase in responsibilities. Improvements in local government statistical policy can be made, for example, by acquiring available indices, setting policies and procedures for consultants, and deciding on a small body of strategic data. Steps that the Federal government can take include: 1. Provide resources and technical assistance to local governments to answer questions about data structure, 2. Work toward maximum uniformity in definitions and procedures, 3. Devote more resources to small areas and categories, 4. Consider a quinquennial census, and 5. Provide assistance for the implementation of geocoded systems.

we believe is still applicable. The third and last exhibit is an abstract discussing a local government's view of statistical policy and its relationship to federal data.[29]

Possibly the most significant issue in any economy is that of economic growth, and the most watched variable is gross domestic product (GDP) or GDP per capita. These series are tied, by definition, to other key economic variables, including employment and unemployment numbers. Several analysts and legislators think that the GDP of the U.S. has been consistently inflated. One of the critics, Alan Sindlinger, claimed in a rather exhaustive analysis that the Department of Commerce misled both the public and government leaders by using data that yielded too high a figure for employment. According to him, there was a discrepancy of about 1.4 million workers between the Bureau of Labor Statistics' household survey and its establishment survey.

The almost identical issue surfaced again in 1991-92 when the BLS discovered an atypically large difference between the employment levels as measured by its monthly survey of a sample of business establishments, and as measured by unemployment insurance reports gathered from the universe of the same businesses about a half year later (the two series are called Current Employment Statistics and Unemployment Insurance). A discrepancy of 650,000 was found between the two, with the CES reporting the higher numbers.

An analysis by the authors is shown in Figure 9 on the next page. This shows the total impact of the revisions from January 1989 to May 1991. The 12-month moving average is a good indicator of the cumulative impact of the revisions. The Bureau of Economic Analysis used the CES employment data to issue its GNP estimates.

In light of the above, government statisticians have an opportunity to take a rather aggressive approach to defend both the integrity of the federal statistical system and the general accuracy of the underlying data. Others have used the situation to call for an advisory committee and still others want to establish a new, centralized statistical agency. Certainly, a window of opportunity exists now to strengthen the federal statistical system while it is under attack. One good way of accomplishing the task is to rethink which surveys, which series are needed, which censuses can be reformed, and which can be eliminated in favor of samples. We must certainly get beyond

---

29. J. Bozeman and B. Bozeman, "How to Lie with Statistics," *Public Productivity & Management Review,* Fall 1989.

---

## Figure 9

## Labor Force
**Change in Monthly Estimates**

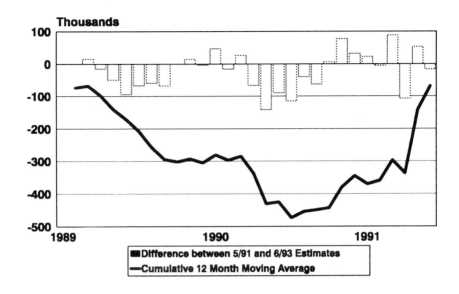

the census approach and recognize that well-designed samples can do the job in many cases.[30]

How can government agencies do more with less? According to many experts, the key lies in information technology for improving both the quantity and the quality of their work. Simply put, modern electronic and optical devices are ready to assist government statisticians in doing a better job of collecting, analyzing, and disseminating the data.[31] The imperative is to move away from the mountains of paper and into electronic filing, CD-ROM storing/retrieving, and a vast array of other electronic, optical imaging, and networking systems, which will assist in the task. Evidence is at hand that information technology has finally come of age and that it can aid in handling the billions of data bits.

## Threats

The gravest threat to government statistical systems would be the refusal to cooperate on the part of individuals and businesses. This is a distinct possibility if the forms and questions get longer and if there is more invasion of privacy. While government authorities could rely on the stick (lawsuit, regulation, etc.), the carrot (shorter forms, electronic filing, sampling rather than census/universe count) will always work much better. A well-designed marketing program showing tangible benefits may range from the serious (feedback, appeal to patriotism, promise of no call-backs, etc.) to the light (specialty promotions, e.g., stickers, coins, pamphlets, etc.). Certainly short questions, fewer surveys, easy responding, and electronic filing will go far in this regard.

A second threat is the possibility of further budget and staff cuts in government bureaus as taxpayers balk and as legislators look for easy ways of "holding the line." However, there is a sense now that like certain other categories of public service (e.g., customs, immigration, drug licensing, air traffic control), data collecting is both a proper activity for government and has definite benefits for all sectors of the economy. In short, no other body is equipped as well for gathering statistics and the process is of much benefit to enterprises and individuals.

Members of major data collection agencies, such as the Bureau of the

---

30. Joseph W. Duncan, "The Numbers are Starting to Lie: Restructuring Economic Statistics," *Leaders Magazine,* Vol. 15, No. 3, July, August, September 1992, pp. 44-45.

31. See Henry Kelly and Andrew Wyckoff, "Distorted Image," *Technology Review,* February/March 1989, pp. 53-60; and many others.

---

Census, BEA, BLS, and others do need to step forward, however, and begin to do a better job of "marketing themselves" to Congress, the private sector, and the public at large. This means not only defending the accuracy and integrity of the data, but also patiently explaining the nature and the value of surveys undertaken. Pruning outdated censuses, starting new ones, switching to sampling, instituting new ways of filing, and so forth, also require publicity and indeed a "selling job" in specific terms. The responding organizations and individuals will be especially receptive to simpler forms and elimination of duplication. Automation can go a long way toward easing the burden and may even allow more frequent surveys.

Those providing the data to government statistical bureaus are often concerned with issues of privacy and secrecy. The concerns can extend from the way a census enumerator introduces himself/herself to a reminder phone call from a staff member of a regulatory commission, from the way a question is formulated to the manner in which reassurance is given that the answers will not be shared with other authorities. Both the human element and the design of the paper/electronic format must reassure the participants that strict privacy and secrecy will be observed. *Whole surveys and individual questions must be rethought along two lines: Are they really necessary? Will they offend the participant in any way?*

Setting up a "proper" system of social statistics that probes sensitive areas is fraught with more danger than is the case for economic data systems. Included here are such topics as education, ethnicity, race, religion, health, aging, disability, and welfare. Each of these is treated at some depth in the excellent volume already referred to, *The Politics of Numbers*.

## Data from the Private Sector (The Individual Firms)

We can distinguish two major categories of data coming from profit-making enterprises. Both are important, and both are useful in their own rights and as complementary statistics to those gathered by the international, governmental, and nonprofit agencies. These are:

1. the statistics about the organization itself, usually published in its own annual and quarterly reports, news releases, and the like; and

2. the facts and figures gathered about organizations by outsiders, such as information service companies, market research firms, think tanks, or trade/industry associations.

We shall deal with the former here; the latter will be discussed briefly in the next section of this chapter and in the following chapter.

### Strengths

Corporate data, which are often complex and multifaceted, can be highly useful. The macrodata of an economy (be it a large or small nation) really rest on the foundations of microdata. We argued recently that statistics are an important part of civic responsibility of corporate officials and ordinary citizens.

*The business economist and others concerned about the quality of government data should work with accountants, controllers, and others in the company to make sure that the internal data are in order and that government forms submitted provide an accurate picture and a sound estimate of the information being requested.* A well-designed data base can help communication with employees on the inside and with suppliers and customers on the outside. And it allows for comparison with competitors.

In the electronic age, even the smallest company can have good records available on instant notice. Cost, price, product shipment, and other figures should be accessible to the relevant employees. Many firms have in the U.S. and elsewhere solid accounting standards and meaningful information systems. The advent of desktop computing and networks allows the interchange of information within the company and even, as and when appropriate, with vendors and customers through dedicated tie-lines (known as EDI, or electronic data interchange). The central issue within a company is usually about proper cost allocation, especially in regard to overhead, rather than (as is the case for public agencies) about accuracy and integrity. The challenge is to have a data environment that provides easy access, pertinent data, and user-friendly devices or interfaces.

### Weaknesses

While some small firms are confronted with gaps in their data base, others struggle with statistical and information overload. A major weakness of both small and large organizations—reminiscent of government agencies—is the inertia to continue bookkeeping, accounting, and hence maintaining old-line time series—much as they have done in the past. Once-a-year spring cleaning may be a great idea for corporate data. Companies, like government agencies, struggle with inaccurate data, figures that will require revisions sooner or later.

## Opportunities

Small and large firms have a veritable statistical gold mine on their hands—if they will only use it wisely. Quite often consultants who undertake a task for a company find that the necessary data for managerial decisions are already present, but that they are partly hidden or scattered in a variety of forms and locations. Organizations that keep streamlined statistics on their production costs, sales, purchases, or payroll find themselves far more effective and far more competitive.

Enterprises should have good statistics on their employees, suppliers, and customers. This is not invasion of privacy; this is sound business practice. In this fashion, they can analyze major alternatives in human resource allocation, purchasing, and selling. A detailed data base on employees can result in far better policies in regard to promotion, transfer, retirement, rotation, and so on. As firms do more and more outsourcing, knowledgeable vendors will be even more crucial. Statistics should include delivery records, fulfillment rates, refund records, etc. The customer base can yield insights on where they are, how often and how much they buy, how they react to price promotions, and the like. Far-sighted companies know not only their customers, but also their customers' customers.

Certainly, any company's key edge comes in serving its client base and watching out for customers' customers. Enterprises have developed two kinds of reporting systems for analytical purposes: macro and micro. Corporate data play a large role in both. Macro reports provide an overview of total business operations and act as general monitoring devices alerting management to changes in the firm's environment. Micro reports are used to narrow the analytical focus to the specific areas of operation in order to identify causes of problems and to assist in day-to-day functions. An example of each, using data for decisions, is shown in two short accompanying exhibits. The next two Figures (10 and 11) show in general terms the manner in which data input levels can be organized and then the way in which such data input serves as a base for macro and micro report generation.[32]

## Threats

The most vital step a company must take is to protect its corporate data base from physical destruction. Elaborate electronic protection is normally required for files on computers along with physical protection for print format. Backup tapes and backup files, sometimes at a remote location, can serve

---

32. Andrew C. Gross et al. *Business Marketing.* Boston: Houghton-Mifflin, 1993, pp. 618-623.

## Figure 10

## A Macro Report Pinpoints Sales Problem

A large U.S. multinational active in Canada noticed a decline in its central division current-month sales when in fact the commodity market in which it sold was known to be expanding rapidly. An investigation down to the branch and customer group levels discovered that a number of the retail customers in specific branch trading areas were being offered extremely favorable prices by another U.S. producer attempting to gain a foothold in the central division. Because the market threat was quickly pinpointed by geographic trading area and customer group, the multinational was able to respond immediately by instituting price cuts that countered the market-penetration strategy of the potential invader. The report system in this instance told management which customers and trading areas were most vulnerable to competitors, thus allowing the firm to undertake specific price cuts without generally depressing margins throughout its national distribution system.

Source: Andrew C. Gross, "The Information Vending Machine," *Business Horizons,* January/February 1988, p. 32.

## Figure 11

## Use of Micro Report Could Have Saved Company $47,000

The sales analyst of an integrated forest product producer became suspicious when reviewing the purchasing profile of one of the branch's largest customers. Historically, the industrial user bought only the vendor's premium quality products for remanufacture in his plants. The purchasing pattern changed dramatically, and the client suddenly began to concentrate on the vendor's poorest and cheapest grades of lumber. Branch and head office personnel ignored this change because sales volumes continued to remain large and current credit checks indicated no financial problems. The sales analyst's requests for further investigation were ignored. With virtually no warning the customer was placed in receivership by a competitor, and the vendor suffered a bad debt in excess of $47,000. The sales analyst's company now routinely reviews marked changes in customer purchasing behavior, having discovered that even relatively current credit checks can provide dated information.

Source: Andrew C. Gross, "The Information Vending Machine," *Business Horizons,* January/February 1988, p. 32.

this function. Companies must be on guard against both employee pilferage of data and outside intrusion. Passwords may need changing frequently.

Since most organizations realize how valuable their statistical data base is, there is little danger of budget cuts threatening the existence of such foundations. However, as the number of files grows, even in electronic format, it will cost more and more to keep them orderly and to make the data readily available to those needing access to them.

While many firms recognize the need for both physical protection of data and for streamlining the statistical system, relatively few have a good handle on how statistics and information in general should be managed. The reason? They cannot manage the politics. In the words of authors who analyzed the situation at length in several companies: "As information becomes the basis for organizational structure and function, politics will increasingly come into play. The most information-oriented companies are least likely to share the information freely."[33]

## Data from Statistical/Information Industry Firms and Nonprofit Agencies

In addition to statistics emanating from international agencies, national governments, and individual enterprises in the private sector, there is a fourth major category that is a rich source of business data. This is the world of information or statistical service organizations: market research companies, business consultants, not-for-profit think tanks, and a host of industry, trade, professional, and technical organizations. As is the case for individual businesses, these vary greatly in size, expertise, focus, client base, etc.

Their common characteristic is that they collect data on a small or large scale and make that data available either on a fee basis or as a matter of course to their membership (on-request, single fee, or on-subscription basis). The statistics that can be obtained this way are truly extensive and varied. They can range from a single table to vast printouts containing many time series.

---

33. J. McGee et al. *Managing Information Strategically.* New York: Wiley, 1993, p.152.

## Strengths

The flow of figures from the profit-making statistical service firms and from the many nonprofit organizations is much more focused than is the case for the data emanating from international agencies or the national government bureaus. The reason is that the mandate of the former is much more specific.

For example, because of long-time tradition, Dun & Bradstreet emphasizes its vast data holdings on the credit-worthiness of large and small companies. Along these lines, it developed expertise in the collection of data on a wide range of business attributes that can be analyzed by region, by industry, by size, etc. Its subsidiaries, including Dataquest, IMS, and A.C. Nielsen, offer statistics and focused information on the electronics, medical prescription, market research, and television fields.

A host of poll-takers (including news weeklies, electronic media, et al.) gather nationwide statistics on economic, social, and political patterns. In the case of nonprofit organizations, the trade/industry/technical groups also built up impressive credentials in their specific areas—from aviation safety records to zoo attendance, from generic drug sales to oil rig fires. Often, the information is available for many industrialized countries.

## Weaknesses

Like other organizations, the statistical service firms and nonprofit associations can lose their "agency" role (representing the interests of their clients, employees, members) and take on an institutional-type role (enhancing their own power, bureaucracy, status). However, competition from the marketplace or vocal complaints from the membership should steer the organization back to its "correct path." Another potential source of problems is the bias underlying the work of the enterprise. For example, consultants may give optimistic figures if they think that is what the client wants to hear, or may recommend a course of action extending their time of service to generate more fee income. In the case of think tanks and nonprofit trade groups, the bias is often well known (e.g., Brookings Institution is a more liberal think tank. American Enterprise Institute is a more conservative one. We expect the Pharmaceutical Manufacturers Association to take the interest of Merck or Pfizer).

One major weakness of an industry or a professional association may be that it is not a true cross-section of the group that it purports to represent. For example, only about one half of all U.S. physicians now belong to the American Medical Association compared to about three fourths some decades ago. In the same way, many of the manufacturing and service/trade associations may not include a host of new and small firms, and remain spokesmen only for large entities. Thus, statistics coming from them may not be indicative of industry trends and may even be misleading if the new/small firms are where the innovation is taking place. In the case of the statistical service firms, it is advisable to be familiar with the underlying methodology and collection procedures to judge clearly if the statistics have integrity and accuracy.

### Opportunities

The sky is the limit! Well, not quite, but given the thrust toward the information society, the enterprises that belong in this section should prosper and their data bases should be much in demand. We expect that both large and small statistical service firms, left or right of center think tanks, and the various trade and professional associations will be doing well during the coming decades. Given the advent of electronic data bases, networking, and existing plus proposed "information highways," the future is assured for those organizations that provide data to their clientele, readers, or members. They have an opportunity to expand abroad and to marry domestic with foreign data for an enhanced data base.

The crucial aspect, in our view, is the manner in which they carry out their research and the subsequent data processing. The dissemination will be relatively easy and, most likely, profitable. Validity and reliability are and will continue to be the two cornerstones. The underlying representativeness, the integrity of data gathering, and the accuracy of the figures must be assured. Above all, client needs must be paramount.

### Threats

We do not see a struggle between the public and private sector. There will always be friction as to which sector and which specific agency is best suited to collect data. There will also be conflict, undoubtedly, about pricing, access, privacy rights, and so forth. *But the pluralistic, diverse foundation of the statistical information domain should reassure us that various views will prevail and that negotiations will take place.*

A greater danger is that the budget constraints of government bureaus and the profit-seeking nature of statistical service firms may result in the neglect of certain topics. However, we think that even this is unlikely as the rise of many consumer, charitable, environmental, and "public interest" groups attest. These nonprofit associations seem able to raise needed funds to gather the statistics that meet their needs.

## Conclusion

In this chapter, we have conducted a SWOT analysis of four major categories for organizations that provide business and related statistics: international agencies; national government bureaus; the individual business enterprise; and the host of profit-making statistical service companies and both for-profit industry and professional associations. Our emphasis, as in other chapters, was on U.S. data and on the federal statistical system, but we have examined the broad spectrum of public and private providers of statistics.

Specifically, we looked at the strengths and weaknesses of the underlying data sets; i.e., the factors that make the existing statistics strong or weak in the eye of the users. We then moved from the question of "what is" to "what can be"—the opportunities and threats the data sets face and the manner in which their collection, processing, and dissemination are likely to unfold. It is, of course, not always possible to separate the data from the data collector. But our emphasis in this chapter was on the statistics themselves. In part two of the next chapter we focus more on the institutional role of the producing enterprises rather than on the characteristics of the data which they publish.

# Chapter 3

# Elements of the Statistical System— The Stakeholders and Interactions

It is a misnomer to call the statistical system a system. But despite the lack of order in the world of statistics there are many critical interactions among users, producers, and distribution channels. Often from different perspectives the users may also play the role of producers or distributors. There is no central control point or regular feedback mechanism that is characteristic of most systems. Yet the term "statistical system" is widely used as a descriptor of the sum of the various players in the process of developing the statistical information that serves as the cornerstone of modern decision making in public and private activities.

In this chapter we will discuss some of the important characteristics of

1. Uses and Users of statistics

2. Products and Producers of statistics

3. Collection, Presentation and Dissemination of statistics

The purpose of this discussion is to review some of the key elements that must be considered if we are to encourage the development of even better and more relevant statistics for decision making in the future. The following three sections deal with each of these sets of stakeholders in the development of statistical information.

## Section 1
## Uses and Users

At one point during long Congressional negotiations a few years ago, Senator Daniel P. Moynihan, Democrat from New York, said in frustration, "Look—everyone is entitled to their own opinions, but they're not entitled to their own *facts*."

Of course, as the Senator himself later ruefully recognized, the "facts" about the economy, as with other issues, are often hedged about with ambiguity, and very much subject to quite diverse interpretation, depending on the purposes of those who need and use them. The other chapters in this report deal directly with shortcomings and needed improvements in the information that is provided to users. In this section, we will look at the uses and the users of economic data. In particular, we will look at:

- Who are users of economic statistics;

- The different purposes—therefore, the different perspectives and interpretations—that different users bring to their use of economic statistics;

- Some of the unique, inherent complexities attached to information as a "product," including the famous problem that statistics can easily—too easily—"lie"; and

- Some of the promises, the problems, and the bottlenecks of on-line technologies to bring the information "products" more quickly and conveniently to the end-users of those products.

## Information Users

Whatever else the Information Age means, it certainly implies not only that there is more information available, but also that there are more users of information, including the quantitative information called statistics.

Statistics did not refer to the quantitative information that tracks economic and other movements and dimensions, but as the name suggests—to any facts or information about the state.[34] Scholars have traced its current quantitative sense back to 17th century England and to the book by William Petty called *Political Arithmetick*, which was a comparison of the military and economic resources of England, France, and Holland. The purpose of the book was to show the superiority of English power in both those arenas. A commentator from that time summed up the purpose of such statistics like this: "To help any ruler to understand fully that strength which is to guide and direct."[35]

Today, government remains simultaneously the largest producer and the

---

34. Paul Starr, "The Sociology of Official Statistics," in *The Politics of Numbers* (William Alonso and Paul Starr, Eds.). New York: Russell Sage Foundation, 1987, p. 15.

35. Ibid., p. 15.

---

largest consumer of statistics. Steven Kelman has pointed out that throughout our history, American legislators advanced arguments supporting statistical research that are consonant with the reasons advanced in 17th century England: first, statistical information is an important aid to the formulation of legislation and government policy; second, statistical information can serve as an important source of patriotic pride; third, information about particular groups within society can serve as an important signal to those groups of societal recognition; and fourth, information gathering by the state makes an important statement about the value of knowledge.[36]

In 1982, the Chairman of the Committee on National Statistics of the National Academy of Sciences, testifying before Congress, cited political administration as the primary reason for the gathering and use of statistics by government: "The executive branch and Congress use statistical data to aid the preparation of legislation....Statistics provide the infrastructure for government decision-making."[37]

While government has remained the primary user of statistical information, over time other user groups have emerged and gained greater prominence. In fact, in democratic societies, the wider spread of statistical information came to serve as a curb on the growth of governmental control. As Peter Buck put it, statistical information moved from being "a scientific prospectus for the exercise of state power" to "a program for reversing the growth of government and reducing its influence."[38]

Moreover, Kenneth Prewitt has cited research that shows, rather counterintuitively, that voters in the United States pay more attention to the economic statistics that track the economy in making political choices than they do to their individual economic circumstances.[39] (Jimmy Carter understood this point when he first fashioned the so-called "misery index," which he successfully used against Gerald Ford in 1976—and which was used successfully against him by Ronald Reagan in 1980.)

In recent decades, the largest growth in the user base of statistical infor-

36. Steve Kelman, "The Political Foundations of American Statistical Policy," in *The Politics of Numbers* (William Alonso and Paul Starr, Eds.). New York: Russell Sage Foundation, 1987, p. 276.

37. Ibid., p. 300.

38. Paul Starr, "The Sociology of Official Statistics," in *The Politics of Numbers* (William Alonso and Paul Starr, Eds.). New York: Russell Sage Foundation, 1987, p.15.

39. Kenneth Prewitt, "Public Statistics and Democratic Politics," in *The Politics of Numbers* (William Alonso and Paul Starr, Eds.). New York: Russell Sage Foundation, 1987, p. 263.

mation—a growth that is both cause and consequence of the "information revolution"—has been in the sector of private companies. The uses of information vary widely in private industry, as suggested by a partial listing of some of the roles that statistical information now plays:

- credit information used to evaluate both customer and suppliers;

- marketing information of all kinds  (about 1 million pages of scanner-based information provided each day to the customers of the world's largest market research organization, A.C. Nielsen);

- information used for stocking shelves;

- information for transferring funds;

- information about passenger loads in airlines; and

- information about credit card purchases.

This, obviously, is but a short illustrative and impressionistic listing of the ways that statistical information is currently used in private industry. Drawing on work from Fritz Machlup, Mark Porat, and Andrew Gross, Figure 12 on the next page presents spatially both the industries and the occupations in the private sector that are the heaviest users of information in the private sector.

Like all users of information, the private sector's differing needs give them differing priorities in terms of the speed with which they need information delivered. Those priorities, in turn, lead them to different modes of information delivery. Figure 13 ranges different users' needs for speed on one axis against the speed of delivery of different modes along the other.


## Information Anomalies

Different uses spur a variety of perspectives, and the object that is perceived from these different vantage points is, in any case, anomalous. After all, information is not a physical object nor can it be described, measured, or assessed as if it were. For one thing, unlike most products, information is not used up over time. In fact, the same information can be used an unlimited number of times without any deterioration in its value. On the other hand, the value of information can sometimes be very closely related to time: to know the winner of the Kentucky Derby thirty seconds before the

**Figure 12**

## Spatial Map of Information Content

**high**

*extent of information content - function*

Research development
Customized transactions
Marketing
Finance
Inventory
Accounting

Agriculture
Forestry
Mining
Construction
"Simple" manufacturing
Government
"Complex" manufacturing

Trade, wholesale &
retail
Nonprofessional ser-
vices
Financial, business
services
Sophisticated, profes-
sional services

**low** ——————————————————————— **high**

*extent of information content - industry*

Journals, newspapers
Newsletters
Abstracts, indexes
Shows, exhibits
Books, reports, monographs
Archives

**low**

Source: *Business Horizons*, January/February 1988.

Figure 13

## Spatial Map of Information Delivery

**high**

Automatic alarm/response
Face to face
On-line
Teleconference
Videotext

*speed of delivery*

Skill improvements
Retrospective search
General business news
Knowledge of industry
Information on distribution channel
New product knowledge
Pricing decision

Promotion, ad campaign
Competitior's action
Market expansion or contraction
Shift in sales, inventory
Purchase transaction
Credit rating
Medical, military action

**low** ——————————————————————————— **high**

*urgency or immediacy of need*

Journals, newspapers
Newsletters
Abstracts, indexes
Shows, exhibits
Books, reports, monographs
Archives

**low**

Source: *Business Horizons*, January/February 1988.

race begins is exceedingly valuable; to know the same thing three minutes later is virtually worthless. The same piece of information can have very different value, depending on the persons using it and their purposes.[40] The value of a given piece of geographical information, for example, might vary, depending on whether it is used by a driller looking for oil or by a land developer assessing the stability of the land.

Because of the time sensitivity of some information, a rough and ready estimate delivered sooner can sometimes be more valuable than exceedingly precise information delivered later. In other circumstances, inaccurate or bad information is much worse than no information at all. Indeed, that is why governments spend billions of dollars on "disinformation." Moreover, without prior purposes in mind, no information would ever be gathered for the simple reason that there would be no guiding criteria for what should be gathered.

*The key point from a user's perspective is that without prior purposes that suggest the shape of the answers needed, there are no questions, no research, and no gathering of statistical or any other kind of information.* Simon Kuznets noted, for example, the impossibility of measuring Gross Domestic Product without making philosophical choices about the end purpose of economic activity.[41] This point was stressed in Chapter 1.

Whose purposes, whose questions? A simple answer is: "Whoever has the power." We are familiar with the truth that "knowledge is power," that more information usually leads to more influence and greater power. It is equally true, but much less well understood, that power confers information.

Raymond Vernon has pointed out that politicians and policy makers are in charge of the technicians who gather statistics. "What such politicians and policy-makers share in common is an interest in using the data—sometimes, too, in suppressing or modifying them—to promote their national or international objectives."[42] Mark Perlman stated that "economic data are constantly used in the interpretation of economic events and the formulation of economic policies by both government and the private sector. But

---

40. Joseph W. Duncan, "The Worth and Value of Information," in *Critical Issues in the Information Age* (Robert Lee Chartrand, Ed.). Metuchen, NJ: The Scarecrow Press, 1991.

41. Paul Starr, "The Sociology of Official Statistics," in *The Politics of Numbers* (William Alonso and Paul Starr, Eds.). New York: Russell Sage Foundation, 1987, p. 51.

42. Raymond Vernon, "The Politics of Comparative Economic Statistics: Three Cultures and Three Cases," in *The Politics of Numbers* (William Alonso and Paul Starr, Eds.). New York: Russell Sage Foundation, 1987, p. 71.

which data are collected and how they are manipulated and analyzed depend on the underlying objectives of a statistical system."[43]

In the U.S., a great deal of information is gathered about both the agricultural and the manufacturing sectors of the national economy. Not nearly as much information is collected about the services sector, despite the fact that the services sector has become the fastest-growing, and by many measures the largest, sector of the American economy. Moreover, while we have a lot of data that describe large organizations, the amount of information available on smaller companies is much less exhaustive, even though smaller companies are playing a larger role in the economy, especially in the employment picture.

The difference in information about these economic sectors follows from the historic differences in power among them. Paul Starr pointed out that different political presuppositions or commitments by users often take the form of different statistical methods: The classic dispute about the national income accounts concerns the practice of not attributing any economic value to non-market services, such as those traditionally provided by women within the family.[44]

Moreover, as Starr indicated, "in determining the poverty rate, conservatives want to include in-kind income....On the other hand, advocates of the poor want the income cut-off for poverty raised because the original basis assumed that food was one-third of income," and multiplied by three the dollar value of a subsistence level of food to arrive at the poverty level. Reformers argue, however, that food no longer consumes as much as one third of the income of the poor, so that the multiplier should be greater than three.[45]

It is not just power in the political, economic, or social sense that guides the gathering and formulation of statistical research. It is also the power of encrusted habit and the on-going power of assumptions that are embedded "out of sight" in procedures. For example, historically, the Consumer Price Index (CPI) has been relatively slow in adding new items to its "market basket." For example, the CPI added cars in 1951 and pocket calculators in 1978. By the time each of these items had been added to the CPI's market

---

43. Mark Perlman, "Political Purpose and the National Accounts," in *The Politics of Numbers* (William Alonso and Paul Starr, Eds.). New York: Russell Sage Foundation, 1987, p. 133.

44. Paul Starr, "The Sociology of Official Statistics," in *The Politics of Numbers* (William Alonso and Paul Starr, Eds.). New York: Russell Sage Foundation, 1987, p. 47.

45. Ibid., p. 48.

basket, their prices had fallen dramatically, a price fall that was not immediately captured in the CPI.[46]

Moreover, Walter Wriston and others have pointed out that U.S. accounting methods for the deficit do not reflect "capital accounts"—that is, money spent for future investments. As Wriston put it, "everything from a 25-cent pencil to billions of dollars worth of bridges, roads and other productive assets is expensed." Who can doubt that the built-in assumptions of these statistical methods unconsciously shape national debate and, therefore, national policy making? Nikita Khrushchev is reported to have complained that in Russia it has become the tradition to produce not beautiful chandeliers to adorn homes, but the heaviest chandeliers possible. This is because the heavier the chandeliers produced the more a factory gets, since its output is calculated in tons.

In sum, the purposes of users determine the shape of information gathered and interpreted. That information, in turn, often determines the relative power of the users, and the kinds of policy that gets debated and enacted—often unconsciously.

## Methods of Information Delivery

In the preceding section, we reviewed the history of the past few decades, which has seen an explosion in the uses of statistical information by the private sector. Unquestionably, that use in the private sector has been made possible by new technologies that have not only allowed for the convenient and compact electronic storage of enormous amounts of data, but also have allowed for the data to be downloaded easily into the customers' own systems. Customers have the option to mix and meld the data with their own proprietary information, and then easily manipulate them to derive highly customized solutions to their own individual problems. This has also resulted in the formation of a number of private companies that have added value to the data that are routinely provided by the federal government for sale to customers.

In recent years, the Securities and Exchange Commission has been working on its so-called EDGAR Project, an electronic system that will allow companies to file their mandated 10K and 10Q reports electronically. This project would also allow private firms, as customers, to download those

---

46. Ibid., p. 50.

same reports without ever having to deal with hard copy.

The National Academy of Sciences now allows private parties, through the Internet services, to use their computers to conduct experiments and test hypotheses. It is easy to see that a similar kind of arrangement might allow for private concerns to use powerful government computers to carry out complicated econometric studies of economic inputs and outputs—computations requiring the simultaneous solutions of thousands of equations.[47]

Other new information technologies are coming onstream virtually every day. For example CD-ROMs now contain the most recent U.S. Census results replacing the cumbersome magnetic tapes associated with the 1960 and 1970 Census distribution effort. In sum, the extraordinary increase in the technologies of information, like the increased numbers of private players, is both cause and consequence of the so-called Information Revolution.

## Section 2
## Products and Producers

In this section, we will focus on the organizations producing the statistics about which we are concerned. While this review is not exhaustive, it is intended to illustrate the rich diversity that characterizes the development of statistical information. At times, we will suggest sources for more complete information on aspects of the field of statistical production.

We will enumerate key agencies, companies, or institutions and briefly comment on their past record and current situation. Next, we will take a brief look at how the statistics are generated. Some of the data can now be produced on an automated basis, for example, from bar codes, credit card transactions, and the like. Indeed, in the future, sensors will play a key role in how data are collected. The format of the generated data will be our next topic. Finally, we will consider some key issues ranging from the internal politics of the statistical agencies to the manner in which users are treated.

## Generators of Business/Economic/Social Data

Both government agencies and private businesses have kept tabs on eco-

---

47. Paul Starr and Ross Corson, "Who Will Have the Numbers? The Rise of the Statistical Services Industry and the Politics of Public Data," in *The Politics of Numbers* (William Alonso and Paul Starr, Eds.). New York: Russell Sage Foundation, 1987, pp. 415-447.

---

nomic activities (their own and that of others) since ancient times. The rise of modern statistical bureaus in the public sector and of the library or information center in the corporation is more recent, but can still be traced back over decades or even centuries. Over 200 years ago, the Constitution of the United States mandated a decennial population census. The U.S. Federal government spent approximately $2.6 billion on the 1990 decennial census including the full costs of planning, conducting, tabulating, and disseminating the results.

Most sovereign nations maintain a central statistical bureau for gathering data, with budgets ranging from lean to at least "moderately handsome." The trends cited by Sir Claus Moser[48] have continued. Since data gathering is not a glamorous activity, many public sector bodies find themselves part of the effort to reduce the overhead cost of governments and, as a result, statistical agencies in most countries are working with reduced budgets compared with real levels of 10 years ago.

Intergovernmental organizations that gather data are a relatively new phenomenon. In the 19th century, only a handful came into existence: the Universal Postal Union in 1874, the Metrics Union in 1875, and later the International Copyright Union. It was not until 1930 that the Bank for International Settlement was established. Most of the key agencies are products of the post-World War II period:

1944    *IBRD (World Bank); IMF; ICAO*

1945    *U.N. and its specialized agencies such as FAO, UNESCO*

1947-49 *GATT, OEEC (now OECD), COMECON, NATO*

1957    *EEC (now EC)*

1960    *OPEC, EFTA, LAFTA*

1960s   *UNCTAD, CARIFTA, others*

Since 1960, a host of other regional and international agencies have been created, some with narrow or special missions: for example, the African Timber Organization in 1976 and the International Jute Organization in 1984. We expect there will be more such bodies reflecting commodity interests. Each of these is likely to become a repository and a publisher of its statistics. However, each one will have to rely on cooperation from national

---

48. *Statistical Services in Ten Years' Time*, pp. 6-8 as quoted in Chapter 1.

and/or corporate memberships for its data collection, and often for data processing and dissemination. The combined data from contributors will be only as good as its parts.

Private sector companies and nonprofit associations constitute the final set of producers of statistics. As we pointed out earlier, each company is "king in its own castle" and, subject to accountants, auditors, and regulators, it controls the facts and figures about itself. Often, it is in the interest of the firm to publish data sets widely; other firms, especially those whose stock is not publicly owned, prefer to release as little as possible about themselves. Groups of companies, associations, and institutes develop their own mission. At first, they are directly responsible to their membership. Later on, as observers of corporate culture note, these organizations take on a life of their own, and may well become as bureaucratic as governments or large corporations.

The following quote illuminates the politicization process that public agencies undergo over time, but, in our view, the remarks are equally applicable to the data producers in the private sector and in associations:

"International bureaucrats have the same utility function as national bureaucrats...the economic theory of bureaucracy applies to both of them. Both try to maximize their power in terms of budget size, staff, and freedom of discretion and appreciate some leisure on the job. Both enjoy some freedom to pursue these objectives because in many respects they have acquired an information monopoly and because the politicians need their cooperation."[49]

In short, the statistical activities of organizations are as worth watching as are their other undertakings. Put briefly: Consider the source. *Put differently: Who says it, when, with how much integrity and accuracy, on what basis—and do they have an ax to grind?* In Figure 14 we show an abbreviated list of producers and some of their key statistical publications. The list is a small sample, but it is representative of the three layers discussed above and below.

In the international statistical arena, the dominant producer is the United Nations, especially its Statistical Division (UNSTAT). UNSTAT pioneered in giving the world the first comprehensive global set of data on both per capita national income and industrial production indices. UNSTAT also provided conversion ratios for comparing gross national product between market and

49. R. Vauble and T. Willett, Eds., *The Political Economy of International Organizations.* Boulder, CO: Westview, 1991, p. 39.

**Figure 14**

# Sort List of Producers

## Primary Sources

| | |
|---|---|
| International | *UN Demographic Yearbook* (United Nations)<br>*UN Statistical Yearbook* (United Nations)<br>*World Development Report* (World Bank)<br>*IMF Statistics* (International Monetary Fund)<br>*OECD Countries—National Accounts* (Organization for Economic Development, Paris)<br>*EC Statistics* (European Community)<br>*IDB Annual Report* (Inter-American Development Bank) |
| National | *Statistical Abstract of the United States* (U.S. Department of Commerce)<br>*USDC Census Report* (U.S. Department of Commerce)<br>   *Census of Manufactures*<br>   *Census of Service Industries*<br>*Survey of Current Business* (U.S. Department of Commerce)<br>*U.S. Industrial Outlook—Annual* (U.S. Department of Commerce)<br>*U.S. Tariff Commission Reports*<br>*Canada Yearbook* (Statistics Canada)<br>*Korea Yearbook*<br>*Statistical Yearbook of Hungary* |
| Company and Institutional | Annual and "10K" reports (especially in the United States)<br>Bank newsletters and reports<br>Filings with government agencies (export/import data, etc.)<br>Trade association surveys<br>Annual reports of nonprofit institutions<br>Research reports from universities<br>Foundation grant reports<br>Scientific and technical societies |

## Secondary Sources

| | | | |
|---|---|---|---|
| General Business Publications | *Business Week*<br>*Fortune*<br>*The Economist*<br>*Forbes*<br>*L'Expansion* | Newspapers | *Wall Street Journal*<br>*Wall Street Transcript*<br>*The Times* (United Kingdom)<br>*Financial Post* (Canada)<br>*Australian Financial Review*<br>*Figyelo* (Hungary) |
| Specific Trade/ Industry Publications | *Aviation Week*<br>*Computerworld*<br>*Coal Age*<br>*Datamation*<br>*Electronics* | | |

## Tertiary Sources and Special Publications

| | | | |
|---|---|---|---|
| Indices | *Business Periodicals Index*<br>*Canadian Business Periodical Index*<br>*Public Affairs Information Index*<br>*Predicasts F & S Indexes* (United States; Europe; rest of world)<br>*Public Affairs Information Index* | Directories | *Consumer Yellow Pages; Business to Business Yellow Pages*<br>*Dun & Bradstreet Million Dollar Directory*<br>*Standard & Poor's List of Companies*<br>*Thomas Register of American Manufacturers*<br>*Encyclopedia of Associations*<br>*Books in Print* (United States)<br>*British Books in Print* (United Kingdom)<br>*Ulrich's List of Periodicals*<br>*Business International*<br>*SRI International* (Stanford Research Institute)<br>*Disclosure*<br>*Value Line*<br>*Standard Rate and Data Service*<br>*Commerce Clearing House*<br>*Euromonitor* |
| Abstracts | *Dissertation Abstracts*<br>*Chemical Abstracts*<br>*Employment Abstracts* | | |
| Databases | On-line Databases (See Figures 16 and 17) | | |

planned economies. The UNSTAT and other agencies publish not dozens but hundreds of books and monographs, including global and regional volumes. To help users with access to the mountains of data, the UNSTAT publishes some guides, primarily its *Directory of International Statistics.*[50]

While UNSTAT and other U.N. agencies (e.g., United Nations Educational Scientific and Cultural Organization UNESCO) for social data can be viewed as "the fountainhead," a degree of healthy skepticism should be maintained vis-a-vis U.N. data. First, the statistics are only as good as those provided to it by the national statistical bureaus. Independent U.N. surveys are a rarity. Second, there are problems with timeliness of the data. For example, the U.N., which is revamping its System of National Accounts, published national accounts data in 1992, but they were data for 1990. Third, comparability over time, among nations, and even for a given country is "a continuing struggle." It is not unheard of to find discrepancies between two U.N. publications.

Like the U.N., other international agencies with a global outlook collect, process, and publish statistics. These include the World Bank, the International Monetary Fund (IMF), the General Agreement on Tariffs and Trade (GATT), and a host of autonomous or semi-autonomous agencies, such as the International Labour Office (ILO) in Geneva and the International Civil Aviation Organization (ICAO) in Montreal. As is the case with the U.N., these agencies also rely on data from member countries that in turn are checked and processed.

However, these groups have at least three distinct advantages: (1) the bureaucracy is somewhat smaller; (2) the subject area is more focused (i.e., labor for ILO, aviation for ICAO, finance for IMF); and (3) some primary surveys are undertaken that act as a check or balance. One of the most comprehensive statistical volumes is the *World Development Report.*[51] In addition to excellent charts and graphs, the volume includes thirty-three statistical tables in the appendix, complete with technical explanations on the construction of data.

Some private sector agencies now publish guides to the plethora of data emanating from the intergovernmental and international agencies. One such reference is the *Index to International Statistics* (IIS), published by the

---

50. United Nations Department of International Economic and Social Affairs Statistical Office, *Directory of International Statistics,* Vol. I. New York: United Nations, 1982, 274 pp.

51. Published by Oxford University Press, New York, for the World Bank, annually.

---

Congressional Information Service. The IIS is usually up-to-date and comprehensive, but it is also expensive. This U.S. firm also publishes the *American Statistics Index* and the *Statistical Reference Index* every month. Yet another reference is *SISCIS: Subject Index to Sources of Comparative International Statistics*. This volume, said to be cumbersome and often dated, is less costly than IIS and does offer a certain form of subject/geography index.[52]

We will discuss the format for data dissemination below. It is worth mentioning now that printed media (yearbooks and other references) are complemented and often replaced by electronic media, specifically traditional magnetic tapes (for computer mainframes), electronic on-line data bases (via networks or small computers with modems), computer readable data bases (in compact disc format, known as CD-ROMs, available in many libraries or for purchase and use in the office or at home), and diskettes. The most comprehensive and most recent guide is the *Gale Directory of Databases*.[53] This directory lists about 1,500 numerical data bases. See Figure 16 for details.

Among regional organizations, the Organization for Economic Cooperation and Development (OECD) is a prominent producer of data. This Paris-based organization is the umbrella group for the two dozen most industrialized nations and a few associate countries. Its key statistical publications include *Main Economic Indicators* and *National Accounts of the OECD Countries*. Its country surveys are also widely followed. The OECD has developed a variety of economic time series and data bases that are published in both comparative format and for individual nations. The OECD data sets are considered among the best, which is not surprising, since, unlike the U.N., the OECD does not deal with the newly industrializing and developing nations whose data collection and processing are incomplete and untimely. Because the OECD deals with far fewer nations than the U.N., it is able to publish more readable formats; e.g., the indicators are often portrayed in easy-to-read bar, line, or pie charts. The OECD also offers data on specific industries or sectors; e.g., pollution control spending, health care, and education.

---

52. Another useful publication is *International Organizations: A Dictionary & Directory*. Chicago: St. James Press, 1986. For an analysis of the agencies and the documents they produce, see another well-crafted volume, P. Hajnal, Ed., *International Information: Documents, Publications and Information Systems of International Government Agencies*. Englewood, CO: Libraries Unlimited, 1988.

53. Gale Research, Detroit, July 1993.

Statistical data bases are maintained by many other international and regional organizations besides the U.N. and its affiliate institutions, the World Bank, the IMF, and the OECD. The Statistical Office of the European Communities (Eurostat) collects, harmonizes, and disseminates statistical information on member countries and affiliates (e.g., the newly emerging Eastern European economies that seek association with the EC). The data availability and formatting have become better in recent years and access has been made easier for users outside the EC. Contents are available in both print and electronic formats.

Three major statistical data bases are available from Eurostat (which is headquartered in Luxembourg). They are:

1. *Chronos-economics statistics*, with over 800,000 time series going back to the 1960s by 25 subject areas. Featuring multilingual descriptions and product codes; three subfiles are available for a number of main indicators: Eurostatus (50 series), Eurostatistics (625 series), and ICG (3750 series);

2. *Comext* - trade statistics, organized by nomenclature, covering over 8,000 products and available by the Harmonized coding system; and

3. *Regio-regional statistics*, offering data on economic and social life in EC regions.

Still other sources of statistics are: the Bank for International Settlements (BIS); various regional banking agencies (e.g., Inter-American Development Bank and Asian Development Bank); various energy agencies (CERN and IAEA); and dozens of major and hundreds of minor industrial or regional bodies, some of which are not governmental but semi-public or indeed industry-affiliated. Budgets and staff size vary greatly, but the politics remain the same as those cited above for the international agencies.

"Are all countries' statistics equally dodgy?" was a question posed by a leading business journal almost two years ago.[54] Its answer was: "No!" The rankings are shown in Figure 15. What makes a good governmental statistical agency? According to the article: coverage and reliability; methodology used in collecting the data; and the integrity and objectivity of the bureau.

---

54. "The Good Statistics Guide," *The Economist*, Sept. 7, 1991, p. 66. See also "The Good Statistics Guide," *The Economist*, Sept. 11, 1993, p. 63.

---

Figure 15

## Number Crunchers Ranked

| Country | 1993 Statisticians' Ranking | 1991 Statisticians' Ranking | Revisions Percentage Points* | Timeliness# |
|---|---|---|---|---|
| Canada | 1 | 1 | 1.0 | 10 |
| Australia | 2 | 2 | 1.7 | 8 |
| Sweden | 5 | 3 | 2.4 | 5 |
| Holland | 3 | 4 | 1.6 | 9 |
| France | 4 | 5 | 1.3 | 6 |
| Germany | 6= | 6 | 3.0 | 1 |
| United States | 6= | 7 | 1.1 | 4 |
| Japan | 9 | 8 | 2.7 | 7 |
| Britain | 6= | 9 | 1.7 | 1 |
| Italy | 11 | 10 | 1.7 | 1 |
| Switzerland | 10 | | | |

* mean absolute deviation between initial estimate of GNP/GDP growth and final figure
# average speed of publication of GNP/GDP, industrial production, consumer prices, and trade statistics
1=fastest, 10=slowest
Source: "The Good Statistics Guide," *The Economist,* Sept. 7, 1991, p. 88; and "The Good Statistics Guide," *The Economist,* Sept. 11, 1993; the most recent article has more detail on the characteristics of governmental agencies than shown above.

Small countries came out on top, not simply because it is easier to collect statistics. Canada, Australia, Sweden, and The Netherlands have the advantage of centralized systems whose independence is carefully guarded. The statistical agencies in these nations were able to protect themselves better against budget cuts (if needed, they would cut selectively, not across the board). The larger countries have decentralized systems; the statisticians report to different ministers and are subject to varying political support. These agencies also find it hard to shift funding and to get extra money for surveys of new industries, such as high tech or services.

*The Economist* in the past has castigated the U.K. Central Statistical Office and labeled it one of the least independent, with "the figures often tasting of fudge."[55] This journal and others have often praised Statistics Canada. In Chapter 1, we commented on the work of the Bureau of the Census and the Bureau of Economic Analysis within the U.S. Department of Commerce and the Bureau of Labor Statistics in the U.S. Department of Labor. Basically, each of the three has a specific mandate and has carried it out quite well (see Chapter 1 and the composite ranking for the United States in Figure 15). *While there is often criticism of the quality of U.S. statistical agencies, in our view the agencies responsible for official statistics in the United States have a high degree of professionalism and integrity.*[56]

Interestingly, what the exhibit and the text above say about smaller Western countries having better statistical bureaus and numbers applies equally to non-Western nations. Specifically, in Eastern Europe, Hungary and other small nations had a better statistical collection system than the former Soviet Union.

As for the former Soviet Union, here is what V. N. Kirichenko, then Chairman of the USSR State Committee on Statistics, admitted in 1990. Elaborating on statistical shortcomings in the former Soviet Union with copious examples, he admitted to number padding, obvious whitewashing, the imperfection of computations, and the tendency to make the data fit the current political tasks. He called for conversion to the U.N. System of National Accounts, but admitted it would be a hard task requiring major effort and much time. Even before harmonizing with the rest of the world, he was hoping to:

"ensure the accuracy of the data...restore the trust in such data on the

---

55. Ibid.

56. For a discussion of integrity, see the special issue of the National Association of Business Economists' Journal, *Business Economics*, July 1993.

---

part of the Soviet and international public. The country can no longer afford to seek the right way with the help of trick mirrors."[57]

A noble undertaking, indeed, but it will not happen before the 21st century. The challenge associated with building a better system of official statistics for the coming century will be to assist the former Soviet bloc countries and the developing nations in implementing new concepts and procedures more in tune with future needs. *It would be a missed opportunity if these countries simply adopted outmoded systems of the market-economy countries.*

As noted above, industry, trade, technical, and professional groups in the U.S. and around the world generate a wealth of data in areas of interest to their membership. As noted by social scientists, these nonprofit organizations, like public agencies, can take on a bureaucratic role as the staff sees and seizes an opportunity and runs with it, at times without the consent of the "governed." It is not unusual to have some turmoil about the directions that an association should take.[58] In our judgment, there are vast differences in both the quantity and the quality of the data among the various associations. *Business economists and managers need to analyze the publications, the integrity, accuracy, timeliness, and coverage of their data—just as they would for data issued by government, the private sector, and universities.*

As a general rule, we find that associations that conduct on-going surveys, with updates as needed, do a better job on data collection and data processing than those that do ad hoc or one-time studies. For example, ADAPSO (which was recently incorporated into the Information Technology Association of America) has done a fine job of collecting statistics for years from its membership which is considered representative of computer service firms across the U.S. In the pollution control field, the Water and Wastewater Equipment Manufacturer Association maintained good directories with indices, but did little data collection, leaving the task to others, such as the federal Environmental Protection Agency and another nonprofit group, the Water Pollution Control Federation.

Professional and technical groups generate some statistics, but these associations are organized much more along occupations and special interests than along industrial lines. This can be an advantage for the business researcher if the focus is on technology, which cuts across several industrial

---

57. V.N. Kirichenko, "Return Credibility to Statistics" *Business Economics,* October 1990 pp. 50-57.

58. For a good overview and running commentary on this topic, see various issues of *Association Management.*

lines. Engineering societies maintain special interest groups (SIGs) that often generate useful statistics. Other groups publish the results of their meetings. For example, the *Chemical Market Research Association Proceedings* (annual) are for sale and constitute a treasure trove on subfields of the chemical industry. The European Society for Opinion and Market Research (ESOMAR) sponsors both an annual congress and special seminars whose *Proceedings* are available for a fee. Many other examples could be cited but the important point is that statistics about industrial and technological trends are available from a rich set of institutions.

Think tanks, university research bureaus, scientific institutes, and foundations represent yet another source of statistical data. Various directories, e.g., the *Research Center Directory*, offer subject indices for the alphabetic or geographic listing of such organizations. This way, one can ascertain quickly the expertise offered. A simple phone or fax call will bring a reply as to available publications and data. For example, the Aviation Safety Institute in Columbus, Ohio, has become an independent and well-respected voice in its field, beholden neither to industry nor to government. Universities on the West Coast specialize in having excellent data on Pacific Rim nations, while those on the East Coast have developed repositories about European countries. Foreign emissaries and consulates are also willing to share data, e.g., the European Community and the OECD maintain information offices in Washington, D.C.

## How and Where Statistics Are Generated

Quantitative information is still largely produced in traditional ways: via surveys, through observations, and rarely from experiments. In the electronic age of the late 20th century and into the 21st century, data will be increasingly collected in an unobtrusive fashion—especially if safeguards for privacy and confidentiality can be provided. The Universal Product Code has made it possible for many firms to track shipments, sales, and retail outlet behavior through analysis of scanner data collected on the basis of these bar codes on packages and documents. Of course, millions of transactions are already routinely recorded as a result of purchases, or even lack of same (e.g., a company may determine that 40% of their long-time clients did not place an order this past month).

"The ability to collect and analyze information about individuals is about to increase exponentially."[59] Information highways, electronic payment systems, smart buildings, and a host of sensors will ease the task of individuals, but at the same time provide "grist" for the "data mill" or data bases of commercial, public, or nonprofit organizations. On the positive side, the marvels of the computer-communication age will allow collection of data on millions of individuals and thousands of enterprises. On the negative side, there may be objections to close monitoring and to the sharing of data by and among the data collecting agencies. For example, several new regulations are being proposed to protect individuals from errors in their files at credit agencies. However, it should be noted that the power of the computer to increase record keeping efficiency will as a natural by-product lead to the development of useful data bases for the corporate decision maker.

As mentioned earlier, U.S. and foreign governments conduct censuses on a regular basis. The mandate to the U.S. Bureau of the Census is to conduct a decennial census of population. It also surveys businesses including manufacturing and minerals, services, construction, retail and wholesale trade, and transportation every five years. Other governments do much the same, such as Statistics Canada conducting its population count in years ending with 1, and also surveying Canadian industries on a regular basis. Given the high level of controversy and legal wrangle about the 1990 U.S. population census, it is quite possible that the Census Bureau may yet turn to alternative modes of data collection; "electronic filing by respondents" may replace census enumerators knocking on doors. An extensive literature is being developed on alternative procedures for the census to be taken in the year 2000.

The collection, processing, and dissemination of the data in both the public and private sectors may undergo radical changes. The next section of this chapter will provide some examples of change in the area of dissemination. For example, all levels of government are dedicated to easing traffic congestion. Necessary data can now be collected via observation posts and sensors rather than asking truckers and motorists to fill out survey forms. Data banks are also being created across interstate lines on crime, weather, welfare, solid waste disposal, electric power use, etc. The challenge will be either to devise representative samples or to conduct censuses in an unobtrusive fashion. There is also extensive literature[60] concerning the use of

59. "No Hiding Place," *The Economist*, August 7, 1993, p. 16.

60. The bibliographic review conducted as background for this study has referenced a number of papers and reports on this topic.

administrative records in the development of official statistics.[61, 62]

In the private sector, credit card transactions serve as the focal point for data collection and analysis. In addition, supermarkets, drug stores, and many other large retail operations routinely collect data via optical scanning of the Universal Product Code. This is useful, but when combined with a consumer identification tag, a powerful marketing tool is born. A. C. Nielsen and other companies are using this combination to build data bases about shopping habits to evaluate promotional campaigns and analyze shoppers, including those who bought and those who did not buy a product. While unobtrusive, this raises privacy issues, so cooperation via signed release forms is normally arranged beforehand and participants in panels are often rewarded for their cooperation.

Surveys will have to be rethought, whether one-time or repetitive. The era of digital television with interactive capabilities is around the corner. Within a few years such capabilities will be in the majority of homes. This will be driven by games and video entertainment, but home information services will be a by-product. As a consequence, it is likely that statistical services, market research, and nonprofit groups will begin to establish ongoing, but rather brief electronic survey forms for participants (print will be an option). In other words, the questionnaire will be flashed on a computer on an interactive television screen and the respondent will be asked to enter numbers or check boxes. To make this easy on survey participants, the forms will be relatively brief because the panel characteristics will be in a related master data base.[63] New questions may be added, old ones can be dropped, but some continuity will be maintained for longitudinal comparisons.

In the meantime, electronic data interchange (EDI) is gaining momentum. This requires common concepts and definitions with a common reporting format being a natural by-product. Most recently, several foundations in the New York and Philadelphia areas agreed to have a single format for grant applications. This trend is likely to spread.

---

61. See William P. Butz, "The Future of Administrative Records in the Census Bureau's Demographic Activities," *Journal of Business and Economic Statistics,* Vol. 3, Iss. 4, 1985, pp. 393-395.

62. See also Thomas B. Jabine and Fredrick J. Scheuren, "Goals for Statistical Uses of Administrative Reords: The Next Ten Years," in *Proceedings of the American Statistical Association,* Section on Survey Research Methods, 1984 Annual Meeting (August 13-16, 1984, Philadelphia, PA). Washington, DC: American Statistical Association, 1985, pp. 66-75.

63. Some particularly innovative experiments on this concept have been conducted in The Netherlands.

## Data Availability: Formats, Time Lag, Prices

The traditional output format of statistical agencies, be they large or small, public or private, has been that of printed matter. The U.S. government has produced massive volumes of data from the various censuses and other countries; central statistical bureaus also opted for books, reports, and monographs. In the private sector, we find yearbooks, occasional reports, etc., in printed form as well. The time delay on these has varied tremendously. Some census reports are available in preliminary form in a matter of months; but it is fair to say that the final volumes often come with a lag of several years. Trade associations, institutes, and other organizations also can vary in making their survey results available in time frames ranging from one month to one year in time lags.

The move away from print is caused by the revolution in on-line and CD-ROM format. Data bases became available electronically toward the end of the 1970s and early 1980s, but the growth has been especially sharp in the past ten years. This is due largely to the advent of the personal computer, the lowered cost of telecommunications, and the resulting linking of terminals into networks. Organizations and individuals now have easy access to vast storehouses of data in a variety of formats and locations.

Figure 16 on the next page shows the recent trends in U.S. data bases by producer status and by format. The role of the private sector has grown and that of the public sector has declined in the past seven years. (This is in line with what has been cited above, namely, that budget and staff of the eight major statistical agencies were reduced by about 13% and 10%, respectively, during the 1980-88 period.) We attribute much of the rise of the private sector to aggressive marketing on the part of data base vendors, such as Dialog, Mead Data Central, Reuters, BRS and others. Now government agencies are also taking a more aggressive stance. Both U.S. statistical agencies and Statistics Canada are actively marketing computer tapes, laser disks, diskettes, and CD-ROM, as well as making data available on-line. Statistics Canada has designed an easy-to-use volume called *The Market Research Handbook*. These and similar steps show that government agencies are becoming user-friendly by offering their data in new and more usable formats.

The most popular form for electronic retrieval is on-line according to Figure 16. However, we expect that many industrial enterprises will follow the lead of college and public libraries and acquire CD-ROM readers for their small computers (or for their information centers). Thus, CD-ROM

**Figure 16**

## Recent Trends in Data Bases

**Part A: Databases by type**

| Class | 1985 no. | 1985 % | 1992 no. | 1992 % |
|---|---|---|---|---|
| Word-oriented | 1926 | 64 | 4925 | 70 |
| Number-oriented | 1084 | 36 | 1533 | 22 |
| Image | | | 272 | 4 |
| Audio | | | 83 | 2 |
| Electronic service | | | 146 | 2 |
| Software | | | 39 | 0+ |
| Total | 3010 | 100 | 6998 | 100 |

**Part B: Databases by medium for access or distribution**

| Type | 1992 no. | 1992 % |
|---|---|---|
| On-line | 4519 | 65 |
| Batch | 320 | 5 |
| CD-ROM | 1088 | 15 |
| Diskette | 557 | 8 |
| Magnetic tape | 481 | 7 |
| Handheld | 33 | 0+ |
| Total | 6998 | 100 |

**Part C: Databases by producer status**

| Sector | 1985 % | 1992 % |
|---|---|---|
| Government | 21 | 15 |
| Commerce/industry | 57 | 75 |
| Nonprofits | 11 | 9 |
| Mix | 11 | 1 |
| Total | 100 | 100 |

Source: K.Y. Marcaccio, Ed., *Gale Directory of Databases, Volume 1*, Detroit: Gale Research, July 1993, pp. xxii-xxvii.

should gain market share from on-line in the future. Here again, public agencies show some initiative; e.g., the U.S. Department of Commerce's National Trade Data Bank now comes on a compact disc rather than as a lengthy printout or book. The U.S. Department of Commerce's bureaus and the U.S. Department of Labor's Bureau of Labor Statistics offer delivery via magnetic tape, diskettes, CD-ROM, microfiche, and electronic news services.

Our experience with electronic format indicates that the time lag in publishing is far less than is the case for the printed format. In many cases, private sector firms and nonprofit institutions make their data available in a matter of several days or a few weeks at the most. Data from Conference Board Surveys, the University of Michigan Survey Research Center's Surveys of Consumers, and the Purchasing Managers Monthly Survey are some examples.[64] Typically, in the 1990s, a study can be conducted on a topic by an agency or association and results are expected to reach all users within a few weeks. For example, shipment data obtained in a survey of machine tool manufacturers conducted by an association in the month of May, is tabulated in June, and findings are reported in an article in the July 1993 issue of *Machine Design*. The abstract of the article, complete with key tables, are available to on-line users by mid-August and to CD-ROM users in September. Some would argue that the print format is still out first. This is true, but there is a tremendous advantage to the electronic form. It affords a concise view of the data and the literature, provides a comparison with other surveys, and therefore gives a better perspective. Furthermore, in some cases, the survey may not even appear in print format; it may be made available to users only on-line, on diskette, or CD-ROM.

Although the CD-ROM format is gaining in popularity (under such names as Wilsondisc or Silver Platter), on-line remains more popular because it allows a broader access to giant data bases stored in vast information warehouse files.[65] The rapid rise of data bases, on-line services, and subscribers in the United States is documented for the 1980s in Figure 17 on the following page. Further growth is expected. Subscribing to an on-line service is relatively simple. All the user needs is a personal computer, a modem, a phone line, and a contract. What is more difficult is to choose

---

64. Indeed, as early as the late 1970s, Predicasts of Cleveland abstracted thousands of articles and tables, transferred the information to magnetic tape, and shipped them via air to Dialog of Palo Alto, which then made the abstracts available on-line. Approximate elapsed time from abstract to on-line availability was less than two weeks at that time. By now, this has been cut in half, though there can be processing delays.

65. For an early overview on this topic, see Andrew Gross, "The Information Vending Machine," *Business Horizons*, Jan/Feb 1988, pp. 24-33.

Figure 17

## Growth of Data Bases, On-line Services and Subscribers in the U.S., 1980—1990

|  | 1980 | 1982 | 1984 | 1986 | 1988 | 1990 |
|---|---|---|---|---|---|---|
| Number of Databases[a] | 400 | 965 | 1,878 | 2,901 | 3,699 | 4,465 |
| Number of Database Producers[b] | 221 | 512 | 927 | 1,379 | 1,685 | 1,950 |
| Number of On-Line Services[c] | 59 | 170 | 272 | 454 | 555 | 645 |
| Number of Gateways[d] |  |  |  | 35 | 59 | 88 |
| Number of Subscribers (thousands) |  |  |  |  |  |  |
| General Interest |  |  | 326.1 | 677.0 | 1,018.6 |  |
| Business/Financial |  |  | 377.1 | 558.6 | 726.6 |  |
| Scientific/Technical |  |  | 229.2 | 345.8 | 404.5 |  |

[a]Databases: Computer-readable collections of data available for interactive access by users from remote terminals or microcomputers. Databases can be "reference" (bibliographic or referral) or "source" (numeric, textual, numeric-textual, full-text, etc.).

[b]Database producers: Suppliers of databases, primarily publishers of print indexes and abstracts journals, but also publishers of other reports who transform and submit the data on magnetic tape to on-line vendors.

[c]On-line services or vendors: Time-sharing firms, network information services, remote computing services, etc., who provide access to databases.

[d]Gateways: Any computer service that acts as an intermediary between users and databases; several categories exist.

Sources: Lines 1-4: *Directory of On-Line Databases, 1991.* New York: Cuadra/Elsevier, 1991, p. v.; Lines 5-7: *Information Industry Factbook 89/90.* Stamford, CT: Digital Information Group, 1989, p. 229.

among the many offerings and to devise an effective search strategy.

Thousands of data bases are available from hundreds of on-line firms, but not all data bases are available from all on-line suppliers. Users must shop around. The producers of data bases (e.g., Wilson for BPI, Predicasts for PTS) sell their output to the on-line services such as Dialog, Reuters, and BRS. The most comprehensive listing currently is the *Gale Directory of Databases*[66] that combines previous publications.

## Selected Key Issues

It is a common view that statistical producers should keep in mind users' needs. What are users' needs and what can the users do to keep the producers on their toes and to get the best value from the output—the statistical system, the time series, the individual data points? To say: *caveat emptor* or *caveat vendidor* (let the buyer beware, let the seller beware) is a cop-out or a cliché. Better to say: "Let both users and producers be alert, aware and awake!"

Alert and awake to what? To each other's characteristics! Users, as discussed earlier, must define or at least describe their activities, needs, desires, and preferences in rather distinct ways if they want producers to be responsive. Know thyself! *As a general rule, users want extensive coverage; ease of access; timeliness, not time delays; accuracy (validity, reliability); clear-cut methodology (consistency and continuity); and integrity of both the data and the source. When the producers of data keep these requisites in mind, the result should be strong demand for the figures.*

Coverage of a statistical system or data base will be defined by its owner or producer—or, as we saw in the case of governments, it may well be mandated. As internal and external conditions change, however, the coverage is likely to be altered to adjust to the new situation. This is fine, but it is necessary for the producers to explain the new, and link up the new concepts with the old. Tables should highlight both the new format and the linkage to the previous set of data.

For example, the Federal Reserve Board just revised its industrial production indices and capacity utilization figures. The coverage is similar to that of the past, basically covering U.S. manufacturing. The specific linkage with previous indices should be made clear, not hidden in footnotes. Similar rules

---

66. Gale Research, Detroit, July 1993.

would apply to other government bureaus and to private sector firms as well as nonprofit associations. Of course, definitions can be a challenge and can affect coverage. For example, what is a computer — a mainframe, a midsize machine, a desktop unit, a portable device, or even a smart terminal? Technology does not wait (e.g., notebook computers and personal message pads), but the data gatherer must make a decision, then live by it, and explain it.

Ease of access implies availability in the various formats, print and electronic, discussed above. Ease of access, just as importantly, implies good indexing, possible use of a thesaurus, an excellent table of contents, friendly-face graphics, and making the data "jump" at the user. Again, linkage with previous sets of numbers would be useful along with methodological explanations in clear terms. On the matter of how to present statistical data, the discussion in the next section provides some suggestions. Finally, the producer should make itself accessible to users by publishing phone and fax numbers. Inquiries should be answered as promptly as possible.

We have already discussed time delays along with format and pricing in the previous section, so we comment on related aspects here. Since the release of federal statistics is closely followed, the clientele is now wedded to specific dates. Some reporters stand by and rush to call in the released data for next-day publication or same-day evening news on radio and television. Of course, major undertakings are often released piecemeal fashion and often require subsequent revisions, as is the case with data from the Census of Population, other censuses, or GDP growth estimates.

Statistics from businesses and associations are also expected on time, but again, some delays or revisions are inevitable. In the words of *The Economist*,[67] "By themselves, revisions are a poor gauge of statistical accuracy. If a country did not bother to revise its figures or if it delayed publication for a year until all the detailed information was in, it would have no revisions, but its statistics would be poor."

As systems are designed for future decision making, we hope the subject of accuracy will get the recognition it deserves. Once again we refer to the pioneer in this field, Oskar Morgenstern in his book, *On the Accuracy of Economic Observations*.[68] Other famous economists, such as Kendrick, Kuznets, et al. also made significant contributions. In the 1950s and 1960s, economics was truly a one-digit science, though few would admit to that.

---

67. *The Economist*, Sept. 7, 1991, p. 88.

68. Oskar Morgenstern, *On the Accuracy of Economic Observations*, 2nd Ed. Princeton: Princeton

Later, as collection and processing methods became more refined, the situation improved. However, even today, we see errors in the range of +20 percent for developing and +5 percent to +10 percent for developed nations (with refinement upon revision). Causes of statistical error include poorly trained poll takers, ambiguous survey forms, misguided classification schemes, deliberate misinformation by respondents, evasion of regulators, and non response.

Past data are one thing, forecasts are another. Economic and business forecasting will continue, because there is much demand for it. A wide variety of qualitative and quantitative techniques are discussed in various business research, marketing,[69] and forecasting texts. In the volume written by co-author Gross it is stated that the best route to follow is to do composite or combination forecasting—because it considers many sources and combines the best features of qualitative and quantitative techniques. The Blue Chip indicators track record previously cited is another testimonial endorsing this thinking. The fearless forecaster has yet another tool; that is, to combine the notion of the buildup and the breakdown method. The former calls for combining shipments of all producers; the latter means ratio analysis from GDP on downward.

For our purposes here, the most interest centers on the track record of intergovernmental and international agencies and national government bureaus in this regard. Figure 18 shows an interesting comparison of OECD and IMF forecast errors. The authors who analyzed these errors,[70] from Indiana University and the Canadian Bank of Commerce, conclude that while in the 1970s there was an optimism bias, in the 1980s this bias disappeared, which is encouraging. Most significantly, they conclude that there is no evidence that the published forecasts of the international organizations are superior to the national forecasts. Partly because of this and partly because some parties gain early access to confidential information, they suggest that the IMF and OECD, et al. refrain from forecasting.

Sound statistical methodology involves more than having extensive coverage, more than being on time, and more than trying to be accurate. At the most fundamental level, the key facets focus on integrity, consistency, and continuity. One final word here in regard to the boundary line between

---

69. Andrew Gross et al., *Business Marketing*. Boston: Houghton-Mifflin, 1993, pp. 163-173.

70. See M. Fratianni and J. Pattison, "International Institutions and the Market for Information," in *The Political Economy of International Organizations* (R. Vaubel and T. Willet, Eds.). Boulder, CO: Westview Press, 1991, pp. 100-122.

**Figure 18**

## OECD and IMF Forecast Errors

**Forecast Error When Forecast was Made in the
First Half of the Current Year**

| | Mean Absolute Error | | | | | |
|---|---|---|---|---|---|---|
| | Real GNP Growth | | Inflation % | | Current-Account Balance (billions of dollars) | |
| | OECD | IMF | OECD (Consumption deflator) | IMF (CPI) | OECD | IMF |
| US | 0.54 | 0.83 | 0.26 | 0.51 | 11.44 | 16.21 |
| Japan | 0.71 | 0.56 | 0.43 | 0.79 | 5.81 | 6.58 |
| Germany | 0.91 | 1.05 | 0.39 | 0.28 | 4.42 | 5.18 |
| France | 0.62 | 0.47 | 0.46 | 0.63 | 2.76 | 3.11 |
| UK | 0.46 | 0.79 | 0.78 | 0.86 | 3.17 | 2.15 |
| Italy | 0.82 | 0.84 | 0.69 | 0.54 | 2.44 | 2.57 |
| Canada | 1.19 | 1.32 | 0.53 | 0.87 | 2.51 | 3.68 |
| G7 | 0.75 | 0.83 | 0.51 | 0.64 | 4.65 | 5.64 |

| | Root mean square error | | | | | |
|---|---|---|---|---|---|---|
| | Real GNP Growth | | Inflation % | | Current-Account Balance (billions of dollars) | |
| | OECD | IMF | OECD | IMF | OECD | IMF |
| US | 0.54 | 0.83 | 0.26 | 0.51 | 11.44 | 16.21 |
| Japan | 0.71 | 0.56 | 0.43 | 0.79 | 5.81 | 6.58 |
| Germany | 0.91 | 1.05 | 0.39 | 0.28 | 4.42 | 5.18 |
| France | 0.62 | 0.47 | 0.46 | 0.63 | 2.76 | 3.11 |
| UK | 0.46 | 0.79 | 0.78 | 0.86 | 3.17 | 2.15 |
| Italy | 0.82 | 0.84 | 0.69 | 0.54 | 2.44 | 2.57 |
| Canada | 1.19 | 1.32 | 0.53 | 0.87 | 2.51 | 3.68 |
| G7 | 0.75 | 0.83 | 0.51 | 0.64 | 4.65 | 5.64 |

Sources: *OECD Economic Outlook*, various issues; *World Economic Outlook*, IMF, various issues.

Quoted in M. Fratianni & J. Pattison, "International Institutions and The Market for Information" in *The Political Economy of International Organizations* (R. Vaubel and T. Willett, Eds.). Boulder, CO: Westview Press, 1991, pp. 100-122.

accuracy and integrity on the one hand, and dissemination and presentation on the other. The business users, like the public at large, tend to be skeptical, and the notion of lies, damn lies, and statistics is hard to overturn.[71] One of the best ways to reassure clients is for producers of the data to make modest claims.

Producers must observe confidentiality and security. How can the producers assure those who cooperate with them that privacy and secrecy will not be violated? This is also a matter of trust, confidentiality, and collaboration. After all, government bureaus, private sector firms, and associations ultimately rely on the goodwill of various respondents, be they in the hundreds or in the millions. Sound public relations can help, but it is even more important to assure and reassure the participants that confidentiality and privacy will be strictly observed.

As more information ends up in government and corporate data bases, a line must be drawn between a public or private organization's need to know and individuals' (and groups') right to privacy. Recently, Prof. H. J. Smith of Georgetown University advanced the idea of the following "audit points" in regard to privacy:[72]

1. scrutinize the sensitivity of personal data being collected (is it needed, could it be obtained otherwise, etc.);

2. avoid deception—claiming to collect data for one purpose, using it for another as well as secrecy—collecting data by hidden means;

3. secure the subject's permission;

4. values and judgment play a key role in ensuring data integrity; make decisions about error levels in an explicit fashion;

5. establish strong organizational controls; and

6. beware of automation, including automated decisions, sensors, etc. In regard to this last point, there is merit in using anonymous procedures as opposed to those that identify individuals (e.g., auditrons or keycards, rather than charge or credit cards).

---

71. D. Huff, *How to Lie with Statistics*. New York: Norton, 1954 and W. Wallis and H. Roberts, *The Nature of Statistics*. New York: Free Press, 1956, both enjoyed good publicity at the time of their publication and were reprinted later in paperback editions. Their warnings are worth reading and heeding.

72. H. J. Smith, "A Matter of Privacy," *Beyond Computing*, July/August 1993, pp. 62-63.

In this section, we focused on the production and the producers of statistics and statistical systems. Although these cannot be separated entirely from the underlying data, we attempted to highlight about "what is" (including what is right and what is wrong) and "what ought to be" in bringing forth the wealth of numbers and in making the output available. Producers and users must and do live together in a close relationship. As noted much earlier, producers at times become users and vice versa. On the whole, we find that the production of statistics has occurred at a high level, though there is room for improvement.

## Section 3
## Collection, Presentation, and Dissemination of Statistics

In this section, we are focusing on the most practical aspects of data processing: how do you collect the numbers, how do you present them, and how do you deliver them to audiences? We have touched on these topics in other chapters and we do not wish to compete with established textbooks in the field. Our remarks are aimed at both the practicing statisticians and business economists to whom these may sound rather familiar (though we hope they too would find some nuggets) and those who "toil in the trenches" in the form of statisticians, analysts, economists, strategists and others who rely upon statistical input. We shall be relying on our experience and past research as well as on works by others in a variety of old and new publications.

To look ahead at our topics, we can sum up the thrust of our remarks in this fashion:

1. Yes, censuses can be useful and at times are mandated, but consider sampling as a realistic alternative at most times and under many conditions;

2. Presentation of statistics involves several diverse facets. All are important: substitutive, statistical, and artistic (graphical); and

3. Dissemination must consider less the publicity needs of the producer group and more the preferences of users and audiences.

Permeating all of the above is modern technology which holds out rich promises and, in some cases, already delivers better sampling, clearer and more exciting presentation, and user-friendly distribution.

## Collection of Data

"What do we know and what do we want to know? The two most fundamental concepts of statistics are those of a sample and a population." So begins Chapter 5 of one of the classic statistics volumes, though it was seldom used as a textbook.[73] They restate the obvious: a sample is not a miniature replica of the population; sample results vary by chance; and the pattern of chance variation depends on the underlying population. So why would anyone want to sample if a complete count can be obtained? There are good reasons.

We turn to sampling when:

1. a complete count is impossible or impractical;

2. the gain in accuracy from a census may not be worth the cost;

3. the individual measurements may not be as accurate for a census as for a sample;

4. the underlying population or universe contains infinitely many items; and

5. the population is inaccessible and no more data can be had from it.

The authors give examples and useful details. For our purpose, point number 3 is worth elaborating here, because the point is so applicable to official or government statistics. In the words of Wallis and Roberts:

"A rather paradoxical example of the effective use of samples is the Bureau of Census' use of them to check on the accuracy of the census. Although sampling error is almost absent from the census, the non sampling errors may be considerable; that is, such errors as those arising from failure to make questions clearly understood, from misrecording replies, from faulty tabulation, from omitting people who should have interviewed. In the sample census {sic}, however, these non sampling errors may be reduced enough to offset the sampling error, for it is cheaper and easier to select, train, and supervise a few hundred well-qualified interviewers to conduct a few thousand careful

---

73. W.A. Wallis and H.V. Roberts, *The Nature of Statistics*. New York: The Free Press,1956.

interviews than it is to select, train, supervise 150,000 interviewers to conduct a complete census of population."[74]

The authors then go on to explain why in the light of the above, nationwide censuses are still taken. The overriding reason mentioned by them (and by us in a previous chapter) is the mandate of the Constitution; another is that information is often required for small groups in a large population; e.g., small towns, ethnic neighborhoods, etc. as well as for the country as a whole.

What is true for government bureaus is also applicable to private firms and to nonprofit groups. Companies must re-think whether it is necessary to poll every employee, vendor, or client or whether a sample would do. In the same way, associations need to ask whether a well-designed sample would serve as well. Certainly, few legal requirements exist in this area. The frequency of census or sample-taking requires careful consideration as well.

## Presentation of Data

The wide range of statistics that are useful for decision making is evident in the number of regular publications on the shelves of planners, analysts and decision makers. In the past, the traditional form of presentation has been tables and text in the print media. Government censuses arrive in massive reports (hardbound or paperback), though early results are promulgated in brochures and flyers. Corporate statistics come in the form of annual and quarterly reports, news releases, and the like. These are the primary forms, while the secondary forms consist of a wealth of tables and text in journals and newspapers. Finally, the tertiary forms, indexes and abstracts, give us an overview and access to the above.

These traditional forms (both their content and their style) changed relatively little until the arrival of the Information Age. By the 1990s, as we saw earlier, the producers of data have committed themselves to the electronic era. Today, central statistical bureaus make available data to users in the form of: magnetic tape for mainframes; diskettes for personal computers; on-line; CD-ROM (compact disk). Statistics from companies are becoming available in the same way, plus, on occasion, in the form of slides, videotape, and even multimedia.

---

74. Ibid., p. 138.

---

On demand or automated delivery are not unheard of. It is possible to download data from large to small computers and to do desktop publishing incorporating public or private data from a variety of databases. Business data are being increasingly presented on television news, especially on such shows as the Nightly Business Report and the business newscasts of CNN.

Proper presentation of statistics requires paying attention to the media through which the figures are likely to be promulgated. But there are additional, equally important questions to be answered: What is or should be presented to what kind(s) of audiences(s)? How can we convey the message best? The first consideration is the actual content, the substance of the topic: Is it GDP or price indices? Is it an employment times series or a single pie-chart on market share? The next question is: what is the appropriate way to deliver this set of data—tables or charts, print or electronic or both? Finally, there is an artistic element in the presentation.

We relied on several books in regard to the above points, but two have proved particularly helpful:

1. Tufte's well known book entitled *The Visual Display of Quantitative Information*[75] and

2. G. Zelazny's book, *Say It With Charts.*[76]

Tufte, a Yale professor and consultant to the Bureau of the Census and large companies, has been called guru of the information design movement. Zelazny is Director of Visual Communication for McKinsey & Company. Both writers consider graphic communication crucial and both hold to the view that information is best conveyed without clutter.

In a more recent book and in an interview article,[77] Tufte expounds on his ideas as to what constitutes good graphics and good design. We are presenting two exhibits from each author. In the words of yet another specialist, Alan Siegel, "people have the right to clarity in what they read" (quoted in "The War on Information Clutter," *Business Week,* April 29, 1991, p. 66). Still other experts are R. Wurman and N. Holmes who create pictorial maps and infographics for popular books and magazines, but also for organizations.

What Tufte, Zelazny, and others have done is to restate D. Huff's classic

---

75. Edward Tufte, *The Visual Display of Quantitative Information.* Chesire, CT: Graphics Press, 1983.

76. G. Zelazny, *Say It With Charts.* Homewood, IL: Business One/Irwin, 1991.

77. See E. Tufte, *Envisioning Information.* Cheshire, CT: Graphics Press, 1991; and P. Patton, "Up from Flatland," *New York Times Magazine,* January 19, 1992, pp. 29-31.

volume, *How to Lie with Statistics,*[78] except their thrust is not how to lie but how to live with (and even how to enjoy) statistics. The field of graphic design or information design has come a long way since Huff's book. Graphs and charts are being refined in layout, plotting, and overall character, while clutter and confusion are being eliminated. Simplification and removal of unnecessary elements are favored over complexity; the goal is to convey comprehension and "make every mark on the page carry a meaning." Otherwise there is no sense in going from text and tables to charts and figures. Excellent small charts can be seen in an increasing number of reports and presentations as a result of the easy-to-use graphing display packages available for desktop computers. These are precisely drawn, yet do not overwhelm; they are easy to recall, hard to forget. Indeed, they are what is called presentation graphics.

But in today's world one must move from the printed to other media. An in-between domain is that of slides. They are not the printed page, but they are not yet video or computer creations either. Of course, with cheaper computing power today we are well beyond slides, and into computer graphics, videotapes, and charts, even on mass media network, local, and cable television. On-line and CD-ROM formats allow featuring tables, but they are not as yet comfortable with charts and figures. Personal computers can convey graphic information quite well, with a high degree of resolution. Color is becoming almost standard both on the screen and even in printouts. Animation can be achieved in a multimedia mode. The whole area of graphics on computer screens is evolving toward more sophistication. At the same time, some graphic artists think that statistics are still best presented in print media.

The most volatile and youngest medium for statistics is television. We see graphs and charts on the news, in the political commentary or even talk shows and, of course, often on business reporting. The same rules still apply, however; indeed, even more so. That is because we are dealing with a moving medium. Thus, the message by definition goes by more quickly; the medium demands charts and figures which are "gee whiz" and that is both the beauty and the danger. The graphs must communicate instantly to the viewer and only two or three points can be highlighted at the most. Line charts, simple pie and bar charts work better than complex histograms or scatter diagrams. In recent years some cable shows are devoting more time to business news and hence to statistical charts with the result that an

---

78. D. Huff, *How to Lie with Statistics.* New York: Norton, 1954.

expanding audience for sophisticated graphic data presentation brings even greater demands for more accurate and timely statistics.

## Dissemination (Delivery/Distribution)

How do the producers of statistics deliver their output to users? We have discussed possible formats above, but we need to do more. Audiences for data (and, for the analyzed version of data, that is, information) need to be identified. After this is accomplished, the needs and preferences of users should be highlighted, including whether their favored mode for delivery is print or electronic, on-line or CD-ROM, tabular or graphical. As a general rule, we find good correlation between urgency of need and speed of delivery. In other words: Those who need statistics or information in a hurry should be and often are willing to pay for it. They need it here and now — fast! Those whose immediacy of need is less pressing can and will depend on the above factors, but also on prices charged (which for certain electronic media tend to drop over time, although some are high or on the rise).

As Figure 13 shows, military and medical personnel demand instant data and usually get it. In the heat of the battle and in the operating room every second counts. In the business world, it is the realm of financial transactions which require split-second execution: deposits, withdrawals, credit checks, currency fluctuations and exchanges. The demand for data may come from a vice president of finance or from a junior assistant executing the transaction. The next level is that of managerial, sales, and accounting personnel who need up-to-date information on their own organization, the industry (e.g., most recent competitive price changes) and the economy (e.g., producer price index changes). To get the latest, the manager - who also nowadays doubles as a researcher - may go on-line, spin a compact disk (the CD-ROM format), engage in teleconferencing, or get on the fax or phone to a distant source. Finally, in terms of in-depth, historical analysis, the business economist or market researcher may settle into the corporate information center, a college library, or the district field office of the U.S. Department of Commerce. A retrospective search may call for weeks of work, possibly in dusty archives, but this is yielding to data bases which offer detailed historical data.

There is yet another audience: the citizens at large, voters, intelligent laypersons, millions eager to hear the latest unemployment figures or consumer price index changes. This is also true for a wide variety of business people and for many small organizations who cannot afford a corporate information center. They will be listening to radio and television news, and special business reports. The networks, cable operators, and local stations want the data, usually in compact form, and on TV as easy-to-view tables and graphs.

What do the above remarks imply for producers, especially for generators of federal (official/government) statistics and for producers of corporate and association data? The first requirement is that the news be newsworthy. There is little doubt that a sufficient number of individuals and organizations are interested in the latest economic data, especially the key indicators (see tabulation earlier in this chapter). Beyond that, however, the releasing bureau must make a decision: How newsworthy is this set of numbers? Who is likely to ask for it, in what format, and under what conditions?

Answers to the above questions need to be thought through, for they will affect mode of delivery (most likely, more than one format), speed of delivery, and prices charged. All three sectors - government, business, nonprofits are leaning now toward charging enough to cover costs, although there are currently complicated debates about what costs should be covered and how the income will fit into the overall governmental budget. Prices charged for some popular and useful volumes are on the rise. Businesses still send out annual reports gratis, but some enterprising firms or intermediaries are starting to charge for them. More valuable publications, such as the *National Trade Data Bank* (in CD-ROM format, from USDC) or membership rosters command much higher prices.

Beyond the audiences cited above, there are some special situations. Thus, for example, the U.S. Bureau of the Census interacts with high profile or high volume users of census data. In the business realm, a company may have a panel known as a user group, key accounts, or lead users. They may get information ahead of other groups. Many public and university libraries are depositories for government documents and may act as clearinghouses for certain associations in the realm of cyberspace, the interactive users who log on to CompuServe, America OnLine, Prodigy, Genie, and others, and academics who participate in Internet and other electronic networks develop into data experts who have special capabilities in their fields of interest.

Many details remain to be worked out, but automation and user fees are likely to be key features to be considered in the design of statistical programs for the 21st century. On-line charges are made on the basis of time used, interconnect fees, and number of "hits" achieved; CD-ROM format may also carry metering devices or sensors, with charges billed automatically when users request the "key" to release and use of selected series. Versatility and flexibility will be crucial for both producers and users.

The age of multimedia and information highways is around the corner. Countless articles have appeared on the topic in the popular, business, and technical press. The notion has even been a popular topic of conversation on television and radio shows, in government buildings, and in company corridors. For the producers of statistics what this age portends is an opportunity to disperse, share and in some cases sell (at a handsome profit) their output. They will have to think of all the possible venues, formats, and outlets which should be approached as enumerated above. Already today, statistics are widely available in print and electronic format. Tomorrow, multi-slide shows, videotapes, user profile faxes, and messages beamed without wires will be the rule.

Users, however, will not want all the information, but only the best. So what the producers of statistics may have to do is go beyond data and get into information. Information is data or statistics with added value through analysis, interpretation, and evaluation.

It is also possible that artificial intelligence, specifically expert systems, will take over some of this assignment. They will assess the incoming data and then dovetail the bits and pieces into a meaningful picture. The results will then be displayed on a portable computer, electronic staff aid device, or message pad. For example, several sources may have estimated the production of organic chemicals in Scandinavia, both past and forecasted. These numbers could then be brought together and displayed. The expert system may even provide an annotation as to whose numbers proved to be correct in the past. Finally, an analysis will be made contrasting such data with capacity utilization and competitors' activities, thereby providing further insights for the decision maker, whose decision will become new grist for the mill. Then, as new numbers are entered, the whole system is enriched and the process starts over again, a journey without an end.

We expect that in the new electronic age, many situations will arise which will call for collaborative schemes or alliances among participants. The competitive spirit will also remain strong; there will be room for large and small entrepreneurial-oriented organizations. Each situation will mean a new assessment on how to proceed. However, we expect that a strong public-private-nonprofit interface will come into being.

## Conclusion

Conclusion or summary is too strong a label for bringing this chapter to a close. We have looked at the manner of data collection (census vs. sampling), at presentation (the notion of graphic or information design) and at the dissemination of the statistics (manner of delivery or distribution). We find that there is much progress, much flux in each area; the coming years will see even more diverse, distinct activities.

We have seen the interactions among users, producers, and disseminators of statistical information as they interact with rapidly changing technology for collection, analysis, and distribution of statistics. We have indicated the growing public interest in statistical information and the likely sophisticated demands of decision makers. These trends certainly support the view that the time is ripe for rebuilding our statistical structure for the future that in many ways is already here.

# Chapter 4

# A Case Study: Health Care Statistics

## Introduction

The discussion of the roles, needs, and actions of various stakeholders can be related to 1993 by taking a look at the formation of public policy in the area of health care. This brief outline illustrates the importance of looking ahead to anticipate emerging issues so that an appropriate data base can be developed to aid the process of decision making.

For a number of reasons, health care statistics make an interesting case study of the ways in which data can be and are used in the formulation of national policy. First, the question of national health care reform has been much in the news lately, with First Lady Hillary Rodham Clinton heading up a task force to tackle this complex set of issues. Second, the statistics that describe the nation's health, health care, and access to health care are intrinsically complex, especially when it becomes a question of generating numbers that show real causal connections. And third, recent revolutionary improvements in health technology, coupled with demographic shifts, have made the challenge of health measurement even more daunting and complex.

## Overview: The Challenge

What is clear at the outset is that in many ways the health statistics that are nearest to hand and easiest to obtain in no way answer the most important questions about the American health care system. But they do pose those questions with an especially sharp focus. Readily available health care statistics show that American spending on health care has skyrocketed over recent decades, from about 6% of GDP twenty-five years ago to 12% at the beginning of the 1990s. In fact, total American spending on health care exceeded that of Canada by 40% and that of Germany by 91%.

Other available statistics make it equally clear that this high level of spending has not translated into better health or better health care for the U.S. population. For example, the U.S. ranks 20th in infant mortality, 16th in female life expectancy, and 17th in male life expectancy.[79]

As the size of this health challenge has come more clearly into public view and debate, a number of speculations have been put forward to explain the discrepancy between the level of spending and the level of health. Here are some of the most prominent:

- third-party coverage obscures the true costs of health care from the consumers of health care;

- the ever-increasing sophistication of medical technologies has driven the general level of health care costs through the roof;

- changing demographics have driven up health care costs;

- the lack of knowledge about the effectiveness of different health care interventions impedes greater cost-effectiveness and productivity; and

- rising expectations of consumers drive up the costs of business.

Given this list of suggested causes, it is no surprise that there has been a matching list of suggested cures put forward, including:

- greater use of Health Maintenance Organizations, or HMOs;

- a shift in Medicare from fee-for-service to diagnosis-related group prospective payment systems;

- imposition of cost controls;

- shifting costs from third parties to patients;

- use of greater ambulatory care rather than in-patient care;

- greater use of "managed care," i.e., HMOs and preferred provider options; and

- close case management of high-risk patients.

Both the causes and the cures outlined above are all in the nature of "best estimates," or educated guesses. Clearly, a full-scale attempt to examine and reform health care in America, like that headed up by the First Lady, requires more systematic and precise information than these speculations.

---

79. Gooloo S. Wunderlich, Ed., *Toward A National Health Care Survey: A Data System for the 21st Century.* Washington, D.C.: National Academy Press, 1992, pp. 20-21.

---

This chapter is designed to suggest some of the complexities encountered when a more systematic research effort is undertaken.

## Some Complexities of Trying to Assess Health Care in America

The largest, and most complex, task is to establish linkages between the process of care and the outcomes of care. The former has traditionally been much easier to measure than the latter. But as the data presented above make unmistakably clear, simply spending more money does not necessarily result in a better national health picture.

Here are just a few of the data series that would be required to assess precisely the connection between causes and effects: better systems for classifying and coding information on a large number of variables, including sites and settings of care;  data on the types of care, with specificity on procedures, drugs, diagnostic tests, and other technologies;  and better data on the costs of care. All of those will require agreements on several issues, including  the minimum number of data elements necessary to convey specific and aggregate cost and expenditures data adequately, and to link the relevant populations, and operational definitions of these data elements.[80]

There are some daunting complexities in measuring health care, including the complexity of defining the issue,  the changing demographics,  and the changes wrought by more sophisticated technology.

Altogether, health status is a complex and multidimensional construct, which reflects significant aspects of an individual's and a population's life, including physical health, mental health, social functioning, role functions, and general health perceptions.[81]

Further complicating factors stem from the subtle change over time in the kinds of health problems that Americans are experiencing, resulting both from the increased technological ability of medications such as vaccines to fight traditional diseases and from changing demographic patterns.

The most significant demographic shift in the U.S. from the point of view of health care, is the trend that goes under the shorthand phrase "the graying of America," as the population gets older. The number of

---

80. Ibid., pp. 22-23.

81. Ibid., p. 27.

Americans over 65 years old will increase from 12% to 21% over the next several years, and the fastest-growing segment of the population today is comprised of those over 85.[82]

All this has led to a shift of the major cause of death in America from infectious diseases to chronic diseases. That means changes in mortality rates are no longer proxies for changes in health status because people are now capable of living with chronic diseases in a way that they could not live with infectious diseases. Moreover, the chronic diseases of the 1990s are more complex than the infectious diseases they "replaced," including much longer asymptomatic stages.[83]

Besides that, for today's chronic diseases the physical and social environments are increasingly regarded as important risk or important protection factors and thus targets for intervention. These two factors of potential risk or protection are difficult to pin down statistically.

Here is an index of the complexity of gauging health and health care in this new more complicated American scene. The government initiative called Healthy People 2000 identifies 100 separate data sources, some of which have multiple parts. It is estimated that all of these will require more than 400 separate statistical series. Yet, for one fourth of the health objectives contained in the Healthy People 2000 project, no baseline data exist.

At the level of the state and local governments, the task is even more difficult. As one report put it, "The main problems that state and local health departments face in developing their own objectives is the unavailability of the data that are needed."[84]

## Two Lines of Inquiry

Assessing health care adequacy in America can be divided into overlapping lines of inquiry, each of them fed by separate data streams: (1) assessing the overall health of the American population; and (2) assessing the access of Americans to health care. Both lines of research are necessary, although they are not fully sufficient to assess the American health care system. We will

---

82. Ibid., p. 30.

83. Michael A. Stoto, *Public Health Assessment in the 1990s*. Washington, D.C.: Institute of Medicine, 1992, p. 61.

84. Ibid., p. 60.

---

look at both in greater detail after a couple of general observations about health care statistics.

In 1989, Michael A. Stoto of the Institute of Medicine formulated a series of criteria for the kinds of health objectives that should be formulated by the federal government: "Objectives (for health care performance) should be presented in terms of a specific, absolute target, such as an infant mortality rate of 9 per thousand. Such a presentation removes all ambiguity, what the objective should be and where it has been met....In turn, that presentation increases the requirement for clear documentation at every step of meeting the objective." Stoto also argues that objectives should be stated in absolute terms rather than in terms of percentages or rates of change, because they are unambiguous, easier to track, and will have a bigger impact on policy makers. Rates, proportions, and averages should be disaggregated where possible into demography, ethnic, racial and socio-economic categories.[85]

## Assessing American Health

In 1990, the Secretary of Heath and Human Services unveiled a national health project called Healthy People 2000: National Health Promotion and Disease Prevention Objectives for the Nation. It defines goals and objectives for improving the health of Americans by the end of this century. Out of that effort also came the Year 2000 Health Objectives Planning Act (PL 101-582), which requires that the Secretary of Health and Human Services implement health surveillance systems, and fund states to monitor and improve the health status of their populations.

There are a number of different information bases for public health assessment. The World Health Organization published a report on the development of health indicators for its Health for All project. A decade ago, the U.S. Public Health Service published national goals in the original *Healthy People* 1990.

In 1987, the National Committee on Vital and Health Statistics reviewed the status of health promotion and disease prevention data. The Centers for Disease Control and Prevention and the American Public Health

---

85. Michael A. Stoto, *Statistical Issues in Formulating Health Objectives for the Year 2000.* Washington, D.C.: Institute of Medicine, 1989.

Association, in conjunction with other health associations, developed Model Standards for Community Health. And the Public Health Foundation developed core data sets for reporting on state public health activities. The National Health Official's APEX program also developed methods for assessing public health needs and resources.[86]

Out of that plethora of possible data, a committee was appointed, Committee 22.1, to adopt a group of desired characteristics and selection criteria for the indicators of public health. The committee agreed on the following as the criteria for a good set of health indicators:[87]

- There should be a relatively small number of them (10 to 20);

- They should allow for a broad measure of community health;

- They should include general measures of community health (such as morbidity, mortality, and quality of life);

- They should include specific measures of community health;

- They should contain a subset that is consistent at the federal, state, and local levels;

- They should be easily understandable, even self-evident;

- They should be measurable, using available or obtainable data;

- They should imply specific interventions compelling action. They should be so closely linked to public health status that changes from past patterns signal the need for response; and

- They should be outcome oriented.

Guided by those goals, the committee developed eighteen indicators to help measure health status outcomes, and the factors that put individuals at increased risk of disease or premature mortality. In the end, the range of topics in the Healthy People 2000 project is extensive: it includes personal behavior and risk factors, including physical fitness and activity, nutrition, and the use of tobacco and alcohol.

Here are the eighteen indicators, each listed with the sources from which the data can be gathered to measure them:

---

86. Michael A. Stoto, *Public Health Assessment in the 1990s*. Washington, D.C.: Institute of Medicine, 1992, p. 60.

87. Mary Anne Freedman, "Health Status Indicators for the Year 2000," *Statistical Notes* (U.S. Dept. of Health and Human Services), Vol. 1, No. 1, 1991.

---

1. Race and ethnicity-specific infant mortality as measured by the rate (per 1,000 live births) of deaths among infants under one year old (Data source: National Vital Statistics System);

2. Motor vehicle crash deaths per 100,000 population (Data source: National Vital Statistics System);

3. Work-related injury deaths per 100,000 population (Data source: National Vital Statistics System);

4. Suicides per 100,000 population (Data source: National Vital Statistics System);

5. Lung cancer deaths per 100,000 population (Data Source: National Vital Statistics System);

6. Female breast cancer deaths per 100,000 (Data source: National Vital Statistics System);

7. Cardiovascular disease deaths per 100,000 population (Data source: National Vital Statistics System);

8. Homicides per 100,000 population (Data Source: National Vital Statistics System);

9. Total deaths per 100,000 population (Data source: National Vital Statistics System);

10. Reported incidence of acquired immunodeficiency syndrome per 100,000 population (Data source: CDC HIV/AIDS Surveillance System);

11. Reported incidence of measles per 100,000 population (Data source: National Notifiable Disease Surveillance System);

12. Reported incidence of tuberculosis per 100,000 population (Data source: National Notifiable Disease Surveillance System);

13. Reported incidence of primary and secondary syphilis per 100,000 population (Data source: National Notifiable Disease Surveillance System);

14. Prevalence of low birth weight as measured by the percentage of live infants born weighing under 2,500 grams at birth (Data source: National Vital Statistics System);

15. Births to adolescents (ages 10-17 years) as a percentage of total live births (Data source: National Vital Statistics System);

16. Prenatal care as measured by the percentage of mothers developing live infants who did not receive care during the first trimester of pregnancy (Data source: National Vital Statistics System);

17. Childhood poverty, as measured by the percentage of children under 15 years of age living in families at or below the poverty level (Data source: Census of Population, Detailed Population Characteristics, U.S. Department of Commerce, Bureau of the Census); and

18. Proportion of persons living in counties exceeding U.S. Environmental Protection Agency standards for air quality during the previous year (Data source: National Air Quality and Emissions Trends Reports, Annual Reports from the Environmental Protection Agency.)[88]

While carefully drawn up, this list has certain weaknesses, as commentators have pointed out. Michael Stoto, for example, has pointed out that different pictures can easily emerge, depending on which year is used as a baseline or standard for certain diseases: "The 1987 rate (of cancer deaths) is 50 percent higher when the 1990 population, rather than the 1940 population, is chosen as the standard....Neither one of those standards is 'correct' in any absolute sense, but they give quite a different impression."[89]

## Access to Health Care in America

Part of health care reform is measuring health in all its dimensions. Another part is measuring access to health care. The Institute of Medicine (part of the National Academy of Sciences) has concluded that "The nation needs, but currently lacks, an entity to continuously monitor the numerous types of utilization and health status [problems arising from insurance inadequacies, cultural impediments, geographic barriers, or other factors and place

---

88. Ibid.

89. Michael A. Stoto, *Public Health Assessment in the 1990s.* Washington, DC: Institute of Medicine, 1992, p. 65.

---

those problems in the broader context of national health policies]. The four-teen-member IOM access monitoring committee was constituted in February 1990 as a first step toward this goal."[90]

Each of the data sources pertaining to health access has some built-in weaknesses. Beyond that, inferring what each of those data suggests about the question of health care access, as we will see, is inevitably complex and tricky. Here are some of the different data sources with their associated strengths and weaknesses.

*Vital Statistics.* These are derived from birth and from death statistics. The birth certificates are the primary source for information about the use of prenatal care and about low birth weight. But there can be problems deter-mining the number of prenatal visits if, for example, a woman has no, or multiple, providers or when recall of service use is required after delivery. Death records provide mortality statistics. When they are linked to the birth record, they offer insight into the correlation of infant mortality connected to low birth weight. However, some have raised the question of the accuracy of the reports on the reasons for death since, in part, they depend on the judgment of the certifying physician. Moreover, as a measure of access for all age groups, the vital statistics system does not tell whether mortality is a result of a lack of insurance, low income, or some other reason.

*Surveys.* The National Health Interview Survey takes large soundings of households and provides a wealth of information that allows analysts to relate the use of health services and self-reports to characteristics of individ-uals and families. Among its strengths is that it is conducted annually, that its items are well-tested, and that it has a large and well-constructed sample of about 120,000 respondents. However, it is obvious that this method fails to reach some subpopulations with health-access problems, such as the homeless and migrant farm workers. Moreover, these surveys do not track the same family over time to discover how, say, changes in insurance cover-age might change access to health care. The National Medical Expenditure Survey (NMES), undertaken by the Agency for Health Care Policy and Research in 1987 tried to overcome that weakness.

*Hospital discharge data.* Computerized data of patient records organized into state data bases are increasingly available. But the lack of income data on a

---

90. Michael Millman, Ed., *Access to Health Care in America.* Washington, D.C.: National Academy Press, 1993, p. 21.

discharge abstract means that researchers have to use zip code data to appraise the effect of income on hospital use. But that misses the scattered poor, who do not live in a neighborhood of equally positioned families.

*Tumor Registries.* Since many cancers can be defeated if detected early enough, data on deaths by those cancers allow for inferences about the access of those patients to health care. (For example, the inference is that if a person dies of a cancer treatable in its early stages, this person had problems with health access early on.) The major sources of this information are the state and local tumor registries, but they are not established in all states and localities and lack data on income and insurance.

*Reportable diseases.* Some of the health care indicators derive from the data gathered as a consequence of laws that require physicians to report certain communicable diseases. This data source suffers from the drawbacks of both underreporting and misreporting: some physicians fail to understand the importance of constantly tracking these diseases, and do not report on them as conscientiously as they should; other physicians might mis- or underreport due to concern for privacy rights, because of changing definitions and reporting guidelines, or because of the difficulties in recognizing diseases with relatively low incidences.

*Claims data.* Health insurance claims contain important and relevant information about utilization, health status, costs, and so on. But its major drawback is also its most obvious one: these data contain no information about those who are uninsured. Moreover, they are not uniform, which makes them difficult and expensive to analyze.[91]

These are some of the more obvious problems that attach to each separate source for information pertaining to the complex issue of health access. But the issue is complex, which means that it cannot simply or easily be measured along any single or any small set of dimensions. It is a concept that must, in a sense, be inferred from a variety of different indices. And those inferences are never simple or straightforward.

The first part of the task of measuring health care access is formulating a good definition of it. The Committee on Monitoring Access to Personal Health Care Service (part of the Institute of Medicine) tried to formulate a definition that encompassed both the inputs to health and the successful

---

91. Ibid., pp. 25-28.

health results. They defined health care access as "the timely use of personal health services to achieve the best possible health outcomes."[92]

Taking this more comprehensive definition, here are a few of the problems in making straightforward inferences from the various sources of data to conclusions about access. As we saw above, in the cases of some cancers that can be cured if detected early, deaths from those cancers would seem to be a clear indication of lack of access to health care. But not even this inference is entirely justified, because it infers *potentiality* from *actuality* - i.e., it assumes that if someone *did not* use health care it must have been because they *could not* use health care. That inference is not always valid. There might be a variety of barriers - psychologically based, cultural norms, or lack of information - that would keep a person from using health care, even though it is available.

As the Committee's book puts it, "Some people are prone to overuse medical care, while others may underuse it having little to do with access barriers." Obviously, in the cases of cancers or other diseases that cannot be effectively countered in their early stages, no inference to mortality rates from those diseases can be made about health care access.

Another way to measure whether access to health care has been achieved is to look at the frequency of visits to health care facilities. But, again, this dimension by itself will not support a valid inference about access. As the Committee writes, "A poor mother who brings her asthmatic child to a clinic but cannot afford to purchase the prescribed medication may have a visit recorded, but few would consider that she had adequate access. A poor pregnant woman with a drug addiction requires many more services than most middle-class women if she is to deliver a healthy baby. A physician may be reluctant to order an expensive diagnostic test for an uninsured patient while erring on the side of overutilization for someone with adequate insurance. Thus, the poor and uninsured may enter the medical system, but it is difficult to tell whether they receive the services they need."[93]

---

92. Ibid., p. 33.

93. Ibid., p. 37.

## Conclusion

Clearly, health care is one of the most pressing and most difficult social challenges to attempt to measure. It is multifaceted, constantly changing, and subject to differing results from different assumptions and different interpretations.

In the end, it can only be assessed by a process of constantly taking different sightings of the phenomenon from different statistical measurements along each of the separate dimensions, then constantly up-dating, revising, and reexamining them.

# Chapter 5

# Fundamentals — National Income Accounting

## Introduction

In the preceding discussion, many of the context elements for the demands on official statistics have been reviewed. The review was presented because it is important to understand why change in statistical systems is slow, as well as to be aware of the variety of demands that flow from various user groups (both inside and outside of government). It is also critical to recognize the history and functions of the producing agencies, the pressure politics of a newly emerging issue, such as health care, and the changing nature of information systems which will impact on collection, production, and dissemination.

This chapter sets forth some of the basic issues that need to be addressed in a more comprehensive program of rebuilding economic statistics than the one outlined in the specific recommendations contained in this report. Chapter 7, Recommendations—National Accounts and the SNA, provides specific targets for an initial program to help in developing a national income accounting program for better meeting the challenges of the 21st century. Many of the recommendations have been suggested by others, but Chapter 7 attempts to pull together suggestions from a variety of sources, to update recommendations to reflect today's conditions, and to take advantage of the opportunities inherent in revision of the world standard United Nations System of National Accounts.

In the discussion that follows we will review some fundamental work that is needed to update economic theory. *A basic contribution of this chapter is the overview of the System of National Acounts which will give the reader an early look at the potential that lies ahead if the system is fully implemented.*

## Changes in the National Economy

Statistical measurement of national economic systems begins with a theory of economic growth and development. Current theory is still based on the classical theory of the market economy, with modern developments focused on mathematical formulations of changes in production, prices, and the roles of monetary and fiscal policies. Debate frequently settles on topics such as the role and impact of regulation, the measurement and identification of externalities, and the theory of trade and economic development.

Yet the economy of the 21st century is expected to be much different from the economy that has dominated the birth, evolution, and development of classical economic theory. The gains of productivity in agriculture and manufacturing have shifted the basic sources of employment from primary and secondary industries to tertiary and even quaternary economic activities. Issues of measuring outputs in services, such as health, education, and government, have received only limited attention, despite the fact that these sectors are becoming more and more important in the economic structure. Lack of output measures means that productivity in these sectors is not well-defined.

Fundamental work is needed on the theory of economic development as countries try to leap frog the traditional "stages of growth" development theory which proceeds from supply of natural resources to the supply of relatively "low-cost labor," as the basis for transition from a developing to a developed economy. In the 1990s these issues are complicated by the transition of some major economies from socialistic "command" or "planned" economies to market-oriented economies. Such a transition involves simultaneous attention to several major factors including prices, currency convertability, productivity, the legal framework, and public attitudes."[94] To illustrate one of the challenges to theorists, consider the complexity of developing a transition theory (let alone a politically acceptable policy) for dealing with all of the following in a simultaneous system!

---

94. This quote and following explanation are from Joseph W. Duncan, "What does Eastern Bloc upheaval mean for U.S. Business?" *D&B Reports*, January/February 1990, pp. 8, 63.

# Transition of a Command Economy to a Market Economy

The republics of the former Soviet Union and the countries of Comecon must address the following interdependent issues. The solutions must be approached as a total system. The challenge is daunting.

### Prices

The planned economies of the former Soviet Bloc had price levels that were established by state planners, not by markets. Hence, any Western company was faced with artificial costs for the internal goods and services needed to serve Eastern Bloc consumers. Further, while Western products may be superior to locally produced products, the artificial prices of the local products tended to create competitive conditions that were difficult to overcome in attempting to achieve significant market penetration.

Planned economies face great difficulties in stimulating internal economic growth when artificial prices cause misallocation of resources or when they stimulate plant managers to produce only those products that make the greatest contribution toward local production goals. For example, the price of bread remained unchanged in the former Soviet Union between 1955 and 1988. For some farmers, it was cheaper to feed cattle with this subsidized bread than other feed grains.

### Currency Convertibility

The ability of consumers in the countries of the former Soviet Union to purchase imports from the West is still severely limited by the availability of hard currency. Currently, there is limited foreign exchange between the Russian ruble and Western currencies. As a result, Western business managers operating in the former Soviet Union have no direct way of repatriating profits from within the former Soviet Union. While many barter deals have been arranged, there is a very limited set of exportable items from the Russian Republics that are suitable for such arrangements. The problems are not limited to East-West trade, but also extend to trade between the Republics and the Eastern European countries.

The current debate about official vs. black-market exchange rates is a direct reflection of the difficulties of moving in the direction of full convertibility. Immediate convertibility with artificial (centrally planned) prices in the background would clearly lead to economic shortages in some areas and pronounced surpluses in others. The combination of planned prices and the inconvertibility of the currency is at the heart of the economic stress that is challenging former Soviet economists and policy makers.

### Productivity

At the center of planned societies is the concept that the state will provide the basic needs of each household. Thus, state-owned apartments are made available to the workers; the rent is a percentage of wages (per square meter); and there is no possibility of changing apartments unless a direct trade can be arranged. This reduces incentives to maintain or improve properties; shabby living conditions result.

The lack of private ownership has a direct impact on the factory floor. There is no incentive for workers to increase productivity; output is usually evaluated only on gross measures such as number of units produced relative to plan requirements. No adjustments are made to improve the quality of the output. Losses due to pilferage, damage, or other weaknesses in the distribution stream are rarely taken into account by the state-set production quota.

In order for Western firms to build and manage effective production facilities in the former Eastern Bloc countries, it will be necessary to train a new generation of workers and to instill incentives and production measurements that are in sharp contrast to those prevailing. Increased productivity is essential if the poorly performing economy is to be revived.

### Legal Framework

A byproduct of current political reform in the Russian Republics is the rewriting of many basic laws. Much experimentation is under way. Changes are being introduced every month, and there is a very limited number of individuals who understand the new laws. This has resulted in an atmosphere of uncertainty for firms that wish to create joint ventures or open new distribution systems.

The old pattern of the Communist Party overruling current laws when it was expedient to do so is being replaced with new laws and regulations, but the learning curve is steep and there will clearly be many revisions in the legal framework that will be necessary for orderly economic transactions to work smoothly. A reliable legal system is a pre-requisite to the free movement of labor and capital and the building of trade relationships.

### Attitudes

The introduction of market-related prices, currency, production and laws is producing a high level of conflict in public attitudes. Cooperatives are being challenged for generating excessive profits, even though profits are necessary to create the incentives to undertake ventures outside the planned system.

Workers in the planned economy are demanding wages equal to those earned in the new market-driven firms, yet their productivity does not merit higher pay. Inflationary pressures are resulting. As the role of Western and market-oriented enterprises grows, the tension between market-driven activities and planned or state-controlled activities is likely to increase.

### Risks and Rewards

Integration of world markets is indeed the promise of the 1990s. Success will mean higher standards of living and a more peaceful world. But the integration will not be easy. Political and social stress are already evident even in the most advanced areas like the Common Market countries of Western Europe. In the Eastern Bloc, the changes will be even more dramatic and challenging.

U.S. firms cannot afford to adopt a "wait-and-see" attitude. By the time the opportunities are clear and the rules firm, others will be there and entry will be very difficult. Yet building on the oppoortunities in these new markets will require a long-term view, flexibility and an astute reading of rapidly changing internal conditions. The risks are great, but the potential rewards look well worth the effort.

These points summarize some of the challenges that are being faced by the former planned economies that are seeking to transform to market economies. The evolution will be difficult. The reality is that the process is moving forward and the result will be a demand for more market-oriented data. As noted in a number of presentations made in the countries of the former Soviet Union, "Information is the lubricant of the market economy."[95]

## Requirements for National Income Accounting

*The first step in developing a statistical stystem to meet future needs is to update economic theory so that it reflects the emerging relationships within developed economies and among economies at various stages of economic development, and to account for the transition from a planned to a market economy as discussed above.*

---

95. Presentations by one of the authors, Joseph W. Duncan, during the period 1988-1991.

The pressure for such a reexamination of economic theory is most evident in Europe, where the longstanding concepts of market development are now under strain. European political and economic integration have faltered due to stagnant domestic employment growth and the sudden availability of relatively low-cost labor from the Central and Eastern European countries. These conditions have been exacerbated by economic distortions flowing from the failure of massive subsidies of specific companies and industries (such as Airbus and agriculture), and the pressures of massive refugee flows. The countries of the former Soviet Union and the countries in Central and Eastern Europe now face the difficulties of determining a strategy for making the transition to market economies.

The development of a new theory of economic development for these transition countries, as well as the function of their official statistical agencies in developing market-oriented data, is beyond the scope of this report. However, it is important to draw attention to *the need to begin a concerted effort to pull together the best efforts of academic thinking to address these issues.*

The second step is more achievable and, in fact, significant progress has been made in recent years. This area is the development of common statistical definitions, classifications and standards. To assure that international comparisons are meaningful, it is essential that similar statistical concepts be employed. This is obviously difficult since each country has its own policies of taxation, social services, and legal organization. For example:

1. *The Harmonized Trade Classification* - As discussed in Chapter 1 the Harmonized Commodity Description and Coding System has been approved by members of the United Nations. This provides a common system for classifying commodities at borders and in international transport. These classifications will be important in the development of trade data.

2. *Standard Industrial Trade Classification* - Work under the leadership of the Bureau of Economic Analysis and the Office of Management and Budget is focused on developing an improved system of economic classification to use in analysis of industries and various segments of the economy.

3. *System of National Accounts* - This chapter will provide an overview of developments in this area.

4. *Accounting guidelines for nations* - The U.S. Financial Accounting Standards Board and other professional accounting organizations have stepped up efforts to gain more international comparability in basic accounting rules and regulations. While limited by national laws, in the long term these efforts are likely to make more comparability in financial data a reality.

## United Nations System of National Accounts

For economists and for business decision makers, evaluating the economic context for their decisions, the United Nations System of National Accounts[96] is important, even though it is not well known. A brief description of the 1993 SNA revision (the full text will be published in the next few months and implementation will require a number of years) is presented in this chapter to provide background for some of the recommendations for improving measurement of the national economy. The U.S. government has already agreed to implement the revised SNA in coming years.

### Concepts for Measuring National Income

The development of the National Income and Product Accounts (NIPA) in the United States and the SNA have represented a significant effort over several decades to provide a fundamental accounting system for understanding economic development.

The development of the National Income Accounts was accelerated as part of the effort to measure economic activity during World War II. The seminal concepts were developed by a number of individuals in the U.S. Department of Commerce, including significant contributions by Simon Kuznetz, Robert Nathan, Milton Gilbert, George Jaszi, Charles Schwartz, Edward Dennison and Daniel Creamer, as well as many others.[97]

---

96. The development of the System of National Accounts is a joint project of the United Nations Statistical Office, the Organization for Economic Cooperation and Development, the European Economic Communities, the World Bank, and the International Monetary Fund.

97. The concept of national income goes back even further, of course. For example, Sir William Petty apparently prepared guesstimates of the income of a nation in 1665. *The Wealth of Nations* published in 1776 by Adam Smith presented a concept of national income similar to measures used today, except that he apparently excluded many services. For a detailed discussion of the historical evolution of U.S. national income and product accounts, see Chapter 3 of *Revolution in United States Government Statistics, 1926-1976.* Joseph W. Duncan and William C. Shelton, October 1978, published by the U.S. Department of Commerce. The text of the 1993 System of National Accounts is expected to describe the historical evolution of that system.

The Employment Act of 1946 was a major stimulus to the development of economic policy, including the establishment of the Council of Economic Advisers in the Executive Office of the President, and the establishment of the Joint Economic Committee of the U.S. Congress, which has expressed a great interest in improving economic statistics in the years since it was established. For example, as early as 1948, the Joint Economic Committee published a report entitled *Statistical Gaps,* which was instrumental in stimulating many improvements in economic statistics.

The post-war reorganization of the Department of Commerce created an Office of Business Economics (OBE), the precursor of the Bureau of Economic Analysis (BEA), which now has responsibility for constructing the National Income and Product Accounts. The National Income and Product Accounts of the United States obtained a relatively independent status from the SNA recommended by the United Nations. During the past decade, under the leadership of Carol Carson, currently the Director of the BEA, the United States has played a major role in leading the U.N. working group responsible for improving the SNA. Further, as noted earlier, the Bureau of Economic Analysis is now committed to moving the U.S. income accounts toward the newly revised SNA.

The United Nations Statistical Commission adopted the revised SNA at its meeting in New York, February 22 to March 3, 1993.[98] The Commision's resolution "recommends that member states consider using the 1993 System of National Accounts as the international standard for the compilation of their national accounts and statistics, to promote the integration of economic and related statistics, and as an analytical tool." These actions of the Statistical Commission were approved by the U.N. Economic and Social Council in its regular meeting in July 1993.

The move toward the SNA was described in the June 1990 issue of the *Survey of Current Business.*[99] The two main goals of the System of National Accounts are:

1. "to facilitate international comparisons; and

2. "to serve as a guide to countries as they develop their own economic accounting systems."

---

98. See *Economic and Social Council, Official Records, 1993,* Supplement No. 6, Report of the Twenty-Seventh Session of the United Nations Statistical Commission E/CN.3/1993/27.

99. Carol S. Carson and Jeanette Honsa, "The United Nations System of National Accounts: An Introduction," *Survey of Current Business,* Vol. 70, No. 6, June 1990, pp.20-30.

---

The article further noted that most countries with market economies currently use the SNA as a guide in the design of their statistical systems. The goal is to record the nature of stocks and flows that are part of the economic system. The framework is designed to group transactions and transactors in an accounting system that is meaningful for economic analysis, forecasting, and policy.[100]

Since the SNA is different from the NIPA, which is so widely known among U.S. economists and statisticians, and since the SNA provides an important framework for elaboration and improvement of international economic statistics, this chapter presents a brief overview of the SNA and planned developments. Business economists and other users who rely upon economic statistics should, of course, read the more detailed working papers that are being prepared by the BEA, as well as the text published by the United Nations, since a major objective of the SNA is to develop international comparisons in economic statistics. Much of this chapter is taken from draft materials which, while subject to some change, are not expected to change the fundamental concepts presented.[101]

If the reader wants immediate background materials on many of the important methodological issues, information can be gained by reviewing the fundamental methodology papers that document the conceptual framework of the NIPA. Unfortunately, many users and analysts of economic statistics are unfamiliar with the details of these papers and, as a consequence, the richness of the current system is not fully appreciated. For more details on the system, see the methodology papers in Figure 19.

### Overall Concepts of the United Nations System of National Accounts

The United Nations System of National Accounts (SNA) is designed, as noted earlier, to record all of the stocks and flows of transactions that are part of the economy. Initially adopted in 1953, the SNA was substantially extended in 1968 to include input-output accounts, flow of funds accounts, and balance sheets. Consequently, the SNA framework includes measures of production, income, saving and investment, and wealth. It incorporates both domestic and foreign activities, financial and nonfinancial transactions,

100. For a discussion of the principles of economic accounting in the United States, see "An Introduction to National Economic Accounting," Allan Young and Helen Stone, in the March 1985 *Survey of Current Business.*

101. Documents used in the preparation of the balance of this section on the System of National Accounts include the draft guidelines reviewed by the U.N. Statistical Commission and internal working papers prepared by BEA. We are grateful to Carol Carson and her staff for making it possible for us to present this layman's version to readers of this report.

**Figure 19**

# Methodology Papers

See Bureau of Economic Analysis, "Users Guide to BEA Information," *Survey of Current Business,* January 1993, pp. 47-71. The methodology papers currently available include:

*An Introduction to National Economic Accounting* (NIPA Methodology Paper No. 1). An introduction to the concepts of the U.S. NIPAs that places these accounts within the larger framework of national economic accounting. This paper shows the step-by-step derivation of a general national economic accounting system from the conventional accounting statements used by business income and product accounts, the capital-finance accounts, and the input-output accounts—the major branches of national economic accounting in the United States today. Also appeared in the March 1985 *Survey of Current Business.* (1985) Available from the National Technical Information Service (NTIS): Accession No. PB 85-247567, price $12.50 (paper copy), $9.00 (microfiche).

*Corporate Profits: Profits Before Tax, Profits Tax Liability, and Dividends* (NIPA Methodology Paper No. 2). A description of the concepts, sources, and methods of the corporate profits components of the NIPAs. (1985) Available from NTIS: Accession No. PB 85-245397, price $19.50 (paper copy), $9.00 (microfiche).

*Foreign Transactions* (NIPA Methodology Paper No. 3). A description of the preparation of estimates in the NIPAs of net exports (both current- and constant-dollar), transfer payments to foreigners, capital grants received by the United States, interest paid by government to foreigners, and net foreign estimates in the NIPAs and those in the balance of payments accounts. (1987) Available from NTIS: Accession No. PB 88-100649, price $19.50 (paper copy), $9.00 (microfiche).

*GNP: An Overview of Source Data and Estimating Methods* (NIPA Methodology Paper No. 4). Basic information about GNP, including the conceptual basis for the account that presents GNP, definitions of each of the components on the income and product sides of that account, and a summary, presented in tabular form, of the source data and methods used in preparing estimates of current- and constant-dollar GNP. Also provides an annotated bibliography, with a directory of more than 50 items over the last decade that provided methodological information about GNP. Appeared in the July 1987 *Survey of Current Business.* (1987) Available from NTIS: Accession No. PB 88-134838, price $17.50 (paper copy), $9.00 (microfiche). The summary of source data and methods was updated in the July 1992 issue of the *Survey* (tables 7 and 8, pages 25 through 41).

*Government Transactions* (NIPA Methodology Paper No. 5). Presents the conceptual basis and framework of government transactions in the national income and product accounts, describes the presentation of the estimates, and details the sources and methods used to prepare estimates of federal transactions and of state and local transactions. (1988) Available from NTIS: Accession No. PB 90-118480, price $27.00 (paper copy), $9.00 (microfiche).

*Personal Consumption Expenditures* (NIPA Methodology Paper No. 6). Presents the conceptual basis and framework for personal consumption expenditures (PCE) in the NIPAs, describes the presentation of the estimates, and details the sources and methods used to prepare annual, quarterly, and monthly estimates of PCE. Includes a bibliography, definitions, and convenient summaries of estimating procedures. (1990) Available from U.S. Government Printing Office: Stock No. 003-010-00200-0, price $4.50.

*The Underground Economy: An Introduction* (reprint). A discussion of the coverage, measurement methods, and implications of the underground economy. Part of the discussion features the relation between the NIPAs and the underground economy: Illegal activities in the context of NIPAs, three sets of NIPA estimates sometimes misunderstood as being measures of the underground economy, and the effect on NIPA estimates of possible misreporting in source data due to the underground economy. Articles appeared in the May 1984 and July 1984 issues of the *Survey of Current Business.* (1984) Available from BEA: Accession No. 53-84-10-001, price $5.00.

and attempts to provide for both current- and constant-dollar measures.

The 1993 revision begins with the foundation of the 1968 SNA. A notable improvement is the objective for providing more attention to the role of services in the economy. For example, the revised SNA "describes the production of storage services and recognizes that services, as well as goods, may be produced over more than one accounting period.[102] Further, the revised SNA establishes criteria for delineation of the financial corporate sector and for the treatment of financial instruments in light of the many innovations in this field."[103] The 1993 SNA revision has been designed to define many of the rules of economic accounting such as the principles of valuation, time of recording, and grouping by aggregation, netting and grossing as a method for reducing the complexity of this comprehensive accounting system. The revised SNA also has been harmonized with the Balance of Payments Manual of the International Monetary Fund (IMF), bringing to fruition a goal that was set forth by the U.N. Statistical Commission in the early 1970s. There have been attempts to reconcile the U.N. and IMF definitions over the years, but it is just finally being realized with the adoption of the new SNA guidelines. Harmonization with the IMF data should, in future years, eliminate much of the confusion in international accounting statistics (a topic which is discussed later in this book).

Of particular significance is the fact that the revised SNA now incorporates "satellite accounts" to provide additional flexibility. The satellite accounts have the attribute of providing a framework for testing new extensions of economic accounting, in particular, environmental accounting.

The revised SNA includes an extraordinary amount of detail which is needed to provide sufficient guidelines to national statistical offices. To introduce you to the forthcoming report describing the SNA, the following material has been prepared on the basis of "A Readers' Guide to the Draft Revised United Nations System of National Accounts" which was developed as an aid to BEA staff. The following sections are organized in order of the proposed outline for the forthcoming manual and, of course, the concepts are subject to some change when the final version of the U.N. text is published.

---

102. Bureau of Economic Analysis, in an article entitled "New International Guidelines in Economic Accounting," pp. 44-45.

103. Ibid., p. 43.

## Basic Definitions within the SNA

The fundamental elements of the SNA are incorporated into an accounting structure. Figure 20 on the next page is a diagram that illustrates some of the basic relationships between flow accounts and the balance sheets. In order to make this an integrated system, *the SNA strives to apply the same concepts, definitions, and classifications to all accounts and sub-accounts.* For example, all dwellings are treated as assets used to produce goods and services. Thus, all housing services, whether sold or consumed by the owners, are included within production, and all of the corresponding income originating from the production of housing appears in the accounts using the same definitions and classifications.

The objective of national accounting is to record economic flows between two dates and the resulting stocks. Flow means that the situation has changed between the transactors (buyer or seller). In the analysis of the SNA, the fundamental question of economic links tries to respond to the question "**Who** does **what**, by **what** means, for **what** purpose, with **whom, in exchange for what**, with **what** changes in *stocks?*"[104] The classifications that structure the system involve the following:

- institutional units and sectors (**who?**);

- transactions and other flows (**what?**);

- assets and liabilities (**what stocks?**);

- activities, establishments, products (other aspects of **who** and **what?**); and

- purposes (**what for?**).

The elaboration of the system quickly generates considerable detail. For example, on the question of institutional units and sectors—the who—there are a variety of players including:

1. Nonfinancial corporations: institutional units principally engaged in the production of market goods and nonfinancial services;

2. Financial corporations: institutional units principally engaged in financial intermediation or in auxiliary financial activities;

3. General government: institutional units which, in addition to ful-

---

104. This formulation was developed by the U.N. Working Party and is presented in the introduction to the Overview-Chapter 2 in the draft Manual.

**Figure 20**

# A Simplified Sequence of Flow Accounts and Balance Sheets[105]

| | | |
|---|---|---|
| **Opening Balance Sheet** | | **Balance Sheet** |
| | *Net worth* | |
| **Production Account** | | |
| *Value added/GDP* | | |
| **Generation of Income Account** | | |
| *Operating surplus* | | |
| **Allocation of Primary Income Account** | | **Current Accounts** |
| *Balance of primary incomes* | | |
| **Secondary Distribution of Income Account** | | |
| *Disposable income* | | |
| **Redistribution of Income in Kind Account** | | |
| *Adjusted disposable income* | | |
| **Use of Disposable Income Account** | | |
| *Saving, net* | | |
| **Use of Adjusted Disposable Income Account** | | |
| *Saving, net* | | |
| **Capital Account** | | |
| *Netlending (+)/Net borrowing (-)* | *Changes in net worth due to saving and net capital transfers* | |
| **Financial Account** | | |
| | *Net lending (+)/Net Borrowing (-)* | **Accumulation Accounts** |
| **Other Changes in volume of Assets Account** | | |
| | *Changes in net worth due to other changes in colume of assets* | |
| **Revaluation Account** | | |
| | *Changes in net worth due to nominal holding gains/losses* | |
| **Closing Balance Sheet** | | **Balance Sheet** |
| | *Net worth* | |

---

105. Prepared by the Bureau of Economic Analysis as an aid to this discussion.

filling their political responsibilities and their role in economic regulation, produce principally nonmarket services (possibly goods) for individual or collective consumption and redistribute income and wealth;

4. Households: All physical persons in the economy, the institutional unit in the household sector consisting of one individual or a group of individuals. The household of the owner of an unincorporated enterprise is not considered an institutional unit (except under certain conditions). The principal functions of households are the supply of labor, final consumption, and, as entrepreneurs, the production of market goods in non-financial (possibly financial) services;

5. Nonprofit institutions (NPIs) serving households: legal entities which are principally engaged in the production of non-market services for households and whose main resources are voluntary contributions by households.

This listing illustrates how the system builds fundamental concepts which are then subdivided into conceptual definitions which are further refined to define the overall tests of activities in the economic system.

The second classification of importance is the consideration of stocks. In essence, assets and liabilities are components of the balance sheet of the total economy and its constituent institutional sectors. In contrast to economic flows, the balance sheet shows the stocks of assets and liabilities held at a point in time. Clearly, stocks are connected with flows, and the essence of the accounting system is to provide a definition of those interrelationships.

In market economies, accounting rules focus on double entry bookkeeping. The SNA strives to follow that procedure, but in fact, since most transactions involve two economic agents/institutional units, transactions are recorded twice by the two transactors involved, leading to a principle of *quadruple entry.* For example, a social benefit in cash paid by a government unit to a household is recorded in the accounts of government as:

1. a use under the relevant type of transfer;

2. a negative acquisition of assets under currency and deposits in the accounts of the household sector;

3. a resource under transfers; and

4. an acquisition of assets under currency and deposits.

Complexity of the system is quickly recognized when it is necessary to collect information from diverse sources with differing definitions and make statistical decisions concerning such things as the timing of transactions, the valuation of transactions, appropriate consolidation of transactions, and evaluation of the consistency between volume measures and real measures. Thus, one of the merits of the SNA is to standardize measurement concepts.

### Transactions in the SNA

The SNA, in looking at transactions, considers four types which are cross-classified by sector, industry and product, or purpose. The four types of transaction are :

1. transactions, goods and services, which show the origin and use of goods and services;

2. distributed transactions, which show how the value added generated by production is distributed into labor, capital, and government, as well as the redistribution of income and wealth through taxes and transfers (current and capital transfers are distinguished);

3. transactions and financial assets, which show the net acquisition of financial assets or the net incurrence of liabilities for each type of financial instrument; and

4. other accumulation entries, which cover transactions and other economic flows not taken into account elsewhere that change the quantity or value of assets and liabilities.

### Balance Sheets in the SNA

Balance sheets are a familiar business concept. They can be applied to national income accounting as well. Up to this point, the discussion of the SNA looked at the current accounts and the accumulation accounts, which record transactions and other flows that occur over time. Balance sheets, on the other hand, are a stock concept. Stocks are a position in, or holding of, assets and liabilities at a point in time.

Stocks are connected with flows: They result from the accumulation of prior transactions and other flows, and they are changed by transactions and other flows in the current period. Stocks result from a continuum of entries and withdrawals (accounting for some changes in volume or in value) occurring during the time a given asset or liability is held. In the SNA there is an Opening Balance Sheet—which for all practical purposes is the Closing Balance Sheet from the previous accounting period; a Balance Sheet of Changes—which recapitulate the accumulation accounts via their balancing items (i.e., changes in net worth); and a Closing Balance Sheet, which is derived from these two accounts.

Net worth, which is the balancing item for the Balance Sheet, is defined as the value of all the nonfinancial and financial assets owned by an institutional unit or sector less the value of all its outstanding liabilities. Although this definition places emphasis on assets and liabilities and the Changes in Balance Sheet Account draws further attention to the accumulation accounts by recapitulating the "changes in net worth due to..." balancing items, most changes in the accumulation accounts only rearrange assets and liabilities if current account activity (i.e., saving) is excluded.

### Transactions Accounts in the SNA

Transactions accounts show the flows associated with a given kind of transaction or group of transactions for each sector (or industry) involved. These accounts specify the kinds of transactions and show the resources and uses for each sector, that is, they show "from whom" for the total flows for each sector (and the total economy). However, they do not show the specific "from whom/to whom" information of the transactions. Because they do not show "from whom/to whom," they are classified as dummy, or screen accounts. Transactions accounts balance resources and uses without the use of balancing items.

The Goods and Services Account is a transactions account that shows, for the economy as a whole (or for groups of products), the total resources and total uses of goods and services. Taxes and subsidies on products are included on the resources side of the account. This reflects the recommendation that output be valued at basic prices and uses be valued at purchasers' prices. The account is balanced globally—for all resources and uses—but not for each kind of transaction. When the Goods and Services Accounts shows type(s) of product, output is shown by industry of origin and intermediate consumption is shown by industry of use. To facilitate analysis for accounts where all sectors may have resources and uses, it is useful to also have accounts that detail the "from whom/to whom" flows.

### The Assets and Liabilities Accounts

The assets and liabilities accounts detail stocks of assets and liabilities at the beginning and end of an accounting period and record the transactions and other flows that explain the changes between the balance sheets.

The transactions and other flows detailed are:

1. transactions recorded in the Capital Account, by type of transaction;

2. transactions recorded in the Financial Account, by type of transaction;

3. other flows recorded in the Other Changes in the Volume of Assets Account, by type of change; and

4. holding gains/losses recorded in the Revaluation Account, by type.

These accounts are presented for each type of asset or liability, at a greater level of detail than in the sequence of accounts for institutional units or sectors.

### The Rest of the World Account

The Rest of the World Account shows transactions between resident and nonresident institutional units and the related stocks of assets and liabilities. The rest of the world plays a role in the accounts similar to a sector, and therefore, the account is established from the point of view of the rest of the world. That is, a resource for the rest of the world is a use for the total economy, and a use for the rest of the world is a resource for the economy. Positive balancing items are a surplus for the rest of the world.

Current transactions are recorded in only two accounts:

1. The External Account of Goods and Services shows imports of goods and services as resources and exports as uses. Its balancing item is the external balance of goods and services;

2. The External Account of Primary Income and Current Transfers shows income flows between the total economy and the rest of the world. Its balancing item is the current external balance.

Accumulation accounts are also relevant for the rest of the world, although only for a limited set of transactions—primarily financial transactions. The External Assets and Liabilities Account is equivalent to the financial assets and liabilities of the total economy's Balance Sheet, with reversed signs. National resident institutional units are created to register the ownership of most other domestic (nonfinancial) assets owned by foreigners.

The Rest of the World Account, unlike the balance of payments, is drawn up from the perspective of the rest of the world. In this way it can be treated as if it were a sector in the System. It is not drawn up from the perspective of the total economy—that is, measuring the total economy's claims on the rest of the world—because, by defining balancing items on the left as claims on the total economy by the rest of the world, the overall balance of the System is maintained.

## The Aggregates

The aggregates are totals for sectors of either balancing items or particular transactions that measure the result of economic activity considered from a particular point of view. Some prominent ones include the following:

*Gross domestic product* (GDP) is the sum of the gross value added of all producer units plus any taxes, less subsidies, on products that have not been included in the valuation of output. GDP is also the sum of the final uses of goods and services, measured in purchasers' prices, less imports of goods and (nonfactor) services. GDP is also the sum of primary incomes distributed by resident producer units.

*Net domestic product* is equal to GDP less consumption of fixed capital. Neither it, nor gross product, are measures of welfare or sustainable income.

*Gross national income* (a concept of primary income, not value added) is equal to GDP plus net primary (factor) income flows to and from the rest of the world. It is the sum of gross primary incomes distributed to resident institutional units.

*Gross national disposable income* is equal to gross national income plus net current transfers received from the rest of the world.

No aggregate measure of welfare is provided by the System.

## The Integrated Economic Accounts

The Integrated Economic Accounts (IEA) array the full sequence of accounts of the total economy, including balance sheets, in a presentation which presents the principal economic relations and the main aggregates. The presentation shows the general accounting structure of the System and presents a set of data for the institutional sectors, the ecomony as a whole and the relations with the rest of the world. The objective is to be flexible so that different dimensions of economic transactions can be portrayed. The IEA is highly aggregated in order to be manageable. In principle, however, specific subsectors can be shown in additional columns, or further detail on the various line items can be shown in additional rows to provide information on topics of interest.

The detailed analysis of production by industries and flows of goods and services by kinds of products is an integral part of the integrated central framework. The detailed analysis of production activities and goods and services balances is made in the input-output tables. The central input-output table of the System presents:

- the resources and uses of goods and services for each type of product, and

- the production and generation of income accounts for each industry according to kind of economic activity.

### Other Tables

In addition to the input-output tables, the System provides for a number of tables outside of the IEA to allow greater detail to be presented. One set—of financial transactions and financial assets and liabilities—provides greater detail on financial transactions. Another set—of integrated balance sheets and assets and liabilities accounts—shows, for each type of asset, the value of the asset on the opening and closing balance sheets as well as the various sources of their change in value. A third set is detailed breakdowns of various categories of expenditure by function such as outlays of government by function.

### The Integrated Central Framework and Flexibility

The SNA does not seek to imply any order of priority or frequency for implementing national accounts. Countries are encouraged to adapt the SNA according to their particular needs and abilities. Three possible ways of applying the SNA flexibility are described in the manuals.

The first way is by using the flexibility within the system itself to vary emphasis by:

- using the System's classifications of sectors, industries, products, transactions, and sequence of accounts at varying levels of detail—including additional ones;

- using different methods of valuation;

- using different priorities and frequencies;

- rearranging results; or

- introducing additional elements.

The second way is by using a social accounting matrix (SAM). The SAM is a presentation of the SNA in matrix terms that incorporates topics of special interest, such as the link between income generation and consumption. A SAM is usually prepared with emphasis on an item or component of special interest to the user, indicating a greater degree of detail than shown in the SNA.

The third way is by using satellite accounts. Satellite accounts are recommended when alternative economic concepts need to be used or if the central framework would become overburdened with details in performing the analysis. Tourism is a good example. Various aspects of producing and consuming activities connected with tourism may appear in detailed classifications of activities, products and purposes. However, specific tourism transactions and purposes appear separately in a very few cases; thus, satellite accounts can provide the needed detail.

### Concluding Discussion of the SNA

This brief discussion is designed to present an overview of the SNA and does not convey the full richness of the System. In fact, it requires a careful study of the various definitions, concept tables, and accounting rules to fully appreciate the comprehensiveness of the integrated accounts. In the U.N. Manual there are chapters describing tools, the current accounts of the central framework, the accumulation accounts and balance sheets of the central framework, other accounts, and associated measures. Each of these topics is complex but the crucial element is the integrated nature of the concepts and classifications applied to all of the accounts.

Understanding how an economic system functions requires an identification of the participants or transactors who exist within the system and an understanding of the activities in which they engage. This is the essential objective of dealing with the questions mentioned earlier in which the entire system is a response to the fundamental links: "**Who** does **What**, by **What** means, for **What** purpose, with **Whom**, in exchange for **What**, with **What** changes in *stocks?*"

An earlier definition of institutional units illustrates that the fundamental units are entities capable of owning assets, incurring liabilities, and engaging in economic activities and transactions with other institutional units. Five types of institutional units identified earlier are mutually exclusive sectors of the economy. They, of course, may be further subdivided into subsectors for purposes of analysis and, as the SNA concept provides alternative methods of subsectoring, may be used for various purposes, so long as the total economy is the sum of the resident sectors.

In this global economy, it is also essential to deal with the rest of the world. In SNA terms, the rest of the world is comprised of all nonresident institutional units that enter into transactions or have economic links with resident institutional units. In fact, the framework provides for describing the rest of the world as though it is a sector. The Rest of the World Account shows the transactions in other flows between resident and nonresident units and the stocks of financial claims that each makes on the other. The Rest of the World Account is divided into current, accumulation, and balance sheet sub accounts. Thus, as noted earlier, it is appropriate to consider the Rest of the World Account as a sector of the system.

The integration of the SNA with the IMF balance of payment account is particularly crucial for analyzing the Rest of the World Account. As noted elsewhere in this report the flows and assets in terms of global transactions require considerable work to take account of newly emerging data flows and transaction types. In the SNA framework there are only two types of subaccounts. They are:

1. the external account of business services which shows the exports and imports of goods and services and the resulting external balance of business services; and

2. the external account for primary incomes and current transfers, which shows the compensation of employees, taxes less subsidies on production imports, property income (including reinvested earnings of direct foreign investment enterprises), and the current transfers receivable from or payable to nonresident units.

The system also provides for four accumulation subaccounts in the rest of the world sector and a balance sheet. The four subaccounts are:

1. the capital account, which shows capital transfers receivable and payable by nonresidents and the net acquisition of nonproduced, nonfinancial assets by nonresidents;

2. the financial account, which shows transactions in financial assets of all types with nonresidents, including the equity ownership of resident institutional units;

3. the other changes in volume of asset account include such flows as uncompensated seizures of assets, write-offs of bad debts, and classification changes;

4. the re-evaluation account, which shows the holding gains or losses on financial assets and liabilities of nonresidents.

The balance sheet that results shows the stocks, the financial assets issued by residents and held by nonresidents, and the liabilities of nonresidents to residents.

This integration of the national accounts with international flows is destined to be of growing significance with the evolving integration of the world economy.

## Applications for Users

There are many concepts for elaborating and applying the SNA. The documents developed by the designers include several suggestions. To summarize from the earlier discussion they include:

*Functional applications.* Four tables provide an alternative view of recording certain transactions—a classification by function. Outlays are classified by functional purpose for general government, producers, and nonprofit institutions serving households. Consumption (divided into individual consumption expenditure and social transfers in kind) is classified by purpose for individuals. These alternative views provide users with an expansion of analytical tools in selected areas.

*Applications of the integrated framework to various circumstances and needs.* Countries differ with respect to their stage of development, economic and social structure, legal organization, and so forth. The SNA is, consequently, constructed as a general framework that provides enough flexibility so that countries may use the framework to meet their specific requirements without departing from the standards that promote international comparability. Countries may utilize this flexibility to emphasize important sectors or activities, by using various levels of the SNA's classifications of transactions and transactors, by rearranging the results, or by introducing complementary classifications or additional levels of classifications. They may focus on an important activity by identifying it as a "key activity" and establishing accounts for a "key sector" in addition to those for the recommended sectors. This chapter in the U.N. Manual provides examples of how the integrated framework can be adapted to meet such specific needs, including a detailed analysis of the household sector. It also discusses special problems of accounting during periods of high inflation and includes an annex that provides an illustration of alternative treatments of nominal interest for economies that experience high inflation.

*Social accounting matrices.* A Social Accounting Matrix (SAM) presents a sequence of accounts in a matrix that elaborates linkages between a supply and use table and sector accounts. It places special emphasis on interrelations between the structure of the economy and the distribution of income and expenditure among households. In a SAM, each account is represented by a row and column pair, with the convention that incomings are shown in rows and outgoings in columns. A transaction is represented by a single entry, which, in the case of an aggregate matrix, can be viewed as the grand total of a sub matrix in which categories of transactors are presented.

As explained above, the detail shown in a SAM may be expanded or contracted as appropriate to the subject being considered; typical subjects include income flows by characteristics of recipient, employment by characteristics of population, and combinations of monetary and non monetary data. SAM's may be constructed as, or in conjunction with, satellite accounts. The SAM approach, with its multiple sectoring, is useful for reconciling and integrating disparate but detailed basic source data, as well as allowing the introduction of a regional dimension where it is relevant and feasible. SAM's are also useful for policy analysis and modeling in which the structural features of an economy play an important role, such as applied general equilibrium models.

*Satellite analysis and accounts.* Although the central framework of the SNA may be used in a flexible way, there are limits to this flexibility. Greater flexibility may be achieved through the use of satellite accounts, which permit the SNA to be expanded for selected areas of social concern without overburdening or disrupting the central framework. Satellite accounts generally make use of classification schemes and concepts that are complementary or alternatives to the ones used in the central framework.

A section on satellite analysis illustrates by example various means of broadening the system. These examples include: Alternative classifications of products and concepts of production, enlarged concepts of transfers and disposable income, expanded concepts of capital formation, a broadened scope of assets and liabilities, and an expanded treatment of transactions by purpose. Another section presents in detail a framework for functionally originated satellite accounts. A final section discusses, as an example, how natural resources could be treated as capital. It is largely based on the United Nations Handbook on the System of Environmental Economic Accounts that will be presented in the Handbook on Integrated Environmental and Economic Accounting. It is just one of the frameworks in which environmental accounts could be developed.

## Conclusion

This brief discussion does not do justice to the technical detail and sophistication of the new United Nations System of National Accounts. However, we hope that interested readers will follow U.S. developments as reported in the *Survey of Current Business* published by BEA. For those interested in the full detail, the forthcoming United Nations text, the technical papers of the U. N., the Organization for Economic Cooperation and Development, the European Economic Communities, the World Bank and the International Monetary Fund, and studies by other experts will be useful.

# Chapter 6

# Global Interaction

## Introduction

The inter-dependence of the world economy has increased dramatically and will intensify in the future. Unquestionably, international commerce will be increasingly important. As noted in Figure 3 in Chapter 1, the volume of trade in OECD countries has increased even in periods of economic weakness. This is evidence of the reorientation of major business organizations such that both inputs to production and marketing of products and services are approached on a global basis.†

In a statistical sense, linkages among countries are captured in the balance of payments accounts of individual countries, which reflect trade, services and capital flows. The U.S. has one of the most comprehensive systems of collecting data, and plays a large role in helping other countries develop their programs of international statistics. With differing legal systems for banking regulation, with different taxing systems, and with variations in trade policy there are many difficulties in building the type of information system that will adequately meet the needs of public and private decision makers involved in international commerce.

U.S. balance of payments data, even with present shortcomings, are probably the most comprehensive in the world. Many other industrial countries also have sophisticated data collection procedures, whereas, data collection in the developing countries is often haphazard.

The need for substantial improvement in international statistics is clear from the following: The individual categories in the world tabulation of the balance of payments should, in principle, sum to zero (a $5 deficit in one country should be offset by surpluses equal to $5 in others). In actuality, there are large imbalances in many categories, indicating errors or biases. The IMF has addressed many of these questions in two major studies: *Report on the World Current Account Discrepancy*[106] and *Report on the Measurement of*

---

† The authors wish to acknowledge the contributions of Marsha A. Kameron to this chapter.

106. *Report on the World Current Account Descrepancy,* Washington, DC: International Monetary Fund, 1987.

**Figure 21**

## Summary of World Balances

(billions of dollars)

|  | 1985 | 1986 | 1987 | 1988 | 1989 | 1990 | 1991 |
|---|---|---|---|---|---|---|---|
| Current Account | -80 | -66 | -49 | -60 | -76 | -112 | -91 |
| Long-term Capital | 16 | 46 | 30 | -55 | 29 | 8 | 190 |
| Short-term Capital | 21 | 46 | 97 | 79 | 25 | 106 | -74 |
| Errors and Omissions | 14 | 29 | -19 | -5 | -15 | 26 | -1 |

*International Capital Flows.*[107]

As shown in Figure 21 the discrepancy in the current account topped $100 billion in 1990 and decreased somewhat in 1991. Errors of this magnitude indicate that many of the world's balance of payments tabulations are subject to considerable errors.

In this chapter we will review some of the challenges in this area with a focus on the U.S. system. Equally important problems are evident in other countries, and the process of improving the international system stands as a major area calling for attention.

In the United States, numerous government agencies have responsibility for collecting and compiling the balance of payments statistics. Since these agencies do not necessarily interact or co-operate with each other, this poses a major obstacle to statistical reform. This chapter reviews some of the major shortcomings of the present system. Recommendations are in Chapter 8, Recommendations - International Statistics.

---

107. *Report on the Measurement of International Capital Flows,* Washington, DC: International Monetary Fund, 1992.

---

## Trade Statistics

This section focuses on the methodology of collecting data, problems which have been previously addressed during the past several years, and the present shortcomings of the data. Merchandise trade, in comparison with other U.S. international transactions, differs in several important respects. Its statistics are compiled from a full tabulation of all transactions, rather than with surveys. A great deal of attention is placed on trade data. As a result they are generally considered to be quite accurate.

### Definitions

Merchandise exports and imports cover all movable goods sold, given away, or otherwise transferred from U.S. to foreign ownership and vice versa. It is assumed that goods moving through U.S. customs change ownership so that the physical position of the goods indicates ownership. For definition purposes, goods shipped between affiliated firms in the U.S. and abroad are assumed to change ownership, even though the change-of-ownership rule may not strictly apply in a legal sense for some of those transactions.

### Methodology

The Customs service is responsible for collecting import and export documents at over 400 U.S. ports of entry and exit. It transmits the data to the Census Bureau via automated transactions and paper documents. The Census Bureau processes, compiles and publishes trade statistics. The data are released to the public about 45 days after the end of the month in question.

### Exports

Within four days after merchandise has been exported, bills of lading containing information on quantities and destination and a summary sheet must be submitted to the Customs Service. The carrier must also present a shippers' export declaration (SED) showing the commodity shipped and its value.

The Customs Service generally gives the SEDs little or no review for completeness or accuracy. They are forwarded to the Census Bureau for processing. This currently accounts for about 60% of the value of exports. SEDs are not required of the companies participating in the Census Bureau's Automatic Export Reporting Program (AERP). Computerized information is sent directly to the Census's Foreign Trade Division. This currently accounts for about 20% of the value of exports.

SEDs are generally not required for U.S. exports to Canada (20% of the value of total exports). The U.S. uses Canadian import data to compile U.S. exports to Canada. SEDs are also not required for export shipments under the U.S. military assistance program.

### Imports

The majority of import transactions are transmitted directly by computer under the Customs Bureau's Automated Broker Interface Program (ABI). This accounts for 86% of the value of imports.

A small percentage of import data is still collected on Customs Form 7501. Importers must submit these forms within 10 days of receipt of the imports. The forms must be accompanied by commercial documents showing the required tariffs. This accounts for about 14% of the value of imports.

Formal quality control measures are applied in the processing stage. This includes a couple of different procedures:

1. A complete review by an import specialist is made of a 2% random sample; and

2. The Census subjects high-value shipments to close scrutiny.

### Recent Innovations and Changes

During the past several years, a number of changes have been made that substantially improved the quality of the trade statistics, especially import statistics which are considered to be complete and accurate.

1. There has been a substantial rise in electronic filing. This streamlines compiling although it does not eliminate the problems of non-filing or errors in keyboard entry;

2. In March 1988, the Census Bureau increased the time period in which monthly data are compiled by two weeks. This has reduced the timing errors so that trade statistics accurately reflect the time period in which they occur;

3. In January 1989, the U.S. adopted the International Harmonized System (HS) for classification of merchandise trade. This brought the U.S. into line with most other countries who use this classification system; and

4. In January 1990, following several years of study, the U.S. and Canada began to use the other country's import data to compile its export statistics.

### Current Problems

Although import data are considered to be accurate, the quality of the export data needs further improvement. Methodological problems include the following:

1. Neither Customs nor Census have systematic controls to ensure that all documents are filed and received for processing;

2. Exporters have an incentive to understate sales to reduce their taxable income and to pay lower importer duties to importing countries;

3. Exporters do not report transactions that are restricted or banned under U.S. law. It is estimated that about 40% of all U.S. exports are subject to at least some type of restriction; and

4. With the growing importance of trade among related parties it is important to get better definition and quality control of data on such relationships.

### Figure 22

## U.S. Merchandise Trade Associated with U.S. Non-bank Multinational Companies

(billions of dollars)

|  | 1989 | 1990 |
|---|---|---|
| U.S. Exports of MNCs | 236.4 | 248.5 |
| Shipped to affiliates | 102.6 | 108.4 |
| Shipped to other foreigners | 133.8 | 140.1 |
| Total U.S. Exports | 363.8 | 392.9 |
| | | |
| U.S. Imports- MNC Associated | 201.2 | 214.4 |
| Shipped by affiliates | 97.4 | 102.5 |
| Shipped to other foreigners | 103.8 | 111.9 |
| Total U.S. Imports | 473.6 | 495.2 |

Source: *Survey of Current Business*, August 1992, p.68.

### U.S. Direct Investment and Associated Trade

A great deal of trade occurs between parent and affiliated companies. As a result, a growing share of U.S. merchandise trade is transacted between affiliated parties. In 1990, trade between affiliated parties accounted for 63% of total exports and 43% of total imports. The high degree of inter-company transactions raises the question of whether goods are appropriately priced at the market or whether non-price factors come into play. The data on the trade of multinational companies are summarized in Figure 22.

## Services

The service accounts (referred to as invisibles) consist of these main categories: travel and tourism; transportation (including freight and port services); royalties and license fees; and numerous other services related to business. U.S. exports of services have nearly doubled over the past six years and account for 25% of the total exports of goods and services. Growth of imports of services has been less rapid, increasing 55% over the past five years and accounting for 16% of total U.S. imports of goods and services.

The service accounts are an important aspect of the current account that is often overlooked. The detailed service accounts are published with a considerable lag. For example, the 1991 detailed service accounts were published in the September 1992 *Survey of Current Business*. Quarterly estimates for the major categories are largely extrapolated from the previous year and are unlikely to capture significant changes that may be occurring.

Data collection for the service accounts has improved considerably, becoming more detailed during the past decade. The system in the U.S. is probably more comprehensive and sophisticated than in any other country. Nevertheless, data on trade in services are not as comprehensive, detailed or timely as merchandise trade. Moreover, numerous questions about reliability suggest that coverage is incomplete and the service accounts are probably understated. Since services are growing in importance and are little appreciated, the definition and estimation procedures for the four major accounts—Travel and Tourism, Transportation, Royalties and License Fees, and Other Private Services are discussed in detail in Appendix 5. The large diversity of the service accounts makes data collection complicated and often unreliable.

Figures 23-26 summarize the trends in the U.S. service accounts over the past six years.

Figure 23

## Exports of Private Services

(billions of dollars)

| | 1986 | 1987 | 1988 | 1989 | 1990 | 1991 |
|---|---|---|---|---|---|---|
| Total private | 77.1 | 86.8 | 100.7 | 118.0 | 138.1 | 152.3 |
| Travel | 20.5 | 23.7 | 29.7 | 36.6 | 43.4 | 48.8 |
| Overseas | 15.7 | 18.0 | 22.3 | 26.9 | 30.8 | 34.5 |
| Canada | 2.7 | 3.3 | 4.2 | 5.4 | 7.1 | 8.5 |
| Mexico | 2.2 | 2.4 | 3.2 | 4.2 | 5.5 | 5.7 |
| Passenger fares | 5.5 | 7.0 | 8.9 | 10.5 | 15.1 | 15.6 |
| Transport. other | 15.8 | 17.3 | 19.5 | 21.1 | 22.9 | 23.6 |
| Freight | 4.7 | 5.1 | 5.9 | 6.3 | 7.2 | 7.2 |
| Port services | 10.6 | 11.6 | 12.8 | 13.9 | 14.7 | 15.3 |
| Other | 0.6 | 0.7 | 0.7 | 0.9 | 1.0 | 1.0 |
| Total royalties and license fees | 7.9 | 9.9 | 11.8 | 13.1 | 16.5 | 17.8 |
| Affiliated | 6.0 | 7.6 | 9.2 | 10.2 | 13.1 | 14.0 |
| Unaffiliated | 1.9 | 2.3 | 2.6 | 2.9 | 3.4 | 3.8 |
| Other services | 27.3 | 28.9 | 30.8 | 36.7 | 40.2 | 46.4 |
| Affiliated | 8.2 | 8.2 | 9.1 | 11.5 | 13.3 | 14.6 |
| Unaffiliated | 19.1 | 20.7 | 21.7 | 25.2 | 26.9 | 31.8 |

Source: *Survey of Current Business*, September 1992, p. 83.

**Figure 24**

## Exports of Other Unaffiliated Private Services

(billions of dollars)

| | 1986 | 1987 | 1988 | 1989 | 1990 | 1991 |
|---|---|---|---|---|---|---|
| Total | 19.1 | 20.7 | 21.7 | 25.2 | 26.8 | 31.8 |
| Education | 3.5 | 3.8 | 4.1 | 4.6 | 5.1 | 5.7 |
| Financial services | 3.3 | 3.7 | 3.8 | 5.0 | 4.3 | 4.7 |
| Insurance, net | 2.0 | 2.3 | 1.5 | 1.6 | 1.8 | 2.2 |
| Telecommunications | 1.8 | 2.1 | 2.2 | 2.5 | 2.7 | 2.8 |
| **Business and professional services** | | | | | | |
| Total | 4.4 | 4.3 | 5.4 | 6.2 | 6.8 | 10.4 |
| Advertising | 0.1 | 0.1 | 0.1 | 0.1 | 0.1 | 0.2 |
| Computer & data proc. | 1.0 | 0.6 | 1.2 | 1.0 | 1.0 | 1.7 |
| Data base and info. | 0.1 | 0.1 | 0.2 | 0.2 | 0.3 | 0.4 |
| R&D and testing | 0.3 | 0.2 | 0.2 | 0.4 | 0.4 | 0.6 |
| PR and consulting | 0.3 | 0.3 | 0.3 | 0.3 | 0.3 | 0.3 |
| Legal | 0.1 | 0.1 | 0.3 | 0.4 | 0.5 | 1.2 |
| Construction | 0.8 | 0.7 | 0.8 | 0.9 | 0.7 | 1.3 |
| Indust. Engineering | 0.1 | 0.3 | 0.3 | 0.2 | 0.5 | 0.5 |
| Maint. and repair | 1.0 | 1.1 | 1.3 | 1.7 | 2.0 | 2.5 |
| Other* | 0.6 | 0.7 | 0.7 | 0.9 | 0.9 | 1.4 |
| Other unaffiliated** | 4.1 | 4.4 | 4.6 | 5.3 | 6.1 | 6.1 |

\* Other consists of such services as accounting, auditing, bookkeeping, agricultural, mailing, management of health care facilities, medical services, personnel supply, sports, performing arts and training services. Medical services is by-far the largest category, comprising about half the "other category."

\*\* Includes mainly expenditures of foreign governments and international agencies in the U.S.

Source: *Survey of Current Business*, September 1992, p. 83.

Figure 25

## Imports of Private Services

(billions of dollars)

| | 1986 | 1987 | 1988 | 1989 | 1990 | 1991 |
|---|---|---|---|---|---|---|
| Total private | 64.5 | 73.4 | 80.3 | 84.1 | 97.0 | 100.0 |
| Travel | 25.9 | 29.3 | 32.1 | 33.4 | 37.3 | 37.0 |
| Overseas | 20.3 | 23.3 | 25.3 | 25.7 | 28.9 | 28.1 |
| Canada | 3.0 | 2.9 | 3.2 | 3.4 | 3.5 | 3.7 |
| Mexico | 2.6 | 3.1 | 3.6 | 4.3 | 4.9 | 5.1 |
| Passenger fares | 6.5 | 7.3 | 7.8 | 8.3 | 10.6 | 10.6 |
| Transport. other | 16.7 | 17.8 | 19.5 | 20.7 | 23.4 | 23.3 |
| Freight | 10.8 | 10.7 | 11.7 | 11.7 | 12.6 | 11.9 |
| Port services | 5.2 | 6.4 | 7.1 | 8.2 | 9.9 | 10.4 |
| Other | 0.6 | 0.7 | 0.7 | 0.8 | 0.9 | 0.9 |
| Total royalties and license fees | 1.4 | 1.8 | 2.6 | 2.6 | 3.1 | 4.0 |
| Affiliated | 1.0 | 1.3 | 1.4 | 1.8 | 2.2 | 2.9 |
| Unaffiliated | 0.5 | 0.5 | 1.2 | 0.8 | 0.9 | 1.1 |
| Other services | 13.9 | 17.2 | 18.4 | 19.1 | 22.5 | 25.1 |
| Affiliated | 3.9 | 5.2 | 5.9 | 7.2 | 8.7 | 9.6 |
| Unaffiliated | 10.0 | 12.0 | 12.5 | 12.0 | 13.8 | 15.6 |

Source: *Survey of Current Business*, September 1992, p. 83.

**Figure 26**

## Imports of Other Unaffiliated Private Services

(billions of dollars)

| | 1986 | 1987 | 1988 | 1989 | 1990 | 1991 |
|---|---|---|---|---|---|---|
| Total | 10.0 | 12.0 | 12.5 | 12.0 | 13.8 | 15.6 |
| | | | | | | |
| Education | 0.4 | 0.5 | 0.5 | 0.6 | 0.7 | 0.7 |
| Financial services | 1.8 | 2.1 | 1.7 | 2.1 | 2.3 | 2.4 |
| Insurance, net | 2.2 | 3.2 | 2.6 | 0.8 | 1.8 | 2.6 |
| Telecommunications | 3.2 | 3.7 | 4.5 | 5.2 | 5.5 | 5.6 |
| **Business and professional services** | | | | | | |
| Total | 1.3 | 1.3 | 1.8 | 2.0 | 2.0 | 2.6 |
| | | | | | | |
| Advertising | 0.1 | 0.1 | 0.2 | 0.2 | 0.2 | 0.3 |
| Computer and data proc. | a | a | a | a | a | 0.1 |
| Data base and info. | a | a | a | a | 0.1 | 0.1 |
| R&D and testing | 0.1 | 0.1 | 0.2 | 0.1 | 0.2 | 0.3 |
| PR and consulting | 0.1 | 0.1 | 0.1 | 0.1 | 0.1 | 0.2 |
| Legal | a | 0.1 | 0.1 | 0.1 | 0.1 | 0.2 |
| Construction | 0.3 | 0.2 | 0.3 | 0.4 | 0.3 | 0.3 |
| Indust. engineering | 0.1 | 0.1 | 0.1 | 0.1 | 0.1 | a |
| Maint. and repair | 0.5 | 0.5 | 0.6 | 0.7 | 0.7 | 0.6 |
| Other* | 0.1 | 0.1 | 0.1 | 0.1 | 1.0 | 0.6 |
| Other unaffiliated** | 1.1 | 1.1 | 1.3 | 1.4 | 1.5 | 1.6 |

[a] less than $50 million

* Other consists of such services as accounting, auditing, bookkeeping, agricultural, mailing, management of health care facilities, medical services, personnel supply, sports, performing arts and training services.

** Includes mainly wages of foreign residents temporarily employed in the U.S. and of Canadian and Mexican commuters in the U.S. border area.

Source: *Survey of Current Business*, September 1992, p. 83.

# INTERNATIONAL CAPITAL FLOWS

## U.S. CAPITAL ACCOUNT

The system in the U.S. was designed when most transactions were conducted in conventional financial instruments and channeled through a few large banks and other financial institutions. Capital markets have changed dramatically since then reflecting the deregulation of capital controls, new financial instruments and the proliferation of transactions. The statistical problems faced by U.S. compilers have intensified and strained available resources.

The next section will focus on the concepts and methodology of the U.S. balance of payments as they relate to portfolio, direct investment, banking transactions, and non-banking transactions.

### Portfolio Capital Flows

During the past decade, large institutional investors, such as pension funds, insurance companies, and investment trusts accounted for most of the growth in international portfolio investment. Large investors shifted part of their assets to foreign managers and often bought and sold securities directly in foreign markets.

#### Methodology

Net U.S. purchases of foreign securities and net foreign purchase of U.S. securities are estimated by the Bureau of Economic Analysis (BEA) on the basis of data from the U.S. Department of the Treasury International Capital Reporting System (TICS). Only long-term stocks and bonds are reported. Filing is required for all banks, banking institutions, brokers, and dealers when total purchases or sales exceed $500,000 in any given month. The BEA adjusts the data to exclude estimates of commissions, taxes, and other charges from the gross transactions. The activity of a large institution reflects the consolidation of many transactions made through the reporting institution. As a result, a small number of reporters account for a large share of the reported total.

Purchases and sales of U.S. securities by foreigners are reported by securities dealers in the U.S. The reports of the dealers are supplemented by reports from corporations that sell bonds directly to foreigners, e.g., Eurobonds. These are not regular reporters.

1. Incomplete or inaccurate data. Money managers and large institutional investors are increasingly maintaining their own facilities for conducting business without dealing with a financial institution that must submit TICS forms.

2. New financial instruments are not reported. Short-term marketable instruments and derivative instruments such as warrants, options, puts and calls are not ordinarily covered on the TICS forms. The TICS covers warrants and options only when the underlying security is a stock or long-term bond.

3. Diffusion of reporting responsibilities. As financial organizations are becoming increasingly complex and the responsibility for reporting becomes decentralized, this obscures the responsibility for reporting.

4. Discrepancies due to foreign exchange conversion. Transactions in foreign currencies are reported in terms of their dollar equivalents converted at the prevailing exchange rate either at the time of the transaction or at the close of the last business day of the reporting month.

5. Sales to third parties. The geographic distribution of the reported data may not necessarily reflect the nationality of the ultimate foreign owner. Transactions in well developed foreign financial markets are done on behalf of third party customers or countries.

## Foreign Direct Investment

During the past decade, there has been considerable concern about the growing globalization of world assets. In the U.S. this was exemplified by the fear that Japan was buying out America. In other countries, there were worries about foreign interests exerting a disproportionate influence on domestic economic policies. Dismantled capital controls and large scale mergers and acquisitions diversified the ownership of assets across national borders. Between 1986 and 1989, net direct investment flows more than doubled to about $200 billion. The value of direct investment measured at book value exceeded $1,000 billion by the end of 1989. (Global data are compiled with a considerable lag.) Since direct investment is largely a function of economic growth, it is assumed that the growth of direct investment decelerated in the early 1990s.

The global presence of U.S. companies has grown dramatically over the past several decades. In 1990, worldwide assets of U.S. multinational companies amounted to $6,522 billion, of which $1,552 billion were assets of foreign affiliates.

## U.S. Direct Investment

The U.S. system and methodology for collecting direct investment data is considered to be one of the most comprehensive systems in the world. Moreover, direct investment capital flows are considered to be more accurate than investment flows related to portfolio or banking flows.

### Definition of Direct Investment
Outward investment or direct investment abroad: A direct investor is a U.S. person (or company) who has 10% or more ownership in a business enterprise located in a foreign country. Inward investment or direct investment in the U.S.: Foreign ownership of more than 10% of a business enterprise located in the U.S.

### Methodology for Compiling U.S. Direct Investment
The Bureau of Economic Analysis conducts many surveys on both direct investment abroad and direct investment in the U.S. Every five years a benchmark survey is conducted which covers virtually all direct investment flows. Annual and quarterly surveys update information for inclusion in the balance of payments statistics.

### U.S. Investment Overseas
The latest benchmark survey covered data up through 1989 and was published in 1991. Reports were required from each U.S. parent and separately for each of its foreign affiliates that had assets, sales or net income greater than $3 million. Greater detail was requested for foreign affiliates that were majority owned.

On an annual basis, BEA collects key information on the operations of a sample of parent companies and their affiliates. Mandatory quarterly reports cover information required for balance of payments purposes.

## Methodological Problems

1. The quarterly and annual data are heavily skewed towards large companies and also towards investors with ownership of 50% or more. For example, the ten largest U.S. parent companies, in terms of the assets of foreign affiliates, owned 32% of such assets. The 100 largest companies accounted for 72% of the total assets;[108]

2. Sizable revisions occur after quarterly reports are revised;

3. Ownership of less than 10% is excluded. Thus, if one party owns 11% and another owns 9%, the 11% is included but the 9% is excluded; and

4. The distinction between direct investment and portfolio investment is often arbitrary. As noted above, direct investment implies that a person (company) has a lasting interest in the management of a business in another country, and this implies a long-term relationship. Portfolio investment reflects primarily short-term activity in financial markets, where the ability to shift funds between countries or financial investments is a major consideration.

## Foreign Investment in the U.S.

The latest benchmark survey covered 1987. Complete reports covering financial, operating, balance of payments and direct investment position data had to be filed if the U.S. affiliate of a foreign company had at least $1 million in assets, sales, or net income.

There are several problems with the surveys of foreign company affiliates. Some of the major problems are:

1. Quarterly surveys are used for the most recent information. They are less comprehensive and only cover a sample of companies;

2. Some data are collected on a fiscal year basis and adjusted to a calendar year for use in the balance of payments;

3. Compliance with reporting requirements is not as good as it could be; and

---

108. *Behind the Numbers; U. S. Trade in the World Economy.* Washington, DC: National Academy Press, 1992, p. 161.

---

4. Late reporting is somewhat of a problem.

## Impact on the U.S. Balance of Payments

Direct investment has a sizable impact on both the current and capital accounts. Direct investment receipts and payments are captured in the current account as dividends, interest and reinvested earnings. The capital account captures changes in the ownership of assets (net worth) including changes in owners' equity, intercompany accounts and reinvested earnings.

The capital account has two major components. These are investment by the U.S. citizens and organizations in businesses located in other countries, and investment in the U.S. by citizens and organizations from other countries.

### U.S. Direct Investment Abroad

Equity capital consists of changes in U.S. parents' equity in their foreign affiliates. Equity capital outflows are recorded at transactions values, based on the books of U.S. parents. Reinvested earnings of foreign affiliates are total earnings including capital gains and losses, less distributed earnings. Intercompany debt flows consist of the increase in U.S. parents' net intercompany account receivables from their foreign affiliates during the year.

### Foreign Direct Investment in the U.S.

Equity capital consists of changes in foreign holdings of U.S. affiliates. Equity capital inflows are recorded at transactions values based on the books of U.S. parents. Reinvested earnings of U.S. affiliates are total earnings, including capital gains and losses, less distributed earnings.

Because of the special nature of the relationship between a direct investor and its affiliates, there may be cases in which goods, services and technical know-how are provided from parent to the affiliate without any corresponding cash flow. It is estimated that these noncash transactions have increased in recent years.

Direct investment earnings are a major portion of the service account. Income on direct investment is the return that direct investors receive on their investment. The two major components of earnings are distributed earnings and reinvested earnings. Interest on intercompany accounts is a small fraction of earnings. Distributed earnings consist of U.S. parents' receipts less U.S. parents' payments. Data collection in this area presents two special difficulties:

1. Confidentiality — The BEA surveys are confidential and this poses a continuing problem in delivering specific industry information to the ultimate user. Data points are often suppressed because the cell is "dominated" by three or fewer firms.

2. Classification — All activities of foreign affiliates operating in the U.S. are consolidated and classified according to the primary activity of the affiliate. This method of classification overvalues the primary activity of the subsidiary and undervalues any secondary or other activities.

## Bank claims and liabilities

### Methodology

U.S. banks, depository institutions, international banking facilities, bank holding companies, brokers and dealers are required to file TIC B forms. Reporting is mandatory. Data includes information on loans, advances and overdrafts and various other transactions. Data includes operating transactions between U.S. banks and their foreign branches, as well as subsidiaries of foreign banks in the U.S. Reports are required if total claims on, or liabilities to, foreigners are $15 million or more for any month-end closing balance. Reports are either monthly or quarterly depending on the institution involved.

Data is generally assumed to be fairly accurate. Interbanking business between U.S. and foreign banks can be verified with the banking data collected by the Bank for International Settlements.

The following items are excluded from both claims and liabilities:

1. Long-term securities of foreign or U.S. issuers (reported on the S form);

2. Permanent capital invested in affiliated agencies;

3. Contingent claims and liabilities;

4. Gold, silver or currency in transit to and from the U.S.;

5. Interest rate and foreign currency swaps associated with bank indebtedness; and

6. Forward exchange contracts.

## Problems

### Omissions

There are transactions that are not included within the TIC B reporting system. These include direct transactions between nonfinancial lenders and borrowers, with financial intermediaries increasingly acting as agents or arrangers of the deal for a fee or commission.

### Accuracy of Data

There are large daily swings in banks' claims and liabilities vis-a-vis their own foreign offices, particularly between the last day of certain months and the first day of the next month. Swings of $10-20 billion are not unusual.

Data are end-month positions which must be converted to flows for use in the balance of payments accounts. Capital flows for banks are calculated from changes in asset positions. Balances in foreign currencies must be adjusted to reflect changes in various exchange rates. The currency composition of the accounts is not known.

### Data Errors Related to Foreign Banks

The accuracy of data provided by U.S. affiliates of foreign banks has been subject to question. It is not clear whether filing instructions are always fully understood and properly acted upon.

## Non-banking Transactions

This is a small category made up of diverse transactions. Exporters, importers, industrial and commercial firms are required to file TIC C forms on a quarterly basis. Transactions include financial claims or liabilities and commercial claims or liabilities related to the sale of goods and services in normal business operations.

## Problems

### Non-reporting and Reporting Responsibilities

TIC C reporters are not subject to the regulatory authority of the Federal

Reserve Bank and they tend to be less cooperative about reporting. At present, it is believed that only a small fraction of the required transactions are reported. Non-bank transactions are a diverse group that includes individuals and businesses of many kinds. It is extremely difficult to measure transactions in this group.

In some respects, the TIC C reports are a residual report, catching transactions that are not reported elsewhere. They exclude direct investment transactions, securities and custody items reported by banks, brokers and dealers. As a result, there is confusion about reporting responsibilities.

For example, in September 1990, the TIC data on U.S. non-bank financial assets abroad amounted to $65 billion compared with $250 billion reported by the BIS and IMF. Similarly, the TIC data on U.S. non-bank financial liabilities was $80 billion compared with $235 billion reported by the BIS and IMF.

### Capital Flight and Money Laundering

There is a broadly held perception that private non-bank flows are seriously understated. Capital flight, money laundering, and illegal flows are often named as reasons for this problem.

### The Use of the U.S. Dollar Abroad

Foreign holdings of U.S. currency are not included in the balance of payments statistics. It has been estimated that one to two-thirds of the U.S. currency outstanding may be held by foreigners. In many foreign countries, the U.S. dollar is widely used as the most desirable medium of exchange because of hyper-inflation (which makes the local currency worthless). The local currency is not convertible for international trade purposes. The wide use of the U.S. dollar abroad is also a reflection of illegal drug traffic and eventual money laundering.


## INTERNATIONAL ASPECTS OF THE CAPITAL ACCOUNT

The difficulties described in the U.S. capital accounts are compounded when analyzing global capital flows. The IMF Working Party "found that world capital account statistical systems are in a state of crisis."[109]

---

109. *Report on the Measurement of International Capital Flows*, International Monetary Fund, September 1992.

---

Global integration of financial markets reflects the combination of a number of important changes over the past decade. These include: dismantling capital controls, the increasing role of foreign banking in national markets, the internationalization of securities' markets, the development of new financial instruments, and the diversification of institutional investors. Global integration has been made possible because of technological advances.

Because of the growing globalization of capital flows, it is imperative to address questions related to the world financial reporting systems. As the reporting system becomes increasingly unreliable, the monitoring of international capital flows is becoming impaired.

Since relatively few countries account for the major part of world capital flows, these leading countries should be at the forefront of upgrading and harmonizing their capital account statistics. (About ten countries account for 85% of the flows while Japan, the U.S., the U.K. and Germany together account for almost two-thirds of all transactions.)

## Other topics

Other aspects of international capital flows relate to offshore financial centers and the growth of the inter-bank market.

## Offshore Financial Centers

Offshore financial centers are small economies that have set up systems to encourage or promote financial transactions among foreigners through domestic intermediaries. OFCs typically have special classes of business licenses that exempt holders from most forms of domestic regulation provided they do not participate in the local economy and conduct only international business.

The transactions of offshore financial centers complicate the world balance of payments. OFCs do not necessarily report transactions, whereas partner countries are more likely to report such transactions. There is a great deal of ambiguity as far as reporting, and it is likely that some portion of transactions are either not reported or misclassified.

For balance of payments purposes, capital flows are not usually recorded, since the transactions are not related to domestic activity. While OFCs omit such activities from their statements, partner countries report them in their own balance of payments as specific transactions with OFCs.

Often, transactions change form as they pass through OFCs. For example, they may enter as direct investment or interbank flows and leave as portfolio investment transactions.

## The International Inter-bank Market

There has been a tremendous expansion in the scale of net and gross capital transactions among the industrialized countries. The balance of payments capture the net transactions. An even more rapid expansion has occurred in the volume of capital transactions.

The progressive relaxation of capital controls, as well as the broader financial liberalization in the industrial countries, has brought about a growing integration and globalization of major offshore and domestic financial markets.

The development of financial instruments has led to increased linkages among financial markets domestically and internationally. The markets for short-term interest rate futures, swaps, forward rate agreements (FRAs) and interest rate options have emerged to complement, and in some cases, to substitute for the traditional interbank deposit and other cash markets. In essence, the interbank deposit markets now basically function as funding markets, while hedging and position-taking have shifted to off-balance-sheet markets.

The derivative markets not only interact with the underlying cash market, but are also themselves deeply inter-connected. For example, securities increasingly incorporate option elements or are swapped into payment flows involving different currencies. Bond issues with a menu of equity-linked elements have become increasingly common.

Figures 27 to 30 give an indication of the scope and size of the international capital markets.

The global inter-bank market more than tripled during the past eight years (Figure 27).

Off-balance-sheet assets have become an increasingly important part of inter-bank assets (Figure 28).

The growth in transactions and notional outstanding positions in derivative instruments had tended to outpace growth in other segments of the market. The outstanding notional volume of derivative contracts on interest rates and currencies as a proportion of international assets of BIS reporting banks has grown from around 25% at the end of 1986 to more than 100% at the end of 1991.

**Figure 27**

## International Bank Positions
## Amounts Outstanding at Year-end

(billions of dollars)

| Parent Country of Bank | Claims | | Liabilities | |
|---|---|---|---|---|
| | **1983** | **1991** | **1983** | **1991** |
| Belgium | 38.2 | 135.1 | 39.6 | 133.1 |
| Canada | 112.9 | 110.1 | 115.2 | 121.2 |
| France | 191.4 | 565.4 | 185.8 | 630.4 |
| Germany | 114.5 | 640.4 | 131.7 | 489.2 |
| Italy | 80.9 | 397.5 | 78.9 | 427.5 |
| Japan | 456.9 | 1935.1 | 414.7 | 1828.1 |
| Luxembourg | 5.2 | 46.7 | 5.0 | 47.9 |
| Netherlands | 62.5 | 199.5 | 59.8 | 178.3 |
| Sweden | 18.2 | 128.9 | 17.2 | 126.1 |
| Switzerland | 79.9 | 408.9 | 67.2 | 398.6 |
| United Kingdom | 178.8 | 282.1 | 181.6 | 333.6 |
| United States | 605.5 | 650.7 | 544.4 | 683.1 |
| Other | 191.0 | 636.6 | 193.5 | 698.7 |
| Total | 2165.9 | 6137.0 | 2034.1 | 6095.8 |

Source: *Recent Developments in International Interbank Relations*, Bank for International Settlements, October 1992, p. 43.

Figure 28

## Comparison of On- and Off-balance-sheet Interbank Assets
### As a Percentage of Total Assets End of 1990

| Banks From | Total | On-balance-sheet | Off-balance-sheet |
|---|---|---|---|
| Belgium | 11.0 | 10.2 | 0.8 |
| Canada | 10.2 | 7.5 | 2.7 |
| France | n.a. | 16.7 | n.a. |
| Germany | 9.2 | 8.3 | 0.9 |
| Italy | 23.5 | 20.4 | 3.1 |
| Japan | 20.4 | 15.0 | 5.4 |
| Luxembourg | 30.0 | 29.2 | 0.8 |
| Netherlands | 20.6 | 18.3 | 2.3 |
| Sweden | 13.3 | 10.0 | 3.3 |
| United Kingdom | 30.7 | 21.5 | 9.2 |
| United States | 7.1 | 3.8 | 3.3 |

Source: *Recent Developments in International Interbank Relations,*
Bank for International Settlements, October 1992, p. 49.

 **Figure 29**

## Selected Derivative Instruments
**Notional Principal Amounts Outstanding at Year-end**

(billions of dollars)

|  | 1986 | 1987 | 1988 | 1989 | 1990 | 1991 |
|---|---|---|---|---|---|---|
| **Exchange traded instruments** | | | | | | |
| Interest rate futures | 370 | 488 | 895 | 1,201 | 1,454 | 2,159 |
| Interest rate options | 146 | 122 | 279 | 387 | 600 | 1,072 |
| Currency futures | 10 | 14 | 12 | 16 | 16 | 18 |
| Currency options | 39 | 60 | 48 | 50 | 56 | 59 |
| Stock market index futures | 15 | 18 | 28 | 42 | 70 | 77 |
| Options on stock market | 3 | 23 | 38 | 66 | 88 | 132 |
| Total | 583 | 725 | 1,300 | 1,762 | 2,284 | 3,518 |
| **Over-the-counter instruments** | | | | | | |
| Interest rate swaps | 400 | 683 | 1,010 | 1,503 | 2,312 | 3,065 |
| Currency and cross-currency interest rate swaps | 100 | 184 | 320 | 449 | 578 | 807 |
| Other derivative instruments | - | - | - | 450 | 561 | 577 |
| Total | 500 | 867 | 1330 | 2,402 | 3,451 | 4,449 |

Source: *Recent Developments in International Interbank Relations*, Bank for International Settlements, October 1992, p. 51.

Figure 30

## Derivative Financial Instruments
### Annual Number of Contracts in Millions

(billions of dollars)

| | 1986 | 1987 | 1988 | 1989 | 1990 | 1991 |
|---|---|---|---|---|---|---|
| Futures on short-term interest rate instruments | 16 | 29 | 34 | 70 | 76 | 85 |
| of which: | | | | | | |
| 3-month Euro-dollar | 12 | 24 | 25 | 47 | 39 | 42 |
| Futures on long-term interest rate instruments | 75 | 116 | 123 | 131 | 143 | 150 |
| of which: | | | | | | |
| U.S. Treasury bond | 55 | 69 | 74 | 73 | 78 | 70 |
| French bond | 1 | 12 | 12 | 15 | 16 | 21 |
| German bond | 9 | 18 | 19 | 19 | 16 | 13 |
| Currency Futures | 20 | 21 | 22 | 28 | 29 | 29 |
| Interest Rate Options | 22 | 29 | 31 | 40 | 52 | 51 |
| Currency Options | 13 | 18 | 18 | 21 | 19 | 21 |
| Total | 146 | 214 | 227 | 289 | 319 | 336 |

Source: *Recent Developments in International Interbank Relations,*
Bank for International Settlements, October 1992, p. 57.

## Conclusion

The large statistical discrepancy in the U.S. balance of payments indicates that there are serious data problems yet to be resolved. Theoretically, improvement of the U.S. balance of payments should be made as a coordinated effort by all the agencies that are charged with collecting and compiling data. In reality, this is not likely to happen. Over the next decade, cost considerations are expected to prevail, so allocation of new funding for improved data collection will be hotly debated. The improvement of the capital accounts should be a top priority.

In the trade off between timeliness and accuracy, the balance of payments is reasonably timely. In assessing quarterly data for 1992, the trade and service accounts were not subject to significant revisions, whereas the capital accounts showed considerable volatility.

The fact that we don't here propose massive overhauls of the entire system should not be taken to imply that we don't think they are needed. On the contrary: the growing importance of the global economy requires that a wide variety of perspectives be brought to bear on the task of constructing a system of statistics that will comprehensively and more perspicuously depict the global market. This chapter was designed primarily to invite that discussion. Some specific immediate recommendations are suggested in Chapter 8, Recommendations—International Statistics.

# Chapter 7

# Recommendations —
# National Accounts and the SNA

## Introduction

This report has outlined the constraints to the reform of official statistics, as well as noting current challenges and deficiencies. Where does this analysis lead us?

The authors take an optimistic approach to looking at the process for developing a statistical system that will meet the needs of the 21st century. It will be a complicated task, yet a number of recent developments offer important starting points for the journey. A few cited are:

- The culmination of a long effort to refine and update the United Nations System of National Accounts (SNA) was achieved when the United Nations Economic and Social Council approved the 1993 SNA revision in July 1993. This chapter outlines some of the elements required for implementation of the proposed revisions.

- The National Academy of Sciences will soon publish a report on international financial flows as a companion to the highly regarded report *Behind the Numbers*.[110] This chapter summarizes key recommendations from the published report and makes a set of independent recommendations in the area of international financial statistics. These key recommendations can serve as the starting point for redesign of the increasingly important global system of statistics about economic relations among nations.

- The Federal Economic Classification Policy Committee (ECPC)[111] is at work addressing the critical questions of developing a classification system that will reflect the economic structures of today (and, hopefully, the future). This effort can be a rallying point for

---

110. Anne Y. Kester, Ed. *Behind the Numbers; U.S. Trade in the World Economy*. Washington, DC: National Academy Press, 1992.

111. This committee is chaired by Jack Triplett of BEA. The Committee will report to the Office of Management and Budget with a target set of recommendations to be adopted in March 1996.

careful consideration of the needs for statistics that will be evident in the next two decades.

- Work is now underway to examine the structure and process for the population census to be taken in the year 2000. While funding for this effort is fragile (since some congressional cuts have been proposed in the current work plan), this fundamental review also provides a framework for addressing the needed improvements and for bringing about change.

While it is easy to be skeptical about fundamental changes emerging from these bureaucratic efforts, it should be noted that the professional statisticians supporting these efforts operate with a high level of professional competence, dedication, and understanding of the deficiencies of the current system. The impediments to change are largely broad in scope and not related to any specific proposal. These impediments include:

1. the resistance of administrators to become champions for causes that will not yield fruit on their watch;

2. a reluctance of the executive branch to propose funding research and new statistical (overhead) programs in a time of chronic budget deficits;

3. public resistance to supplying information to governments including problems with the paperwork burden discussed earlier;[112]

4. the tendency for legislative bodies to micromanage statistical agencies and to ignore the long-term effects of statistical program changes; and

5. the lack of a political constituency for statistical improvements.

With these barriers that have been so well-defined and recognized, why make recommendations for improvement? We suggest several reasons.

First, we believe that this report can be a starting point for the development of a practical "vision" of future directions. *If enough discussion and debate are fostered, the resulting consensus could be a starting point for building political pressure for change, not only within the statistical community but, also more important, in the user community (both public and private).* A cost-benefit analysis of improved data for better decisions versus status quo and weakening data for future needs should be a compelling case for change.

---

112. See discussion in Chapter 1

Second, the resistance of executive branch decision makers and legislators can be overcome if the case is presented in a long-range, well-documented manner. *We believe that trying to solve these issues with "incrementalism" has proved to be a failure.* A "comprehensive" program has more potential for getting attention and for yielding measurable and understandable results.

Third, the issues of "reporting burden" and public resistance to "big brother data banks" belong to another era. When the available technology for electronic data interchange, for encoding and protecting electronic files, for scanning and optical character recognition, is combined with the rapid evolution of computer accessibility, enormous expansion of cpu power in desktop and handheld computers, and the availability of inexpensive data storage and telecommunications systems, *the opportunity to collect, analyze, and disseminate better information is at hand. We simply need to appreciate the opportunities and design new systems of collecting the information that is available throughout our society.*

Fourth, *a set of new and improved national statistics will invariably lead to a set of new and improved national goals.* For example, the current economic dogma places a high priority on balancing the trade deficit. Using alternative, more precise data may indicate that this goal is much closer to being achieved than previously recognized or the data may uncover problems not currently appreciated. The power of economic statistics to shape economic policy recommendations can never be underestimated.

Further, other nations are already making rapid progress in these same areas. Their progress makes it important for the U.S. to show the path toward the 21st century with the recognition that this statistical framework can be replicated throughout the developed world and, later, in the developing world.

## Future Direction for the U.S. National Economic Accounts

As discussed earlier, key aspects of the U.S. national economic accounts need strengthening. This section recommends nineteen major improvements to enhance the relevance of the accounts for use in economic analysis during the balance of the 1990s and into the 21st century.

These recommendations are based on a review of budget and technical papers of the Bureau of Economic Analysis (BEA), Bureau of the Census, Bureau of Labor Statistics (BLS), Internal Revenue Service (IRS), and the

Office of Management and Budget (OMB).[113]

The papers contain actual and proposed improvements for economic statistics included in BEA, Census, BLS, and IRS budgets during the early 1990s through fiscal year 1994; reports and articles on technical subjects; and an accounting of the agencies' actions on the recommendations of the Creamer Report (the *Gross National Product Data Improvement Project Report*). Current programs, future plans, and new ideas were discussed with officials and staff of the above agencies. Discussion also focused on the new Joint Program in Survey Methodology of the Universities of Maryland and Michigan, and Westat, Inc. The Census, BLS, and IRS undertook a systematic review of their actions on the Creamer Report recommendations expressly for the review that served as background for this book; the BEA had previously done this. *Four of the nineteen recommendations in this report are non-implemented Creamer Report recommendations.*

The conceptual design of the accounts requires that a vast array of economic transactions be summarized into usable statistics for economic analysis, balanced by the limitations of data collection costs, by the lack of appropriate data in business records, and by reporting burdens involved in obtaining the necessary data to convert the concepts into actual statistical measures. *The conceptual evolution will continue in the second half of the 1990s when BEA converts the national income and product accounts (NIPA) to the United Nations' System of National Accounts (SNA).* In preparing the accounts, BEA relies heavily on data from other federal agencies and, to a lesser extent, on data from private and international organizations.

The recommendations in this chapter address three broad areas:

1. The statistics underlying the accounts provided by the Census, BLS, and IRS which account for the bulk of the data base;

2. The preparation of the accounts by BEA; and

3. The infrastructure of economic statistics in the public and private sectors that affects the accounts.

The following chapter includes specific recommendations for addressing problems with international statistics which were dicussed in Chapter 6, Global Interaction. There is some overlap in the SNA because it also deals with Rest of the World interrelationships as discussed in Chapter 5,

---

113. This review was undertaken by Norman Frumkin, currently an economic consultant and writer. He formerly worked as a consultant in the early 1970s to the *Gross National Product Data Improvement Project Report* (The Creamer Report) which was published in 1977.

Fundamentals. Let us now turn specifically to recommendations concerning NIPA and the SNA.

## Specific Topics of the National Accounts

This section highlights four aspects of the national accounts: (1) quarterly Gross Domestic Product; (2) real output; (3) input/output tables; and (4) satellite accounts.

### Quarterly Gross Domestic Product

The gross domestic product (GDP) estimates, which are prepared on a current basis every quarter, are the bedrock of the accounts. They are used in cyclical analyses of the economy and in formulating fiscal and monetary policies. Three GDP estimates are prepared every quarter: the "advance" figure is published roughly 25 days after the reference quarter ends, and subsequent revisions are published in the "preliminary" figure 55 days after the quarter and in the "final" figure 85 days after the quarter.

Two aspects of the quarterly estimates are discussed: new data collections and the statistical discrepancy.

### New data collections

New data collections to improve the GDP data base are recommended for the following components: personal consumption expenditures, purchases and total expenditures of state and local governments, employee compensation, and corporate profits.

*Personal consumption expenditures:* Quarterly personal consumption expenditures for services are based on extrapolating annual levels by the movement of wage payments in service industries from the monthly BLS survey of employer payrolls to estimate approximately 30% of total services expenditures. Personal service outlays totaled $2.3 trillion in 1992. The Census Bureau greatly expanded the annual and quinquennial coverage of service industries in its surveys and economic censuses during the 1980s. There is, however, no quarterly coverage of important service industries, such as health care and auto repair. Outlays for services are subject to wide cyclical fluctuations, contrary to the common notion that they move steadily in one direction.

## Recommendation

Our recommendation in Chapter 9 is to eliminate the 85-day estimate. If a decision is made to continue publication of the 85-day estimates, the Census Bureau should collect quarterly data on sales of service industries for use in the final 85-day GDP estimates. In planning this survey of service industry establishments, Census should examine the ongoing Consumer Expenditure Survey of households that it conducts for the Bureau of Labor Statistics to determine if some outlays reported by households can be used to supplement the industry estimates.

*State and local governments' purchases of goods and services and total expenditures:* Government expenditures include purchases of goods and services which are part of the GDP. In addition to purchased goods and services, expenditures include transfer payments for income maintenance, interest, social insurance funds, subsidies, and other items. Expenditures are used in the derivation of government budget surplus/deficit positions in the national accounts.

There are several gaps in these data. First, quarterly data on purchases of goods and services other than for employee compensation and structures are not available. Thus, purchases totaling $118 billion in 1992 of equipment, supplies, utilities, and services for education, police, health, transportation, housing, welfare, utilities, and other governmental functions are judgmentally extrapolated from earlier annual levels for the subsequent quarterly GDP estimates. Additionally, these purchases are subject to cyclical fluctuation since they are in part governed by changes in tax revenues.

The second gap is in the quarterly estimates of state and local budgets. Here too, trend extrapolation of purchased goods and services is used for some transfer payments. Total expenditures were $822 billion in 1992. Quarterly data on receipts of state and local governments are available.

Third, quarterly source data are not available for about 10% of receipts, primarily contributions for social insurance, and for interest receipts, which are recorded in the NIPAs as negative expenditure. They amount to over $100 billion!

## Recommendation

Our recommendation in Chapter 9 is to eliminate the 85-day estimate. If a decision is made to continue publication of the 85-day estimates, the Census Bureau should conduct a quarterly survey of expenditures of state and local governments for use in both the final 85-day GDP estimates and in the 85-day state and local budget estimates. The survey should cover compensation other than wage and salary compensation, which is the only component currently reported. This is a non-implemented Creamer Report recommendation.

*Compensation of employees:* The employee compensation figures are composed of wages and salaries, social insurance (employer taxes for social security and unemployment insurance), and other labor income (mainly employer-paid private pension, health, and welfare plans). Wage and salary data are based on the monthly BLS survey of employer payrolls. The social insurance estimates are derived by multiplying the BLS wage data by social security and unemployment insurance tax rates. The other labor income figures are extrapolated from annual trends. Employee compensation was $3.5 trillion in 1992 ($2.9 trillion for wages and salaries, and $0.3 trillion each for social insurance and other labor income).

### Recommendation

The Internal Revenue Service should tabulate data from a probability sample of the Employer's Quarterly Federal Tax Return (Form 941) on wages and social security payments for use in the final 85-day GDP estimate. This is a non-implemented Creamer Report recommendation.

*Corporate profits:* The corporate profits estimates for manufacturing, mining, and trade corporations are based on Census survey information in the *Quarterly Financial Report (QFR).* Quarterly corporate profits in the construction, transportation, utilities, finance, and service industries are based on stockholder and regulatory agency reports and extrapolating annual data using industry sales or other measures of industry activity multiplied by trended profit margins. Corporate profits before the payment of income taxes for this latter group of industries were $134 billion in 1991. Corporate profits are a cyclically volatile component of the GDP.

### Recommendation

The Census Bureau should conduct a comprehensive review of the scope of the Quarterly Financial Report (QFR) in consultation with the Bureau of Economic Analysis to determine where it can feasibly remedy major data gaps in the quarterly estimates of corporate profits. Based on an assessment of the quality of the existing data sources used in estimating corporate profits, the review should include the benefits and costs of (a) expanding coverage to the construction, transportation, utilities, finance, and services industries; and (b) expanding the coverage to unincorporated businesses in those industries where sole proprietorships and partnerships are prominent. If some expansion of the QFR is warranted, research and pilot surveys will be necessary prior to operational surveys. The inclusion of banks in the survey would have to be coordinated with the banking regulatory agencies. The FY 1994 Census Bureau's budget includes a request for funds to add the business services industries (SIC 73) to the QFR. We support the request.

### Statistical Discrepancy

The statistical discrepancy is a broad guide of the extent of statistical inconsistencies and statistical error in the national accounts. Specifically, the discrepancy is the GDP estimated from the product side (the sum of all *uses* of income) minus the GDP estimated from the income side (the sum of all *sources* of income). The product side comprises consumer expenditures, private investment, government purchases, and net exports. The income side comprises employee compensation, business profits, rental income, net interest, consumption of fixed capital, indirect business taxes, current surplus of government enterprises, subsidies, and business transfer payments. Conceptually, the sum totals of the product and income sides are equivalent since they both represent the nation's output, only viewed from different perspectives; the product side focuses on markets and the income side on production costs.

When the discrepancy is positive, the product side is larger than the income side, and when the discrepancy is negative the income side is larger. Because the discrepancy is a net figure, it is smaller than the actual statistical inconsistencies and errors among the various items of the accounts because the positive and negative inconsistencies and errors are partly offsetting.[114] Other GDP measures with slightly different definitions or methodology are published: final sales of domestic product, gross domestic purchases, final sales to domestic purchasers, gross national product, and command-basis gross national product.

Figure 31 shows the GDP and the discrepancy during 1988-92 in current dollars. The discrepancy shifted from $-28.4 billion in 1988 to $33.4 billion in 1992, a swing of $62 billion over the period. The discrepancy was 0.6% of the GDP in 1992. It was primarily positive in the past five years, but before 1988 it was often negative and is likely to become negative again because of the misreporting adjustments to wages, profits, and nonfarm proprietors' income, which now total over $300 billion. The 1977 benchmarks for these adjustments were rough approximations, and they are now being extrapolated by less reliable source data. There are no similar source

---

114. Other reasons why the statistical discrepancy understates the error in the accounts can be found in Allan H. Young, "Evaluation of the GNP Estimates," *Survey of Current Business,* August 1987.

---

Figure 31

## GDP and the Statistical Discrepancy

(billions of current dollars)

| | 1<br>GDP | 2<br>Statistical<br>Discrepancy | 3<br>Percent<br>of GDP<br>(1)/(2) x 100 |
|---|---|---|---|
| 1988 | 4,900.4 | -28.4 | -0.6% |
| 1989 | 5,250.8 | 1.1 | 0.02 |
| 1990 | 5,522.2 | 5.4 | 0.1 |
| 1991 | 5,677.5 | 21.9 | 0.4 |
| 1992 | 5,950.7 | 33.4 | 0.6 |

Source: Based on data in the *Survey of Current Business* (spring 1993).

Figure 32

## Real GDP on the Product and Income Sides: Annual Growth Rates

(billions of 1987 dollars)

| | 1<br>GDP<br>Product | 2<br>Statistical<br>Discrepancy | 3<br>GDP<br>Income<br>(1)-(2) | 4 Percent Change from Previous Year | |
|---|---|---|---|---|---|
| | | | | GDP<br>Product<br>(1) | GDP<br>Income<br>(3) |
| 1988 | 4,718.6 | -27.4 | 4,746.0 | 3.9% | 4.0% |
| 1989 | 4,838.0 | 0.9 | 4,837.1 | 2.5 | 1.9 |
| 1990 | 4,877.5 | 4.9 | 4,872.6 | 0.8 | 0.7 |
| 1991 | 4,821.0 | 18.7 | 4,802.3 | -1.2 | -1.4 |
| 1992 | 4,922.6 | 27.9 | 4,894.7 | 2.1 | 1.9 |

Source: Based on data in the *Survey of Current Business* (spring 1993).

data problems of this size on the product side.

Figure 32 shows the differences in annual rates of economic growth obtained when using the alternative product- and income-side GDP measures in constant dollars. The annual growth rates typically differed by no more than 0.2 percentage point during 1988-92, although the differential was 0.6 percentage point in 1989 due to the sharp change in the discrepancy between 1988 and 1989. The growth rates were usually higher for the product-side than for the income-side estimates because the discrepancy became increasingly positive; when the discrepancy becomes increasingly negative, the income-side estimate shows a greater growth rate. On a quarterly basis, the differentials in growth rates are sometimes larger than in these annual figures.

The disconcerting aspect of the discrepancy since 1990 has been the noticeable increases in 1991 and 1992. The increases may reflect problems with a few large items or with several small items. Furthermore, the nature of the discrepancy is that it only indicates changes in the magnitude of statistical problems; it does not identify sources of the problems.

The discrepancy also may increase when particular improvements in the data base affect the product side or the income side more than the other. This should not inhibit incorporating data improvements when they become available. It is impractical to wait for comparable improvements to be made simultaneously on the product and the income sides before incorporating the improvements in the national accounts simply to avoid increasing the discrepancy.

### Recommendation

The Bureau of Economic Analysis should examine possible sources of the large increases in the statistical discrepancy in 1991 and 1992 for (a) clues of problems that may be developing in the GDP data base or in the BEA estimating procedures; and (b) the effect of incorporating new data improvements in the national accounts. If the increases in the statistical discrepancy are considered to reflect particular data problems, remedial action is necessary. To the extent the increases are considered to reflect the incorporation of new data improvements, no remedial action is warranted.

### Recommendation

The Bureau of Economic Analysis should publish the GDP as estimated from the income side of the national accounts and the income-side growth rates. This will provide an immediate comparison with economic growth rates based on the product-side GDP. The income-side measure can be calculated using the data published on the statistical discrepancy. However, only sophisticated users are likely to perform this calculation and then also calculate the income-side growth rates. The income-side GDP has the same statistical validity as the product-side GDP.

## Price Measurement and Real Output

Economic growth rates are based on movements of real GDP; that is, GDP in constant dollars. This section focuses on the price indices used to deflate GDP in current dollars to GDP in constant dollars. BEA recently enhanced the measures of economic growth with its new alternative constant-dollar measures in which alternative base-period prices provide different rates of economic growth.[115]

GDP in constant dollars is obtained primarily by using price movements from the Bureau of Labor Statistics' (BLS) consumer, producer, and import/export price indices to deflate GDP in current dollars. Other indices used in the deflation include the Census Bureau's price index of single-family new housing construction, BEA's price index of multi-family new housing construction and its hybrid price-cost index of defense purchases of goods and services, and the Census Bureau's construction cost indices for nonresidential structures.

### Quality Change in High-tech Products

A critical element in preparing price indices is the need to adjust for specification changes in the goods and services items being priced from one quarter to the next. Changes in the specifications of the size, durability, safety, performance, or other characteristics of a product are referred to as quality changes. When there is no change in the quality of a product from one period to the next, the percent change in the market price is incorporated in the price index with no adjustment. By contrast, when the quality is enhanced, an estimate of the cost of the enhancement is subtracted from the market price, and when the quality is lessened, an estimate of the quality deterioration is added to the market price. The percent change between this quality-adjusted price in the current period, and the market price in the previous period is the price change incorporated in the price index.

---

115. Allan H. Young, "Alternative Measures of Change in Real Output and Prices, Quarterly Estimates for 1959-92," *Survey of Current Business,* March 1993.

Adjustments for quality change require estimates of the cost of the quality change from producers of the product. When estimates are not available, the adjustments made by the analyst in preparing the price index become more subjective. The assumption in this procedure is that quality enhancements are associated with price increases and quality deterioration is associated with price decreases.

However, quality improvement is sometimes accompanied by price declines. Thus, the traditional method of using cost estimates of the quality change is problematic. BLS has changed its methodology of pricing computers in the producer price index to accommodate this phenomenon by estimating price changes due to changes in the quality of the product through statistical regressions. This is referred to as the hedonic method. The substitution of these new price indices for computers in the national accounts had a noticeable effect on the GDP growth rate. For example, the annual growth in real GDP during 1982-88 was revised from 3.8% to 4.1% due to the new method of pricing computers.

### Recommendation

The Bureau of Labor Statistics should improve the measures of price change for various high-tech products in the producer, consumer, and import/export price indices. First, it should identify electronic, communications equipment, medical equipment, pharmaceuticals, and other high-tech products in which quality improvements have been accompanied by lower prices. Second, for these high-tech products, it should develop new methods for measuring quality change similar to the hedonic technique it uses for computers in the producer price index. Third, when the same high-tech products are included in two or more of the producer, consumer, and import-export price indices, the new procedures should be included in all of the affected indices.

### Nonresidential Construction Price Indices

The Census Bureau provides cost indices for new construction of nonresidential structures — industrial, commercial, school, hospital and other nonresidential buildings, and utilities, bridges, dams, and other nonbuilding structures. It also provides a price index for road building. The indices are prepared by other federal agencies and by private companies and are compiled by the Census Bureau.

A construction cost index is based on changes in the cost of materials, labor, and equipment inputs used in construction projects. Because it does not include the effect of changes in productivity and profit margins in the construction industries, it is an input index. This differs from a price index, which is an output measure and thus captures productivity and profit margin changes as well as the materials, labor, and equipment inputs. Currently, the only price indices for new construction are for single-family and multi-family housing and for road building.

### Recommendation

The Census Bureau should develop price indices for new nonresidential building and nonbuilding structures. These should refine the presently used input-cost indices if feasible. However, it may be necessary to develop completely new output-price indices for some types of structures. This is a non-implemented Creamer Report recommendation. The FY 1994 Census Bureau's budget includes a request for funds to develop a price index for nonresidential buildings. We support the request.

### Productivity of Government Workers

Government purchases of goods and services are composed of purchases from private industry and of wage and fringe benefit compensation of government workers. Purchases from private industry are deflated for specific items, using BLS producer and consumer price indices and average hourly wages in selected services industries, the Census Bureau's and BEA's construction cost and price indices noted above, and BEA's hybrid price-cost index of defense purchases.

Employee compensation accounted for 59% of government purchases in 1992 — 44% for the Federal government purchases and 68% for state and local governments. The constant-dollar measure of employee compensation of government workers assumes that productivity for workers with the same level of education and experience is constant over time. The only allowance for productivity change is when there is a shift in the composition of workers toward those with more or less education and experience. Estimates of the education and experience of workers are based on the number of employees at different pay scales. If the proportion of employees in the higher-pay categories rises, it is assumed this represents more education and experience and thus a productivity increase; if the proportion of employees in the lower-pay categories rises, it is treated as a decline in education and experience and consequently in productivity; and when the proportion of workers in all pay categories is unchanged, there is no measured change in productivity.

These estimates are an input measure of the change in labor productivity. BEA uses this technique because it is difficult to quantify the output of government workers since it relies on presumed direct linkages of the amount of education and experience with productivity. Input measures do not allow for change in the quality of education, experience, and other factors affecting worker skills and know-how over time. By contrast, an output measure of labor productivity based on the goods and services produced by government workers would implicitly capture all factors contributing to worker efficiency. The currently used input measure probably lowers the growth rate of real GDP since it does not include improvements in worker skills and know-how other than those associated with greater amounts of education and experience. There are no estimates of the effect of this exclusion.

### Recommendation

The Bureau of Economic Analysis should focus on developing output measures of the productivity of government workers. The Bureau of Labor Statistics' studies of the productivity in twenty-eight Federal government functions and services are a major data source for preparing Federal government estimates. These studies may also be appropriate for estimating productivity in related state and local government programs. This is a non-implemented Creamer Report recommendation.

## Input/Output Tables

Input/output tables are used in two major ways: (1) in preparing the quinquennial benchmarks of the national accounts; and (2) in economic analysis, such as in projecting future employment associated with varying rates of anticipated economic growth and in quantifying the regional impacts of proposed military base closings. A benchmark input/output table is prepared at five-year intervals that coincides with the years of the economic censuses (1982, 1987, 1992, 1997, etc.). Abbreviated updated annual input/output tables are prepared in other years.

The benchmark table incorporates the maximum amount of fresh data for each cell of the I/O table largely on data from the economic censuses. By contrast, fresh data for the annual tables are confined to the rims of the table comprising each industry's total output and the final demand and value added quadrants of the table. The intermediate production quadrant is simulated from the most recent benchmark-year coefficients, which are then modified to equate the sum of the cells in each industry row and column to the industry output total.

The average completion time for the benchmark table is seven years after the reference year. This lengthened to over nine years for the 1982 table. BEA's goal is to reduce the completion time to five years. An abbreviated 1987 table is planned for completion in 1993 or early 1994. It will utilize fresh data from the economic censuses and economize in noncensus areas.

Three problems have contributed to the average lag of seven years. First, there is a high turnover of personnel in the input/output program, resulting in a high proportion of the staff with no experience in having worked on a previous input/output table. Second, the estimating procedures have not been sufficiently automated. Third, certain detailed data in the microdata files of the economic censuses, such as those for small companies and central administrative offices, have not been tabulated.

### Recommendation

The Bureau of Economic Analysis should revitalize the input/output program to reduce the completion time of the benchmark tables to five years after the reference year. This includes motivating experienced employees to stay with the program and developing automated procedures for estimating the intermediate production quadrant cells of the table.

### Recommendation

The Census Bureau should tabulate certain data from the microdata files of the economic censuses for use in preparing the benchmark input/output table. Examples of such tabulations are those for small companies and central administrative offices. The FY 1994 Bureau of Economic Analysis budget includes a request for funds to reimburse the Census Bureau for such tabulations. We support the request.

## Satellite Accounts

Satellite accounts are part of the United Nations' System of National Accounts that BEA will adopt in the second half of the 1990s. Satellite accounts extend the national accounts by encompassing an entire field of economic activity. They may be prepared for a variety of activities, such as research and development, natural resources, pensions, housing, health, transportation, and education. Satellites enlarge and enrich the analytical framework for formulating public policies.[116]

Satellites differ from traditional national accounts in several ways, although they are statistically linked to them. For example, in the traditional accounts, elements of research and development are spread among the household, business, and government sectors. In the satellite accounts, these are brought together in one place to give a comprehensive accounting of the activity. The satellite accounts also allow for different definitions of particular activities. In the traditional accounts, research and development are treated as a business expense, a government purchase, or a nonprofit institution consumption item; but in the satellite accounts, research and development is defined as capital investment, albeit intangible investment, with deductions for depreciation in future years. In addition, satellite accounts provide for more detail on the activity including its subcategories, employment and financing.

BEA has been working on satellite accounts for research and development and natural resources, and has proposed to add pensions as a third category. Much of the data base required for the satellites is available from the traditional accounts and other existing data sources. BEA has not developed an inventory of new data needs for the satellites. These needs will become clearer as work progresses on the satellite estimates.

### Recommendation

When it can be foreseen that existing data sources are inadequate to develop the satellite accounts further, BEA should prepare an inventory of high-priority data needs for these accounts. Because the satellites involve the program and statistical activities of other agencies, BEA should consult with these agencies in drawing up the data needs inventory through an interagency committee. Such an inventory will facilitate the planning of future statistical programs by putting them in an overall context.

---

116. Carol S. Carson and Bruce T. Grimm, "Satellite Accounts in a Modernized and Extended System of Economic Accounts," *Business Economics*, January 1991.

---

## Infrastructure of Economic Statistics that Impacts the National Accounts

This section identifies several underlying aspects of economic statistics that affect the accuracy and relevance of the national accounts. Although these topics are less direct, they have both tangible and intangible impacts that accumulate significantly over time. The topics are: BEA consultation with users; standard industrial classification system; funding for economic statistics; reporting burden; college teaching of economic measurement; and private industry uses of the national accounts.

### BEA Consultation with Users

The national accounts are designed and prepared by BEA. BEA refines and expands the concepts, scope, and definitions of the accounts over time to reflect changes in the economy and to enhance the use of the accounts for economic analysis. Recent examples of such enhancements are the alternative measures of real output introduced in 1993 and the ongoing development of satellite accounts noted previously.

Ideas for the further development of the national accounts originate with the BEA staff, from contacts with public and private users of the accounts and from a general awareness of trends in the American economy. Occasionally, outside expert groups, such as the National Accounts Review Committee in the 1950s and the Advisory Committee on Gross National Product Data Improvement in the 1970s, are designated to study the accounts and recommend needed changes in them. BEA participates with other countries in developing the United Nations' System of National Accounts (SNA), and changes in the SNA generate changes in the U.S. national accounts, such as those that will be incorporated in the accounts in the second half of the 1990s.

While these sources of ideas will continue to be important in the future, BEA lacks a vehicle to consult with users on a regular basis. Such a vehicle would have major benefits. First, it would provide a forum for systematically obtaining a range of views on potential innovations in the accounts that originate with BEA or the users. Second, it would assist BEA in seeking advice on handling technical issues of definition, classification, and statistical estimation. Third, it would provide a general benefit from an interactive feedback on a variety of issues on a timely basis. Both the Census Bureau and the Bureau of Labor Statistics have advisory committees that provide a means for consulting with users on a regular basis.

**Recommendation**

The Bureau of Economic Analysis should convene a standing group of users of the national accounts with whom it consults on a regular basis.[117] The group should include representatives from the Council of Economic Advisers, Federal Reserve Board, Congressional Budget Office, universities, private industry, labor unions, and research organizations. The subjects would include conceptual innovations, technical issues, data presentation, or other aspects of the accounts.

**Standard Industrial Classification System**

The Standard Industrial Classification (SIC) is a system for grouping industry data on a consistent basis. The SIC provides a code number for each industry that government and private organizations follow in tabulating and presenting statistical data obtained from surveys, which in turn are incorporated in the national accounts. For example, data on the production, employment, prices, profits, and capital expenditures of the automobile manufacturing industry are always included in SIC 3711.

The SIC system is revised about once every decade to reflect the changing nature of American industry. The revisions typically involve adding new and growing industries, deleting or combining declining industries, and reclassifying industries to reflect more accurately the activities and organization of U.S. industries. The most recent SIC revision was in 1987. The SIC is adopted and published by the Office of Management and Budget after consultation with government agencies and the public.

A comprehensive review of the SIC is underway by the Economic Classification Policy Committee (ECPC). The ECPC is chaired by the Bureau of Economic Analysis with members from the Census Bureau and the Bureau of Labor Statistics with the Office of Management and Budget as an ex officio member. The SIC will be revised in the 1990s based on the outcome of this review.

The ECPC issued a notice for private and governmental comment in March 1993 on two issue papers, "Conceptual Issues" and "Aggregation Structures and Hierarchies," with comments due by the end of May 1993. Other issue papers will be available on request later in 1993 regarding collectability of data, criteria for determining industries, time series continuity, service classifications, international comparability, and detailed product clas-

---

117. This idea has been endorsed by the Bureau. Carol Carson, Director of BEA, commented on the need for an advisory group in *Business Economics*, July 1993.

---

sifications. The work plan includes additional notices for public comment in 1993 and 1995, with OMB adoption of the revised SIC in March 1996.

This timing allows sufficient time for the Census Bureau to incorporate the revised SIC in the 1997 economic censuses, which will be mailed to respondent companies in January 1998. Data tabulations from the 1997 economic censuses will be available in 1999-2000. Monthly, quarterly, and annual survey data that are based on samples of companies drawn from the company lists used in the economic censuses, and which are benchmarked to the economic censuses, will be revised to be consistent with the new SIC codes in 1999-2000. If the targeted completion date of March 1996 for the revised SIC slips more than a couple of months, the new SIC codes will first be introduced in the 2002 economic censuses, with data first available in 2004-2005.

Contrary to previous SIC revisions, this one involves a reassessment of several principles underlying the SIC. One is the method of designating certain activities as industries. The current method primarily classifies industries according to the method of production, which is a supply-side definition; by contrast, an industry classification based on the markets for products would be a demand-side definition. In the current supply-side system, for example, sugar products such as granulated sugar and molasses made from cane sugar are classified in SIC 2061, while the same products made from beet sugar are classified in SIC 2063. Thus, even though the products are perfect substitutes, they are grouped in different industries based on their method of production. The question in this case is whether to maintain the current supply-side definition or to modify or supplement these definitions with demand-side classifications. Among the other issues to be addressed are the under-representation of detailed categories of services industries, the present concept of using business establishments of large companies that are located in specific geographic locations as the linch pin of industry designations, and the method of forming hierarchies of broadly similar products grouped in two-, three-, and four-digit SIC industries.

### Recommendation

The Economic Classification Policy Com-mittee composed of the Office of Management and Budget (ex officio), Bureau of Economic Analysis, Bureau of the Census, and Bureau of Labor Statistics should make a concerted effort to complete the ongoing revision of the Standard Industrial Classification system by its target date of March 1996. This will provide the required lead time for the revised system to be incorporated in the 1997 economic censuses. If there is a slippage of more than a couple of months in this complete date, the revised SIC would first be incorporated in the economic statistics of the 2002 economic censuses.

### Funding for Economic Statistics

Economic statistics are the foundation for decision making information. While information is important for formulating and evaluating public policies, the value of information is difficult to quantify. The Federal government produces massive quantities of economic statistics, yet sometimes there are not enough data or data of the right kind. Or as policy makers say, "When we need a prompt answer to a question, relevant and accurate information is not always available."

Having good information is part of good government. Planning to provide for good information means forecasting the type of data that will be necessary to analyze the wide range of events that may occur in the future. The provision of information also costs money, but presidents, representatives, and senators are elected to improve the daily lives of the population, not for providing good information. Although the availability of good information may be a more certain way of devising successful policies that will help in reelection campaigns, elected officials are not typically staunch supporters of statistical programs.

Persuading elected officials of the need for better data is not easy. It is most convincing when the data are related to concrete problems or issues that currently exist or have a reasonable chance of occurring in the future.

Several recommendations in this paper to enhance the data base and preparation of the national accounts will require additional funding for BEA, Census, BLS, and IRS. It means justifying the need for these improvements at four main stages of the Federal government's budget process:[118]

1. within the statistical agency;

2. within each agency's department such as the Commerce Department for BEA and Census; the Labor Department for BLS; The Treasury Department for IRS;

3. the Office of Management and Budget and the President; and

4. the House of Representatives and the Senate.

---

118. See Figure 4 and related discussion in Chapter 1.

---

**Recommendation**

When submitting their budgets to the executive branch and to Congress, statistical agencies should give more attention to relating the need for the data to existing or potential problems and issues of the nation. Requests should provide an example of how the data will help address a concrete problem, in contrast to explaining the consequences of not having the information. This is particularly important in requests for a new program or to expand an existing one.

**Reporting Burden**

One of the costs of producing economic statistics is the time and money spent by survey respondents in completing survey forms. These costs are borne by private and government respondents. In designing surveys, it is important to limit requests for information to necessary items, to have the forms easily understood, and to use samples of the population to be surveyed (in contrast to the universe) when feasible. In the case of businesses, it is helpful to be familiar with their recordkeeping practices so that questions can be designed that will minimize the burden on the businesses in compiling data. Such efforts in survey design help contain the reporting burden on the public, increase the cooperation of the public in responding to surveys, and raise the quality of the information reported. In addition, statistical agencies have instituted automated reporting technologies such as computer-assisted telephone interviewing and touch-tone data entry that reduces reporting burden.

The Office of Management and Budget oversees the containment of all federal paperwork through its required approval of each survey's forms, frequency, and sampling, the design of tax forms, and similar reviews of other information collections.

Despite these efforts to contain paperwork, there is a societal trend in the U.S. not to respond to surveys. For the most part, federal statistical surveys are voluntary, which means that public cooperation in responding to surveys is vital. The erosion of public participation in surveys diminishes the representativeness of survey data, and additional expense is incurred in recontacting the respondent or contacting higher level people in the organization, finding replacement respondents, or imputing for missing respondents. In some cases, the inability to obtain responses prevents the survey from being based on a probability sample, and thus no measures of sampling error can be calculated. Examples of such nonprobability sample surveys are the Census Bureau's monthly Survey of Manufacturers'

Shipments, Inventories, and Orders and the Bureau of Labor Statistics' monthly survey of employer payrolls and employment, both of which are basic data sources used in preparing the national accounts.

The general decline in survey participation has been exacerbated in the economic statistics by the tendency of some businesses only to respond to mandatory surveys. This stems from two attitudes:

1. there is no penalty for not responding, and

2. if the government thinks the survey is important, it would make it mandatory.

Additionally, some companies state that one way to reduce costs, to accommodate their downsizing or when business is slack, is to eliminate survey reporting.

The policy of only responding to mandatory surveys endangers the representativeness of economic statistics. It is a no-win situation and needs to be stanched. There is a political risk associated with legislation to make certain surveys mandatory. If a few surveys are made mandatory, this only intensifies the response problem for the vast majority of surveys that remain voluntary and in the end the statistical system suffers even more. We propose a positive response to the non-response issue and nearly all readers can play a part as well.

### Recommendation

Federal statistical agencies should make broad-based efforts to raise the response rate on voluntary business surveys. One approach is for the agencies to convene regional or industry conferences of high-level company officials stressing the importance of the data for public policy and the direct or indirect benefits to the company. The officials should be encouraged to institute policies within their companies to ensure that survey forms are completed and that care is given in supplying accurate information. Such private industry groups as the National Association of Business Economists, U.S. Chamber of Commerce and local Chambers of Commerce, National Association of Manufacturers, and National Federation of Independent Business should work with the federal agencies in this effort.

### College Teaching of Economic Measurement

The qualifications and abilities of economists and statisticians working in federal statistical agencies are key to the development of economic statistics. As in all fields, experience gained on-the-job in statistical agencies is vital to performing the ongoing work with increasing efficiency, dealing with problem areas, and designing changes in the content, methodology, and presentation of economic statistics to reflect the evolving changes in the economy. The knowledge and training that the economists and statisticians bring to the job are also critical to the level and quality of their work. Both job experience and education and training interact in determining the usefulness of the output of statistical agencies.

A long-standing weakness in college courses in economics and statistics is that at best they only superficially teach the properties and methodology of economic measurement. In economics courses, glancing reference is given to the concepts and meaning of economic indicators and to the data and estimation techniques used in preparing the indicators. These are treated as something that is learned on-the-job, and, in general, as being lower level and uninteresting. In statistics courses, minimal attention is given to the process of survey design: conceptualizing a topic, designing a survey to collect information on the topic, collecting the data, analyzing the data, and drawing inferences from the analysis. The major emphasis is on analyzing the data through various tests of statistical significance.

The loss to economic intelligence from this lack of teaching economic measurement at the college level is that persons coming to work in statistical agencies do not have the training for sophisticated analysis of the implications of the data programs they work on. It affects their judgments in making everyday decisions, which problem areas they consider worthy of exploration, and the content of research projects they undertake to investigate problem areas.

The new Joint Program in Survey Methodology of the Universities of Maryland and Michigan, and Westat, Inc., is a model for a course program on survey methodology. During the coming year, it will explore expanding its curriculum to include an economic statistics program.

### Recommendation

The federal statistical agencies should work with economics and statistics departments in universities to introduce meaningful courses in economic measurement. These may include interdisciplinary programs between the economics and statistics departments. It will involve convening conferences with college faculties, perhaps through professional organizations such as the American Economic Association and the American Statistical Association, to present the dimensions of the problem and to design appropriate course programs. Follow-up conferences should monitor the progress and modify or expand the teaching programs as experience is gained with them. The new Joint Program in Survey Methodology of the Universities of Maryland and Michigan, and Westat, Inc., would be an appropriate vehicle for organizing the conferences.

### Private Industry Uses of the National Accounts

The national accounts primarily provide the Federal government with the analytic basis for formulating and evaluating fiscal and monetary policies to promote maximum sustainable economic growth with minimum unemployment and inflation. Private industry use of the accounts is far less. And within private industry, large companies are the primary users because they can relate the fortunes of their companies to national trends more readily than small- and medium-size companies that have more limited product and regional markets.

Companies use the annual data in the national accounts more than the quarterly estimates because the annual data provide more product- and income-side detail. This detail in the annual estimates allows some large companies to compare their performance on sales, profits, and labor costs with national product, industry, and labor markets. Less private industry use is made of the price measures in the national accounts because they do not provide sufficient product detail; far more product detail is available in the Bureau of Labor Statistics' producer, consumer, and import/export price indices. There also is little private industry use of the input/output tables. While the I/O tables provide considerable product detail, they are too out-of-date for relevant use.

Overall, private industry makes highly selective use of the accounts because of the weak statistical linkage between economy-wide trends and a company's performance and prospects. This does not mean that the accounts are unimportant to private industry. The accounts are used to formulate and evaluate public policies that create a healthy climate for economic growth and thus have a weighty impact on business sales and profits.

### Recommendation

Private industry companies should reverse their declining participation in government business surveys and ensure that the information they report is accurate. While industry makes only limited direct use of the national accounts, the economic well-being of businesses is significantly influenced by use of the accounts to formulate and evaluate fiscal and monetary policies. Government business surveys are the lifeblood of the accounts, and the accounts underlie basic policies used to create a climate of economic growth in which businesses prosper.

## Actions Taken on the Creamer Report Suggestions

The Advisory Committee on Gross National Product Data Improvement completed the *Gross National Product Data Improvement Project Report* in 1977.[119] Daniel Creamer was the chairman of the advisory committee and staff director. The report contained over 150 recommendations affecting the Bureau of Economic Analysis (BEA), Bureau of the Census, Bureau of Labor Statistics (BLS), Internal Revenue Service (IRS), Departments of Agriculture, Defense, and Health and Human Services, and other federal agencies. It included a six-year plan to implement the recommendations during 1978-83. The highest priority recommendations and those which were relatively easy to implement and required little or no additional funding were scheduled to begin in the earlier years. The total cost of the recommended improvements was roughly estimated at $25 million in 1976 prices.

The Creamer Report provided a coherent framework for shaping federal statistical programs. It is not another advisory report gathering dust. Considerable progress has been made in implementing its recommendations. Selected non-implemented Creamer recommendations are included as recommendations in this paper, attesting to their continued relevance.

### Recommendation

The Office of Management and Budget or the Joint Economic Committee of Congress should sponsor a comprehensive assessment of the national accounts by a non-government group of experts from universities, research organizations, industry, and labor unions. The study would examine the concepts, methodologies, data bases, and data presentation of the accounts to reflect current and prospective needs of economic analysis and policy formulation. The beneficial results of the Creamer Report and the passage of sixteen years since the report was completed underscore the usefulness of having an independent review in the 1990s.

---

119. Office of Federal Statistical Policy and Standards, U.S. Department of Commerce, Report of the Advisory Committee on Gross National Product Data Improvement, *Gross National Product Data Improvement Project Report, October 1977.*

# Chapter 8

# Recommendations —
# International Statistics

Throughout this book we have stressed the emergence of an unprecedented level of global interaction. Our position has been that statistics to meet the needs of the 21st century must have a special capability to deal with global issues. In Chapter 6 on Global Interaction we stressed some of the weaknesses in current data collection efforts. In the previous chapter some recommendations will help meet the need for better international data. This chapter, while not dealing with all of the issues that have been raised, makes recommendations for improving international statistics.[†]

The interdependence of the world economy has increased dramatically and these international linkages are expected to intensify in the future. These relationships are captured in the balance of payments accounts of individual countries with respect to trade, services, and capital flows. Since the conceptual consistency of economic statistics across international boundaries is a principal objective of the statistical improvements suggested in this book, this consistency must start within the realm of international economic data.

The U.S. has one of the most comprehensive systems of collecting data of all types, particularly foreign trade information. For the balance of payments statistics, numerous government agencies have responsibility for collecting and compiling the data. Since these agencies do not necessarily interact or cooperate with one another, this poses a major obstacle to statistical reform. The major shortcomings of the present system have been addressed in Chapter 6.

## Merchandise Trade

Merchandise trade, in comparison with other U.S. international transactions, differs in several important respects. Its statistics are compiled from a full tabulation of all transactions rather than from surveys. A great deal of

---

† The authors wish to acknowledge the contributions of Marsha A. Kameron to this chapter.

attention is placed on trade data and, as a result, they are generally considered to be quite accurate. Moreover, during the past several years, a number of changes have been made to substantially improve the quality of trade statistics.

Still, a number of problems remain. Trade statistics are presently based on the concept of *residence*. A resident is anyone or any business that has a center of economic interest in a given country and resides in the country for more than a year. Thus, for example, trade between a U.S. parent and its foreign subsidiary enters the balance of payments even though a U.S. company is the ultimate owner. When foreign direct investment was minimal and virtually all exports were made by domestic companies, there was little difference between the resident and the owner. With the tremendous growth of multinational companies and joint ventures, a growing percentage of trade involves multinational companies. A considerable portion of trade is not owned by the country in which it is manufactured.

### Recommendation

Use a supplemental balance of payments framework that captures transactions between foreign affiliates of U.S. firms abroad and U.S. parents and foreign affiliates in the U.S. and their foreign parents. This supplemental framework would dramatically change a country's international trade balance. For example, in 1987, the U.S. trade deficit was $148 billion, but computed under a supplemental framework the deficit was $68 billion. For policy purposes and trade negotiations, this dramatically alters the position of the United States. A summary of the supplemental balance of payments is given in Figure 33.[120]

There are, however, several difficulties in collecting these data. First, sales by foreign affiliates are collecterd annually, but data on domestic purchases are not collected at all. Second, data on foreign affiliates of U.S. firms and U.S. affiliates of foreign firms are based on data where ownership is only 10% or more. In the current pattern of interactions ranging from loose federations to controlling ownership, there is a need for more detailed defini-

---

120. Anne Y. Kester, Ed., *Behind the Numbers: U.S. Trade in the World Economy.* Washington, D.C.: National Academy Press, 1992, p. 182.

---

Figure 33

## Net Sales of Goods and Services by
## Americans to Foreigners, 1987[121]
### Cross-border Sales to and Purchases from Foreigners by Americans

(billions of dollars)

| | |
|---|---|
| Exports to foreigners | |
| + U.S. exports of goods and services | $336 |
| - U.S. exports to foreign affiliates of U.S. firms abroad | -87 |
| - U.S. exports shipped by U.S. affiliates of foreign firms | -51 |
| Total | 198 |
| | |
| Imports from foreigners | |
| + U.S. imports of merchandise and services | 484 |
| - U.S. imports from foreign affiliates of U.S. firms | -75 |
| - U.S. imports shipped to U.S. affiliates of foreign firms | -143 |
| Total | 264 |
| | |
| Exports minus imports equals net cross-border sales to foreigners | -68 |

Source: Anne Y. Kester, Ed., *Behind the Numbers: U.S. Trade in the World Economy.* Washington, DC: National Academy Press, 1992, p. 182.

tions of the affiliated relations. This would require agreement on a new set of consistent definitions.[122]

Similarly, the present trade statistics do not differentiate between affiliated and nonaffiliated trade. Under the present methodology, trade statistics are compiled as merchandise crosses the border. Thus, trade between multinational companies and their affiliates abroad is included in the trade balance. No distinction is made between this type of trade and trade between unaffiliated, or unrelated, partners. In 1991, 46% of total U.S. imports were

---

121. The National Academy of Sciences figures used estimates of purchases (basically derived as output less gross domestic product) that could be constructed annually. Companies have indicated that data on purchases are extremely difficult to report.

122. BEA notes that its current definitions are consistent with the IMF and OECD 10% definition. BEA does publish more data on a majority-owned basis for foreign affiliates than for U.S. affiliates, but it says that it can identify majority-owned affiliates of both types, and in the major area of services it has already addresssed supplemental-framework-type issues. Further, although BEA does not publish separate data on affiliated-part trade in the main balance of payments, it does collect and publish annual data on affiliated party trade for exports and imports collected on its annual surveys of foreign affiliates of U.S. firms and U.S. affiliates of foreign firms.

from related parties. Although export data are not publicly available, it is assumed that exports by related parties is also high.

**Recommendation**
Incorporate the annual surveys of multinational companies into the balance of payments accounting. Also, incorporate data from the annual surveys of direct investment for more detailed data on affiliated trade.

No distinction is made between raw, intermediate, or final goods. Components for various products are often imported from various countries and then assembled for export. With the present statistics, it is not possible to derive a value added component.

**Recommendation**
Use universal bar coding to track the components of trade. Such an automated system would produce information about the origin of various factors of production and assist in improved classification.

Finally, although the present system for collecting trade data is extremely comprehensive, there are questions about the usefulness of the data.

**Recommendation**
Simplify the amount of data that is compiled. Although this might involve a loss of accuracy and completeness, the considerable cost savings that would be generated could be used to improve the collection of other international statistics, notably in the capital accounts. Methods for simplification include:

- Limiting publicly available trade data to the aggregate categories. More detailed category breakdowns would be available by special request and the users could be charged for the information they request. Present data are unwieldy and often not in a usable format. Specialized requests could improve the quality and usability of the data;

- Shifting from a full tabulation system to a sample system to collect trade data. The trade-off between accuracy and cost would need to be evaluated; and

- Adopting a data sharing system that U.S. and Canada presently use in which imports of one country are used to compile the exports of the other country.

## The Invisibles and Service Accounts

The invisibles and service accounts are becoming an increasingly important component of the current account. U.S. exports of services have nearly doubled over the past six years and account for 25% of the total exports of goods and services. Although data collection for services has improved considerably during the past decade, data are not nearly as comprehensive, detailed, or timely as merchandise trade. It would be unrealistic to expect the data on the service account to ever approach the accuracy of the trade accounts since this sector is so diverse and much smaller than its merchandise counterpart. With the realization that service information is largely an "estimate," improvements should be made via statistical means to improve the accuracy of the samples.

### Recommendation

Consistent estimation and sampling procedures need to be established. The framework developed by the U.S. should be coordinated with the major industrial countries to develop ultimately a consistent framework for use on a worldwide basis. Using estimates and simplifying the data collection process should be considered a reliable alternative to survey methods with considerable cost savings.

The largest service categories are travel, passenger fares, freight, and port services. There is room for improvement in the data collection from each of these categories.

Tourist expenditures and revenues are calculated based on random surveys of travelers. This method is cumbersome and subject to serious inaccuracy.

### Recommendation

Integrate Immigration and Naturalization Service (INS) data—which are already being collected at the Customs Service—with balance of payments statistics.

Integrate computerized data from airlines on international travel for balance of payments accounting, including data on cost of airfare, number of passengers, and number of days abroad. A system needs to be developed to compile these data into a form usable for the balance of payments. Estimation procedures to determine other costs of international travel such as meals and hotels could be used.

For freight and shipping, the convention is to consider that all payments are paid by the importer. Problems arise because the flag of the carrier often differs from the residency of the operator and because the operator may not be accurately determined.

### Recommendation

Data on imports need to track not only freight, but also the country of origin. A five-year benchmark survey would improve the statistical accuracy of these expenditures.

## The Capital Accounts

World capital flows have increased tremendously during the past decades reflecting innovation, deregulation of financial markets, and elimination of capital controls. At the same time, the resources in the U.S. for adequately collecting data have been shrinking due to budgetary constraints.

The U.S. has made a major effort to revise direct investment data to reflect more accurately market conditions. Portfolio and other capital flows are subject to considerable error in the balance of payments accounts. These errors reflect many factors including purchase of securities directly overseas, use of financial instruments that are not captured in the present system, money laundering and the extensive use of the black market, and use of the dollar as a local currency in many countries throughout the world.

The U.S. system was designed when most transactions were conducted in conventional financial instruments and channeled through a few large banks and other financial institutions. Capital markets have changed dramatically since then reflecting deregulation of capital controls, new financial instruments, and the proliferation of transactions. The statistical problems faced by U.S. compilers have intensified and strained available resources.

The concepts and methodology of the U.S. balance of payments as they relate to portfolio, banking transactions, and nonbanking transactions have been addressed in Chapter 6, Global Interaction.

### Recommendation

It is widely acknowledged that these serious shortcomings exist in the present system as discussed in Chapter 6, Global Interaction.

There are three basic approaches to revising the entire system of capital accounts:

1. Make revisions and changes to improve the accuracy of the present system. These types of changes are the easiest to implement, but the usefulness of such a piecemeal effort is questionable. A marginal improvement in the accuracy of the capital flows would not necessarily be more reliable than what presently exists;

2. Restructure the domestic system entirely and change the method of reporting. This may involve a change to annual statistics via benchmark surveys. The quarterly data are presently so volatile and subject to such tremendous revision that they are of limited use. A more accurate framework that is produced annually would represent an improvement for users, although the intra-year changes in financial conditions could not be well-tracked. It may be true that a full tabulation of international capital flows is not possible. Use sampling techniques which are less costly, but perhaps just as accurate in tracking capital flows. Finally, any new system must have the flexibility to include new financial instruments; and

3. Develop a worldwide system to monitor capital flows. In view of the tremendous linkages of global capital, it is becoming increasingly difficult for the U.S. or any single country to monitor adequately capital flows without international coordination and cooperation. As an alternative to the present methodology, a new system could be developed by international monetary and financial agencies with consistent concepts and definitions. In developing a worldwide system, serious consideration should be given to whether the present classifications are meaningful. Of course, there would obviously be a number of difficulties and objections to a global system, such as enforcing compliance among participating countries, ensuring confidentiality, and managing the huge number of transactions.

Revisions to the present system, or development of a new system, must begin with clarifying and redefining important concepts for consistency. For example, there needs to be an improvement in the interaction between agencies assigned to collect, report, and analyze data. Innovations will require frequent adaptations of reporting systems. The definition of portfolio capital needs to be expanded to include derivative financial instruments.

Before new procedures can be developed, conceptual problems need to be addressed including:

*Defining residence: foreign vs. domestic.* Under the present system, foreigners establishing a local address are no longer considered foreigners. Investors frequently find it convenient to lodge their securities with nominees when investing in overseas markets, and compilers have no way of knowing whether financial intermediaries correctly capture all transactions involving foreign accounts held in nominees' names.

*Classifying transactions.* The present classification system contains many overlapping elements and ambiguities. For example, it is becoming increasingly difficult to distinguish between banking and securities transactions. It is often hard to distinguish between short- and long-term because of the increasing liquidity of many financial instruments.

*Timing.* In principle, the sale and purchase of an asset should be recorded at the same time. In practice, countries may record transactions at different times.

*Deriving flows from stock data.* In many countries, outstanding claims and liabilities are used to derive capital flows. Stocks can change for a number of reasons not related to flows, including changes in market price of assets, changes in exchange rates, write-offs, and expropriations and uncompensated seizures.

*Defining reporting responsibilities.* As the distinctions between banking and the securities business become increasingly blurred, specific reporting responsibilities need to be defined.

*Timeliness vs. accuracy.* There obviously is a trade-off between timeliness and accuracy. There is nothing to be gained from a quick release of information that is not considered reliable and accurate. It would be far more useful to delay reporting for a reasonable amount of time after which the data are considered accurate. Data could include footnotes about confidence bands rather than having an endless revision of data that are seldom used.

*Linking domestic data with the remainder of the global economy.* Despite its shortcomings, the U.S. reporting system is one of the most comprehensive in the world. Most of the leading industrial countries have well-developed statistical systems, whereas many of the statistics of developing countries lack timeliness and accuracy. International comparability is made more difficult in instances where developed countries have not implemented the most recent U.N. revisions of international economic classification.

The individual categories in the world tabulation of the balance of payments should, in principle, sum to zero. In actuality, there are large imbalances in many categories that indicate errors or biases. These are shown in the table below. The IMF has addressed many of these questions in two studies: *Report on the World Current Account Discrepancy*[123] and *Report on the Measurement of International Capital Flows*.[124] The magnitude of the discrepancies involved in global balance of payments statistics implies that any interpretation and analysis should be done at one's own risk.

### Recommendation

Under the present system, countries should adhere to the definitions in the International Monetary Fund's *Balance of Payments Manual* to achieve greater consistency, but there is no realistic way to enforce this. In the future, a total revamping of the international balance of payments is needed to improve timeliness and accuracy. The task of revamping the world's balance of payments system is highly complex and would require global coordination and cooperation. Changes in the U.S. could serve as a model for a new global system that reflects the linkages in the world economy.

Because of the tremendous international linkages and instantaneous communications, there is widespread interest in the economic data of countries throughout the world. It is unclear, however, which international agency should spearhead this effort. The IMF is the best source of international economic and financial data. It publishes country data in a timely fashion, but makes no attempt to assure comparability from one country to the next. For example, comparisons of inflation rates in different countries can be somewhat misleading because the methods of calculation differ in various countries. On the other hand, the Organization for Economic Cooperation and Development is an excellent source of comparative data for its member countries; it imposes a consistent definition for many of its statistics. While the OECD is making an effort to include data on the transition countries in Central and Eastern Europe, it does not provide coverage for developing countries. While the United Nations compiles a vast array of internationally comparable data through its use of consistent methodology and definitions, these data lack timelessness and, hence, usefulness to decison makers. While the United Nations codes have a framework for the development and adop-

---

123. *Report on the World Current Account Discrepancy*. Washington, DC: International Monetary Fund, 1987.

124. *Report on the Measurement of International Capital Flows*, Parts I and II. Washington, DC: International Monetary Fund, September 1992 (Part I) and December 1992 (Part II—Background Papers).

tion of global data improvements, the developed countries in recent years have not been satisfied with U.N. leadership in this area. Consequently, we can expect that the OECD, the IMF, and the Statistical Office of the European Communities (Eurostat) will be playing a larger role within the U.N. system for the development of international data of importance to the developed countries.

# Chapter 9

# Concluding Remarks

The preceding two chapters make a large number of very specific recommendations for improving the base data for economic statistics, both for the System of National Accounts and for our knowledge of international interactions. These recommendations are intended to complement other recommendations that have been presented recently. Specifically, the excellent report on trade statistics, *Behind the Numbers*, and the forthcoming report from the National Academy of Sciences, *Following the Money: U.S. Finance in the World Economy*,[125] offer a considerable number of detailed suggestions for improving the basic series.

As we come to the end of this book the question arises, "Where, exactly, have we arrived?" As the reader will have noticed, this journey has not exactly been a fast trip on a straight and smooth superhighway toward a preordained destination. It might more fittingly be compared with a series of separate exploratory paths that lead from the edges toward the center of a vast thicket of existing statistical systems—rather like a series of dirt roads a forester might make into a stand of old-growth trees to explore, to clear away underbrush, and to try to establish a more rational and balanced system of future growth. Each of the nine chapters in this book represents one such path. Along some of those paths, our primary purpose was to observe and classify; along others it was to clear away the dead wood and the obscuring underbrush; along still others we looked for places to plant anew.

As we said at the beginning, we don't start the reform of statistical systems in a clearing, "from the ground up." Instead, we have inherited a vast, inter-connected system of statistics, whose reform must be done prudently, conservatively, and in the spirit of evolution rather than revolution. As we undertake such change we must be mindful constantly of the necessity both of preserving what is still valuable and of seeking wide consensus for whatever changes are undertaken.

*But there must be changes!* The current system of statistics has fallen woe-

---

125. Anne Y. Kester, Ed. *Following the Money: U.S. Finance in the World Economy*. Washington, DC: National Academy Press, forthcoming.

fully behind the pace of change of the realities those statistics purport to represent. And while a conservative and incremental approach to that change must be the constant watchword, truly effective change can only come about if it is informed by a larger vision: a vision that is clear-sighted in its understanding of the current statistical system, bold in its projections of what a more adequate system will look like, and aggressive in its determination to move all affected and interested parties toward making that vision a reality.

Such a layered and comprehensive vision of the required changes to the statistical system will not—to be effective it *cannot*—spring full grown from the mind of any single individual, nor from any single agency, bureau or institution. But it must be "housed" in one place which can serve as a sort of "clearing house" to accumulate, sort and disseminate the best ideas among all interested parties. The role of that kind of "clearing house" will be not to pre-empt a wide-ranging conversation about needed reforms, but to facilitate it.

It's a job for the Office of Management and Budget (OMB). Such a task is not new for OMB. While we have noted frequently in these pages that OMB in recent years has lost the largest parts of its resources for economic statistics, there was a period—during the 1940s and '50s—when OMB was willing and able to co-ordinate the gathering and analysis of statistics, devoting a full third of its staff to that task. We are suggesting that OMB should reprise that central role: it's a role that belongs in the Federal Government, which is simultaneously the biggest producer and the biggest user of statistics, and has the longest history of any player in both those roles. Within the Federal Government, that task belongs in the Executive Office.

Quite simply, it belongs in OMB. But that is not to say that it is the sole responsibility of the OMB. On the contrary, we have pointed out throughout this monograph the large and ever-increasing number of producers and users of statistical information. In fact, most large producers are also large users and vice versa. Each of them has a crucial stake, a unique perspective, and a valuable contribution to make to the discussion of how our statistical systems should be changed and improved. Those stakeholders include, besides the Federal Government:

- Both large and small private companies (special attention should be given to smaller businesses whose importance and input are still under-represented in statistics despite their growing importance in the economy itself);

- Academicians;

- State and local governments;

- Trade associations;

- Unions;

- Environmentalists; and

- Interest groups.

This is but a very partial listing of the plethora of groups who have important interests and perspectives on the reform of our statistical system. They should all have a voice and a place at the table as reform efforts are considered and go forward. How can that be accomplished? Over the years, there have been many proposals for combining or reorganizing statistical agencies. The simple premise is that if all statistics were collected by a central agency, it would be easier to make them uniform in concepts, definitions, and implementation. We have argued in this book that the pluralistic system brings considerable strength to the statistical information base. Therefore, we believe that statistical reorganization is not the answer to improving the statistical system. Rather, work needs to be done on identifying what should be measured, how it should be measured, followed by periodic evaluation of the statistical activities (a recommendation that repeats work of the 1970 President's Commission on Federal Statistics).

We recommend the creation of a permanent Advisory Committee to consult on a continuous basis with the OMB. It should be comprised of representatives of each of the groups listed above, each of whom would have staggered but long-term tenure on it in order to preserve some institutional expertise and memory within it. While it would have no official power, this Committee would meet regularly—and publicly—to consider the broad range of suggestions for change and improvement. Its statutory powers would be non-existent. Its powers of persuasion could be limitless.

There are a number of topics that could be addressed by this advisory committee in addition to the "vision" for the statistical system. It could assist in reviewing existing statistical programs to see if priorities can be altered to reallocate existing resources more efficiently. Second, it should investigate issues of information policy as it relates to statistics, including questions of reporting burden, the role of statistical agencies in dissemination, and the development of mechanisms for fostering approved governmental and private sector cooperation in the development of information systems.

Throughout *Statistics For the 21st Century*, there have been numerous comments about revisions and conflicting information. It is noted in Appendix 3 that the estimates of growth in Gross Domestic Product show little change between the first, second, and third preliminary estimates (when compared with the more complete estimates provided by the July revisions).

We strongly endorse the recommendation of earlier studies, including Cole, Federal Reserve Bank of Boston, and Fleming, who have recommended that the early revisions be simplified to one. Specifically, we recommend publishing only the first (the 25-day) estimate and dropping the 55- and 85-day estimates. Instead, the resources of the Bureau of Economic Analysis could be better utilized in refinements that contribute to the July revisions.

The need for improvement is clear. No less clear is the need for mechanisms and motivation to involve all of those interested in the statistics that define us and shape our hopes for the future. That's the reason for this book—to sound a sentinel's early signal about the need for change and to invite others to join the process of reform.

The authors welcome—in fact we *request*—that you send us your reactions to the topics treated in this book, as well as to the ways we have treated them. To repeat: we intend here not to have the last word but to send a first signal, not to end the discussion but to begin it. We will not only learn from your reactions in order to improve our future efforts, we will also gladly send on your suggestions to OMB or to others who can benefit from them.

We have spoken of the institutional lethargy that can impede statistical reform. There is a counterpart in individuals: It is a sort of *psychological lethargy*—a tired pessimism which ruefully accepts the status quo as the best that can be done, a despairing sense that this is how things have to be, a feeling that no meaningful reform is possible given budgetary restrictions and territorial disputes.

This book was written because we disagree with that pessimism; we passionately believe that meaningful change in our statistical systems is both necessary and possible. But such a book is only the first step.

The next steps are up to you!

# Guidelines for Bibliography Development

## Overview

In the development of this report, a detailed bibliography was prepared to provide references to selected source materials on the subject of improving U.S. official statistics.[†] This monograph is designed to provide a perspective on creating an integrated framework for evaluating priorities for proposed improvements in official statistics. The literature provides some guidelines for specific criticisms and recommendations for improving the overall quality of statistical indicators. In keeping with the objective of the present report, the full bibliography focuses on identifying literature on:

1. the evaluation of statistical indicators;

2. proposals for modifying or improving them; and

3. recommendations for the collection of new data series.

In the Bibliography at the end of this book is a sample list of documents drawn from the full bibliography. For interested readers, we will publish the entire bibliography of over 2,200 items on CD-ROM early in 1994. The electronic version of the bibliography will feature author, title, subject and source indices coupled with search and report generation functions so that it will be possible to select material relevant to each reader's specific area of interest. In the interim, readers may contact the authors for tailored searches of the data base.

The remainder of this appendix presents the perspective guiding selection of documents for the bibliography, an overview of our library search process, and an introduction to our classification concepts.[††]

---

[†]This appendix discusses procedures for our research on developing a bibliography on suggested references concerning problems and solutions for improving individual statistical series. A **sample** of the bibliography that was developed is in the bibliography at the end of this book.

[††]The authors wish to acknowledge the contributions of Information Resources Management Associates of Madison, Wisconsin and Seattle, Washington to this chapter.

---

## Basic Perspective

The perspective adopted by this monograph is that of a private-sector decision maker. We recognize that official statistics are first and foremost developed for public policy purposes. From a social perspective, however, these statistics are also used by citizens, businesses, and other decision makers. This report and bibliography, therefore, concentrates on the need to provide a broader view of statistical information required for sound decision making.

This bibliography of over 2,200 references also supports a second theme of the report. Documents have been selected that discuss statistical series required for accurate, timely, and relevant information about a wide array of policy questions regarding investment in our infrastructure and our role in a global economy, including human and physical capital and the environment. Documents describe statistical series classified broadly as pertaining to a "System of Economic Accounts," "System of Social and Demographic Accounts," or "System of Environmental Accounts." Coverage of statistical series is therefore not intended to be truly comprehensive since many specific topic areas were excluded.

The bibliography emphasizes concepts, definitions, and methodologies for statistical measurement. The principle that guided development of the bibliography was that a document would be included if it evaluated a current series or, either explicitly or implicitly, identified needed or proposed revisions or improvements. Documents are included that describe revisions to statistical series when the description includes reasons for the revision (e.g., gaps in coverage, known biases in published estimates, structural changes in the economy that require new data collection or modifying existing classification systems, evidence of a new disease that results in new definitions, and so forth).

Documents are included that evaluate, present, or recommend alternative techniques for improving published estimates. The bibliography also includes documents that describe techniques that have relevance not only for a particular statistical series, but whose evaluation or recommended solution may improve the quality of other statistical series (e.g., correcting undercoverage bias in telephone health surveys also has relevance for known coverage bias in other series). These techniques include the application of computer technology for data collection, such as computer-assisted telephone or personal interviewing (CATI or CAPI). However, documents that only describe a quality control or assurance program designed to improve the quality of statistical data, for example, were not included if the document did not also present an evaluation of those data.

Documents that have been included explicitly address a particular statistical series and offer suggestions that are deemed potentially relevant for improving the quality of the series or statistical series in general. For example, the bibliography includes articles that present alternative statistical or technical approaches to data collection, non response adjustment (weighting and imputation), and new interviewing techniques to improve respondent recall.

Although model building and econometric and statistical techniques are utilized as part of the process of evaluating the quality of statistical series, relatively few documents on these subjects are included in this bibliography. Computer matching or record linkage techniques or evaluations, as well as the literature on disclosure avoidance, have been excluded, although it is noted in the report that these are important topics.

Furthermore, although the institutional structures and processes of government are critical for producing quality statistics, this bibliography does not include a large number of documents published during the 1980s through the early 1990s that evaluate or recommend political or structural changes in the governmental statistical system. As noted in the report, the key issues are conceptual and methodological, not organizational. For example, the bibliography excludes important findings reported by the U.S. General Accounting Office on information resource management, as well as observations reported by individuals participating in legislative hearings.

Extensive evaluation and research related to the U.S. Census of Population and Housing was conducted during the 1980s. This bibliography contains only a small number of documents relevant to evaluation and recommended changes in the Census. For more information, the reader should consult additional publications of the U.S. Bureau of the Census, including the *1980 Census of Population and Housing Evaluation and Research Report* series and Congressional hearings.

The time period covered by this bibliography is limited to documents written between 1978 and 1993. *A Framework for Planning U.S. Federal Statistics for the 1980s* summarizes governmental agencies' recommendations for improving the federal statistical system as a result of ideas suggested prior to 1976.[1A] Thus, documents contained in this bibliography may be considered an "update" to the "Framework" report in terms of suggestions for improvement in individual statistical programs.[2A] Indeed, as this bibliography demonstrates, many of the recommendations contained in the "Framework" continued to be on the agenda of programmatic changes for the federal statistical system throughout the 1980s.

There are, however, some exceptions to the time period covered by this bibliography. The first exception relates to developing a "System of Social and Demographic Statistics" (SSDS). Recommendations for developing a system of social accounts appear in published form during the early 1930s and again during the 1960s. These recommendations were never formally implemented, although the U.S. government issued several reports labeled "social indicators" between the middle 1970s and early 1980s. The second exception relates to developing a "system of environmental accounts." Work on a system of environmental accounts was begun in the early 1970s, but recommendations were never implemented. Thus, in these two areas, documents published before 1978 have been included.

Coverage of documents related to systems of social and environmental accounts is not complete. A large literature on "social indicators" exists, but this bibliography includes only those documents that evaluate the concept of a system of social accounts or that make recommendations for specific statistical series to be included in a system of social accounts. To the extent possible, published and unpublished documents on a system of environmental accounts were located, but coverage is not considered complete.

Although the U.S. official statistical system is formally linked to international statistical organizations, harmonization of domestic and international classification systems is a requirement for operating in a global economy, and a large amount of data for private decision making is essential for public decisions, this bibliography is nevertheless limited to documents about official statistical series of the U.S. federal statistical system. There are three exceptions to this rule.

---

1A. One of the co-authors, Joseph W. Duncan, was responsible for development of and publication of *A Framework for Planning U.S. Federal Statistics for the 1980s.* Many of the proposals of that earlier report are relevant to this report, but there has been no attempt to review or duplicate the approach of the "Framework." The Framework started with governmental needs for data. This report, as noted earlier, is concerned with the general needs of society and consequently is not driven by the needs of governmental agencies for program planning or evaluation data, although clearly those needs will weigh heavily in the ultimate determination of new statistical programs and priorities.

2A. Ibid.

---

The first exception is those documents that describe needed improvements in international or non-U.S. statistical systems that supply critical information to U.S. decision makers about the United States and its linkages, relationships, and commitments in the international arena. For example, recommendations issued by the United Nations or Eurostat were included if they were deemed relevant to the globalization of economic activity, including production, markets, and international trade. This bibliography also includes documents that focus on requirements for statistics on the global environment, ecology, and energy, whether the document originates in the United States or elsewhere, because these issues are not limited to the political jurisdiction of the United States and because statistical data are needed for informed policy decisions regarding the long-term causes and consequences of global environmental change.

The second exception is that there has been much intellectual exchange of ideas and methodologies between the U.S. and other national statistical agencies, including Canada and The Netherlands, for example. This bibliography includes documents written by statisticians in other countries, especially Canada, when the subject matter is relevant to the U.S. statistical system. A few documents by Dutch economists on measurement of subjective well-being and by The Netherlands and other Central Statistics Bureaus on computer-assisted telephone or personal interviewing have also been included.

The third exception is corporate statistical data that are obtained by federal agencies to assist them in policy planning and evaluation (e.g., the U.S. Small Business Administration obtains Dun & Bradstreet Corporation business data files; the U.S. Department of Energy obtains petroleum and gas reserve information under contract from private producers). Thus, selected documents that describe private-sector data used by U.S. statistical agencies for public policy are included.

## Search for Documents

Documents were located in four ways. The first was through a review of the principal sources of publications about statistics, including journals, proceedings, and monographs. The second was through literature searches in relevant data bases and indices. The third was through targeting references cited in the documents reviews. The fourth was through contacts in various governmental agencies.

For a comprehensive retrieval effort, literature searches began with the following four steps:

1. The *Current Index to Statistics* by specific subject;

2. Indexes to U.S. Government publications, primarily the *Monthly Catalog* and the *American Statistics Index*;

3. Monographs in the library catalogs of the University of Wisconsin-Madison and the University of Washington; and

4. Articles on statistics in the leading index of the discipline (e.g., *Economic Literature Index, Enviroline, Energyline, Education Index*).

It should be noted that sources of materials relevant to this report are widely scattered, and no single agency, association, or index is primary. This was particularly true for documents on the environment, natural resources, and energy, which is why we caution the reader about the incompleteness of coverage in these subject areas.

More than sixty journals and other annual series are represented in this bibliography. Papers published in five proceedings have received in-depth coverage here as well. These are: the *National Bureau of Economic Research Conference on Income and Wealth, Proceedings of the American Statistical Association Business and Economic Statistics Section, Proceedings of the American Statistical Association Survey Research Methods Section, Proceedings of the American Statistical Association Social Statistics Section, Proceedings of the Annual Research Conference* (sponsored by the U.S. Bureau of the Census), and *Proceedings of the Symposium on Statistics and the Environment* (co-sponsored by ASA and other organizations).

## Indexing the Documents

### Citations

In general, citations have been entered for whole works. However, for monographs and all proceedings, the bibliographers also entered citations for individual chapters or articles. Citations for individual chapters were indexed separately and linked to the parent document if an initial review of the document revealed a high level of complexity and it was also believed that the reader would benefit from the detail provided by separate indexing. For example, citations may be found both to the entire monograph and individual chapters and appendices of the National Research Council monograph, *Behind the Numbers*.

### Subject Indexing

The bibliographers provide detailed indexing to reflect the statistical subject area under discussion, as well as the nature of improvements being considered. To express this another way, this approach will provide the best support for writing about a subject area and its related concerns, or about a methodological concern permitting the reader to cite examples from a multitude of subject areas.

Every document in the bibliography is indexed according to its subject matter to enable the user to locate articles on a particular topic. Each document is linked to one or more of the broad categories and assigned as many of the specific index terms as are relevant. The indexing vocabulary was derived from the language employed by the author of the document, with an attempt to impose coherency or standardization to the language of description. Where two or more terms are commonly used for one concept, one term was chosen as the primary index term, and index entries for alternative terms are linked by "see" references to the preferred term. This practice was also used to link abbreviations such as GNP to full terms such as Gross National Product. In instances where concepts overlap, the related terms are brought together by "see also" references in the index.

The structure of the subject headings was, however, standardized. The broad subject headings have a maximum of two subfields, while the specific subject headings may have up to three subfields.

The broad subject headings are composed of a term for the general category of indicator and this may be followed by a term for the subset of the category. Thus, the structure is:

TERM—Term.

For example:

Economic Indicators—NIPA

The broad subject headings used are:

Census of Population and Housing

Economic Indicators

Environmental Indicators

Methodology

Social Indicators

The specific subject headings may consist of up to three subfields, i.e.

TERM-Term-term.
with the following pattern:

**TERM**: The first level comprises the statistical topic area under discussion, such as NIPA, Wealth, Mining and Minerals, Health, Contagious Diseases, Work Force, Immigration, and so forth.

**Term**: The second-level term is the focus of the evaluation or recommendation, such as Concepts, Conceptual Issues, Definitions, Data Requirements, Data Quality, Methodology, Measurement, Data Sources, and Timeliness. The terms "Methodology" and "Measurement" were often used interchangeably by authors; the bibliographers attempted, however, to distinguish the meaning of these two terms (see below, section on "Definitions of Second Level Subject Terms"). As we note below, individual citations also confused "concepts" and "definitions," but the bibliographers attempted to distinguish between the two in their classification of a document.

**term**: The third level is somewhat more open-ended, including format terms (History, Bibliography, Maps, Satellite Imagery); narrower topics as subsets of TERM or Term (Income Flows, Cost Weights Composite Estimation, 1987 Revision, Sources of Error); and agency names or place names (DOD Purchases, USGS Monitoring), and so forth.

A document may have multiple subjects associated with it, if more than one topic was covered. For example, a document may have addressed issues regarding capital investment in industry (concepts), balance of payments (data quality), and needs for new data associated with capital investment. Every document is classified by one or more primary terms that represent the general subject matter (e.g., economic indicators or social indicators), and is further classified by the specific terms (topics) discussed in the document (e.g., capital formation, economic well-being, poverty).

The specific terms may be further delineated by a methodological term, if relevant. Thus, a document might have the following terms assigned:

Economic Indicators—Capital

Capital Investment, Industry—Concepts

Capital Investment, Industry—Data Requirements

Balance of Payments—Data Quality

The reader should note that individual statistical series are neither identified nor indexed. To have done so would have increased enormously the size of the index and subject bibliographies. In addition, many of the documents referred to general categories of statistical series or were devoted to discussions about many series. The title of the document often indicates the statistical series under discussion, however.

### Definitions of Second-Level Subject Terms

The second-level subject term represents a classification of the methodological focus or type of evaluation that a document describes. Nine subject terms have been applied to reflect the contents of a document: data requirements, conceptual issues, concepts, definitions, measurement, data sources, methodology, data quality, and timeliness. A document will be classified by one or more of these terms. We define below each term and provide examples.

### Data Requirements

The term "data requirements" refers to a document that addresses the issue explicitly or implicitly: "Are we asking the right questions?" The document recommends improvements in or revision of a current statistical series, development of a new statistical series, or application of different methodology(ies) in order to respond to social, economic, or environmental change or to policy initiatives for which a current series is inadequate. Many documents do not explicitly make a recommendation, but it is nevertheless implicit in the author's analysis.

Example: Some documents included in this bibliography discuss the need to revise official industrial and occupational classification systems to reflect structural changes in the U.S. or global economy. Although these documents are classified by the bibliographers with the subject term "data requirements," the policy need for modifying a classification system is rarely explicitly stated by the author as the reason for revising the classification system.

Example: Hammel's (1980) article identifies some of the policy needs for timely, accurate, and reliable labor force statistics (e.g., increase of women in the labor force and their impact on labor markets, data on structural imbalances and labor market deficiencies, allocation of federal funds, and new program initiatives for assisting the unemployed) and discusses the failings of the *Current Population Survey* (CPS) and plans for its revision.

Example: Vaughan (1989) notes that work undertaken in the 1970s to model the tax and transfer system using data from the *Current Population Survey*, while yielding useful results, also identified problem areas with these data that related to benefit types (p. 223). These included, for example, being unable to distinguish between retired worker and widow benefits for widowed women and between disabled worker and childhood disability benefits.

### Conceptual Issues

This term refers to what statistical series "are about." Documents classified in this way are often general, more theoretical, discussions.

Example: Sheifer (1978) writes that "Ideally, the Employment Cost Index should reflect only increases unrelated to improved performance. It should measure changes in rates of pay for specific jobs, not the individuals filling those jobs. But how in a mass survey operation does one identify those in-grade wage adjustments for individuals—regardless of whether they are labeled longevity or merit increases—which are pay adjustments in the desired sense?" (p. 684).

Example: Groves et al. (1981) specifically addresses "conceptual issues in the measurement of victimization," stating that ambiguous criteria are used to determine "when distinct victimization exists or whether events are part of a single crime" (p. 1). The authors then analyze a variety of response error issues in measuring victimization.

Example: The bibliography includes chapters in books that are general discussions about what should be included in environmental indices.

### Concepts

*Webster's Ninth New Collegiate Dictionary* defines "concept" as an "abstract or generic idea generalized from particular instances."

Example: According to Tibbetts (1978), the first step in designing a new approach to industrial price measurement is to "specify an economic concept for integrating both the needs of the producing-industry-oriented users of the data and those who need detailed product indexes" (p. 513), which, he argued, is the "production function" combined with the "Theory of the Firm" (p. 514).

Example: The National Health Interview Survey captures data on "morbidity," which is defined as "a departure from a state of physical or mental well-being, resulting from disease or injury, of which the affected individual is aware" (Fuchsberg, 1978, p. 570).

### Definitions

*Webster's Ninth New Collegiate Dictionary* defines "definition" as "a statement expressing the essential nature of something (as by differentiation within a class)" and "a statement of the meaning of a word or word group." Authors often do not distinguish between a concept and a definition, and use the terms interchangeably. The bibliographers did attempt, however, to distinguish between the two words, whenever possible.

Example: Hamel (1980) explains that the Commission that evaluated the *Current Population Surveys* in the late 1970s recommended that members of the Armed Forces be included in the definition of "employed" in the national statistics because military service was now voluntary (p. 104).

Example: Some documents that recommend revising labor force statistics discuss the effect of classifying "discouraged workers" as "outside the labor force," because the current definition excludes certain categories of people who would take a job or have conducted a job market search with the result that the "true" number of unemployed persons is underestimated.

### Measurement

We have relied on *Webster's Ninth New Collegiate Dictionary* for applying the subject term "measurement" to a document. Webster's defines "measurement" as "the act or process of measuring" or "a figure, extent, or amount obtained by measuring" ("measure" is considered a synonym). Measurement is about "operationalizing the concepts." The bibliographers applied the term "measurement," if an author meant this term but employed words like "methodology" or "concept."

Example: In some instances it appeared appropriate to apply the subject term "measurement" to documents that discuss "how to get at" concepts. OECD argues we can measure air quality by recording $CO_2$ emissions, $SO_x$ emissions, $NO_x$ emissions, etc.

Example: Sackley (1978) explains how the Employment Cost Index statistics are computed. He explains that, "The measurement of pay for salaried workers and those paid on a piece-work or commission basis requires reduction of earnings to an hourly average before the occupational average is calculated. This is accomplished by dividing the straight-time earnings payment by the straight-time hours associated with the payment." (p. 689).

## Data Sources

The term "data sources" is applied when the discussion focuses on where the data come from or why data are difficult to collect. This is a topic that arises in the areas of epidemiology and risk assessment where problems such as the long delays in the appearance of symptoms and the subtlety of adverse effects make it difficult to identify affected populations. In the area of labor statistics, there are discussions comparing variability in the unemployment picture that can be linked to the source of the data: employer, worker, unemployment office, and so forth.

## Methodology

This term refers to methods, rules, procedures, and techniques applied from scientific design through analysis, including model-building, forecasting, econometrics, and regulatory compliance testing.

Example: This bibliography contains documents that evaluate the X-11 ARIMA method for seasonal adjustment of labor force statistics and contrasts it with the benefits derived from employing the concurrent adjustment method.

## Data Quality

The term "data quality" refers to a document that addresses issues related to technical adequacy. Technical adequacy means "Are the appropriate methods and measures being employed to produce a statistical series?" Technical adequacy addresses the credibility of the data. Are the statistics accurate and reliable? In this bibliography, a large number of documents address the issue of "technical adequacy," that is, what error has been identified or what contributes to sources of error in the estimates.

Example: We applied the term "data quality" to Groves et al.'s (1981) analysis of the National Crime Survey, which indicated that these statistical series suffer from "major response error" due to the failure to report a victimization (p. 3). Their paper then details the ways in which response error results from instrument design, survey design, data collection methods, and underreporting due to failure to recall an event.

## Timeliness

This term means "Is the information released when it is needed?"

Example: The U.S. General Accounting Office concluded that the Operations of U.S. Affiliates of Foreign Companies statistical series released by the Bureau of Economic Analysis (BEA) were very dated by the time published; revised 1986 data were not published until 1988 (U.S. General Accounting Office, 1989).

# The General Accounting Office's Role in Federal Statistical Activities and Related Reports on Statistical Policy Issues

As funding for the collection, analysis, and dissemination of statistical information by the Federal government has been sharply curtailed, the Government Accounting Office (GAO) has tried to take up some of the slack. But, the GAO is, by its mandate, a *reactive*, rather than a strategic planning institution. Its job, established by Congress, is to respond to Congressional requests for research and investigation into how well different federal institutions are working, rather than to take the initiative in planning and coordinating government activities.

Nevertheless, over recent years, the GAO has increasingly come to focus on federal statistics. In conducting research and investigations, the GAO assists Congress in its responsibilities for monitoring the federal agencies carrying out the programs that Congress has approved and funded. In recent years, GAO activities have increasingly focused on federal statistics. For this task, it has approximately ten professional staff members in the information and statistical policy area, with two or three in its office of the Chief Economist and one or two in its Seattle office. This is more staff than the Office of Management and Budget (OMB) has allotted for its statistical policy responsibilities. The GAO has completed a number of separate studies of federal statistics.

## Overview

This section[3A] presents the GAO perspective on three areas of federal statistical activities; lack of adequate funding and funding process, lack of coordination, and decentralization of the statistical functions in the Federal government.

In a stringent budgetary situation faced by all federal programs, there are two options: first, to ask for more funds for statistics or, second, to ask for a rearrangement of the allocations among the statistical agencies depending on priority needs.

---

3A. Part of this section is based on an interview with Bruce Johnson, the GAO Assistant Director responsible for statistics and information policy.

---

The Congressional budgetary process, which allocates funds for statistics as part of each department's or agency's budget, does not realistically permit a consideration of optimal allocation of funds for statistics across the agencies, or offer to give up some funds in one department to get more funds in another.

As a result, funding for meeting federal statistical requirements is continued in the budgets of over seventy agencies or organizational units having $500,000 in allocation for more statistical activities.[4A]

Coordination of statistical activities among the federal agencies needs to be strengthened. OMB has the responsibility for government-wide statistical coordination, but OMB has only five professional staff members, down from a level of about twenty-five or thirty staff, who carried out both paperwork reviews and statistical policy coordination a couple of decades ago. Since any large increase in staff at OMB for statistical policy is unlikely in this budgetary environment, the crucial question becomes "What priority items should OMB be doing?"

The largest task must be in the area of budgetary review, taking a crosscutting approach that transcends the politics of agency budgets and looks toward shaping a government-wide perspective on federal data needs. The Boskin Initiatives for improving economic statistics is an example of such crosscutting planning. In implementing these initiatives, OMB coordinated the President's budget request for improvements in the economic statistics programs of the Bureau of the Census, the Bureau of Economic Analysis, and other agencies. Unfortunately, Congress has not funded this initiative at the requested level.

Another important coordinating task for OMB is to review the Decennial Census, with a view to asking which data should be collected as part of the Census of Population and Housing and which could be collected by other surveys. This review, which requires trade-offs among competing agency interests, has to be led by OMB.

Third, the de-centralized nature of federal statistics gives rise to problems of coordination among the agencies. A number of different studies have called for greater centralization. A recent policy proposal called Mandate for Change argued for the creation of a national information agency, bringing

---

4A. See Office of Management and Budget, *Statistical Programs of the United States Government, Fiscal Year 1993*, which is the required Paperwork Reduction Act report to Congress on budgets for statistical activities.

together the Census, BEA, and others.

This is neither a new issue nor a new proposal. For example, President Carter undertook a statistical reorganization project. After some study, the Carter group decided the disruptions that would be caused by greater centralization were too great for the advantages that might be gained. Other studies have come to much the same conclusion.

Given these barriers to reorganizing the federal statistical agencies into a centralized agency, what steps can realistically be taken toward greater coordination? A primary way is through much greater sharing of data. That, in turn, requires Congressional action to deal with the agencies' statutory requirements on confidentiality of statistical information. There are some bills to that effect currently making their way through Congress.

Of course, to all three of the problem areas identified above, there are quick and simple answers: Invest more money. Beef up the OMB statistical policy staff. Consolidate all the economic statistics in a single agency. We have also seen all the reasons why that will not happen.

In light of these realities, GAO is looking at five areas where it might help the statistical process:

1. Examining ways to enhance the leadership in all statistical areas of the Federal government;

2. Examining economic statistics, especially reviewing the impact of bad statistics and also looking, for example, at what happened to the Boskin Initiatives;

3. Examining the Decennial Census, including assessing its importance to the rest of the statistical system, and the so-called 'Reform 2000' initiatives;

4. Examining which social and demographic statistics should be collected elsewhere rather than in the Decennial Census; and

5. Examining the entire array of information policy issues—including individual privacy, public/private relationships in the supply of information, the role of electronic technology, and the question of pricing.

With the reduced level of funding available for statistical activities, the federal agencies have concentrated more on maintaining data collections and less on evaluating the resulting data series. To some extent, the GAO has filled this void by undertaking evaluations of statistical programs and making recommendations for improvements. The following selected list of GAO reports is representative of its interest in a broad range of federal statistical subject matter.

The GAO has investigated the quality and usefulness of federal data in the following areas:

- The Human Nutrition Information Services 1987-88 Nationwide Food Consumption Survey;

- The U.S. Department of Agriculture's meat forecasts and estimates;

- The 1990 decennial census process, evaluation of results, and 2000 census planning;

- The air pollution monitoring data produced by the Environmental Protection Agency's National Air Monitoring Network;

- The Environmental Protection Agency's hazardous waste data, including the Resource Conservation and Recovery Act reporting system;

- The Environmental Protection Agency's pesticide data, including the Pesticide Product Information System (PPIS), the Pesticide Document Management System (PDMS), and the Federal Insecticide, Fungicide, and Rodenticide Act and Toxic Substances Central Act Enforcement System (FATES);

- The data underlying the Center for Disease Control and Prevention's national estimates of the current and projected size of the AIDS epidemic;

- Federal data on foreign investment in the United States;

- The National Trade Data Bank;

- Education data, including the National Assessment of Educational Progress, Fast Reponse Survey System, and the Common Core of Data; and

- The Energy Information Administration's energy data.

## Economic Statistics

This appendix lists and summarizes sources used for documentation concerning data on economic statistics, the environment, health, international trade, and social and demographic statistical information. In the area of economic statistics, there are several topics of interest. These include agricultural data, trade data, labor statistics, financial data, and a variety of issues about how economic statistics are gathered and assessed.

## Agricultural Data

The report "Initial Report on the Quality of the Agricultural Survey Program" discusses the process used by the National Agricultural Statistics Service (NASS) to continually improve its agricultural survey program. Specifically, it addresses what we know about the quality of the agricultural statistical program of NASS.[5A]

In its report, *Short-Term Forecasting: Accuracy of USDA's Meat Forecasts and Estimates,* GAO concludes that the USDA forecasts and estimates, when looked at over 1983-89, are reasonably accurate. Comparisons of forecasts and estimates to actual production and price figures resulted in total error rates of less than 6%. GAO also found that USDA forecasts and estimates compared well to other available forecasts produced in the private sector. GAO did find, however, that when forecasts were assessed month by month, larger error rates were evident, particularly during the early months of the USDA forecast cycle. Although overall error rates were small, they did have a consistent bias error component (p. 1).

GAO recommends USDA develop a better process to identify, report, and correct bias errors when they occur and to provide better documentation of their procedures and assumptions (p. 7).

- General Accounting Office. *Short-Term Forecasting: Accuracy of USDA's Meat Forecasts and Estimates.* GAO/PEMD-91-16, May 1991. 76 pages.

The GAO review, "Nutrition Monitoring: Mismanagement of Nutrition

---

5A. George A. Hanuschak, *Initial Report on the Quality of the Agricultural Survey Program,* Seminar on Quality of Federal Data. Statistical Policy Working Paper 20, prepared by the Federal Committee on Statistical Methodology, March 1991, pp. 29-39.

Survey Has Resulted in Questionable Data," concludes that methodological problems, deviations from the survey's original design, and lax controls over the collection and processing of the results all raise doubts about the quality and usefulness of the data in the 1987-88 Nationwide Food Consumption Survey. Results from the survey may not be representative of the U.S. population because of low response rates. GAO raises concerns that the data may be biased. In April 1991, an expert panel convened by the Human Nutrition Information Service (HNIS) to assess the integrity of the 1987-88 data concluded that the data presented may represent biased estimates of the nation's dietary intake (pp. 2-3).

The most serious data quality problem in the survey resulted from a low response rate: only 34% of the households in the basic sample provided individual intake data—a response rate so low that it is questionable whether the data are representative of the U.S. population (p. 3).

Since this survey contains the only current data available on household and individual food consumption, GAO thought it important for the HNIS to disclose the data's limitations to the federal agencies and others that rely on the survey to make policy decisions (p. 4).

GAO recommends that before the next survey, HNIS should:

- Demonstrate that efficient survey instruments and procedures have been developed to reduce the burden on respondents, to increase respondents' motivation to participate in the survey, and to meet essential data needs;

- Develop a plan to ensure that the result obtained from the household food use and individual intake data are representative of the U.S. population; and

- Indicate the steps to be taken and the quality controls to be followed so that future surveys will not repeat mistakes of the past (p.5).

## Budgets for Statistics

The following hearings and reports addressed the adequacy of agency budgets for statistics and the impact of the budget cuts and personnel trends on the quality of the statistical programs:

- U.S. Congress. House of Representatives. *Impact of Budget Cuts on Federal Statistical Programs.* Hearing before the Subcommittee on Census and Population of the Committee on Post Office and Civil Service. March 16, 1982. Washington, D.C., U.S. Government Printing Office, March 16, 1982. 481 pages.

- U.S. Congress. House of Representatives. *An Update on the Status of Major Federal Statistical Agencies, Fiscal Year 1986.* A Report Prepared by Congressional Research Service of the Library of Congress for the Committee on Government Operations. Washington, D.C., U.S. Government Printing Office, May 1985. 88 pages.

- U.S. Congress. House of Representatives. Committee on Government Operations. *The Federal Statistical System 1980 to 1985.* A Report Prepared by Baseline Data Corporation for the Congressional Research Service of the Library of Congress. Washington, D.C., U.S. Government Printing Office, November 1984. 284 pages.

- U.S. Congress. House of Representatives. Committee on Government Operations. *Reorganization and Budget Cutbacks May Jeopardize the Future of the Nation's Statistical System.* Washington, D.C. U.S. Government Printing Office, September 30, 1982. 18 pages.

- U.S. General Accounting Office. *Status of the Statistical Community After Sustaining Budget Reductions.* GAO/IMTEC-84-17, July 18, 1984. 61 pages.

## Bureau of Mines Data

We have included here the preface and summary list of recommendations from *A Review of the Statistical Program of the Bureau of Mines,* which addresses the improvement in collection, analysis, reporting, and dissemination of data.

- National Research Council. Commission on Behavioral and Social Sciences and Education. Committee on National Statistics. Panel to Review the Statistical Program of the Bureau of Mines. *A*

*Review of the Statistical Program of the Bureau of Mines.*
Washington, D.C., National Academy Press, 1982. 210 pages.


## Economic Statistics

The following materials provide information on the criticisms that were directed at federal economic data in the 1980s and on the Boskin Initiatives:

- U.S. Congress. Joint Economic Committee. *The Quality of the Nation's Economic Statistics.* Hearings March 17 and April 17, 1986. 429 pages.

The next article is based on the evaluation of the GNP estimates required by OMB's Statistical Policy Directive No. 3. This report is concerned with the reliability of GNP data and whether the early current quarter estimates of aggregate GNP provide a useful indication of the estimates that emerge when complete and final source data are available. The article contains information on recommendations to improve GNP source data. Improving GNP data was included in the Boskin Initiatives and plans for these improvements were included in the budget for the Bureau of Economic Analysis, as detailed in the reports, Statistical Programs of the United States Government for FY 1990-FY 1993.[6A]

The next report[7A] identified five high priority areas and made recommendations for improvements:

- GNP estimates;

- Merchandise trade statistics;

- Service sector data;

- Use of business lists; and

- Fees for statistical services.

This was the forerunner of the Boskin Initiatives. (During the Bush Administration an unpublished Economic Policy Council Working Group report was prepared.)

---

6A. Allan H. Young, "Evaluation of the GNP Estimates," *Survey of Current Business,* Volume 67, Number 8, August 1987, pp. 18-42.

7A. Report of the Working Group on the Quality of Economic Statistics to the Economic Policy Council, April 1987.

---

The following paper[8A] draws attention to the gaps and weaknesses in the statistical base for economic policy making. The next article discusses how U.S. government statistics are outmoded, not having adapted to economic and technological changes. As a result, information is inadequate for public policy and business decisions. Inadequate resources for the statistical agencies and poor OMB coordination are targeted for blame.

The article looks at assumptions and definitions used to collect data, and criticizes how long it takes to make data available.

- Kelly, Henry and Andrew Wyckoff. "Distorted Image: How Government Statistics Misrepresent the Economy," *Technology Review*, February/March 1989, pp. 53-60.

The next report evaluates the current state of federal economic statistics, including a review of the level of funding for these data, and makes recommendations for improvements. The report contains an appendix listing articles on federal statistics.

- National Association of Business Economists. *Report of the Statistics Committee*. February 1988. 40 pages.

A perspective on areas where better data would improve economic policy analysis is provided in the next report. It notes instances where the statistical system does not track change well: introduction of new technologies (computers and telecommunications equipment), impact of international trade on the domestic economy, techniques for evaluating the quality of health care and services, etc. The report also comments on the lack of effective statistical coordination by the OMB.

- U.S. Congress. Office of Technology Assessment. *Statistical Needs for a Changing U.S. Economy: Background Paper*. Washington, D.C., U.S. Government Printing Office, September 1989. 40 pages.

The hearings cited below discuss the federal statistical infrastructure and review the recommendations of the Working Group on the Quality of Economic Statistics. Boskin & Darby testified on March 1, 1990. On March 29, 1990, Sar Levitan, Joel Popkin, and James Smith of the NABE testified. Smith also had, as part of his testimony, the February 1988 NABE Statistics Committee Report.

---

8A. F. Thomas Juster, *The State of U.S. Economic Statistics: Current and Prospective Quality, Policy Needs, and Resources*. Prepared for the 50th Anniversary Conference on Research in Income and Wealth. Washington, D.C., May 12-14, 1988.

- U.S. Congress. Joint Economic Committee. Hearings. March 1, 1990 and March 29, 1990.

The next article maintains that economic statistics are unreliable since the numbers are revised regularly. For example, the retail sales report of May 1989 was first reported erroneously and is cited as a case of bad data triggering bad government policy. Examples are cited of reactions to government data and their uses. A complex economy plus budget cuts have had their impact on data reliability.

- Crutsinger, Martin, "Economists Question Accuracy and Value of U.S. Statistics," *The Washington Post*, July 5, 1990, p. D1, D5.

- News release of 2/14/91 from the Council of Economic Advisors, "FY 1992 Economic Statistics Initiative Improving the Quality of Statistics," and related newspaper articles on this release. Also included in this appendix is a Census Bureau staff paper on the FY 1992 Initiative as it pertains to the Census budget.

The hearings cited below were held to discuss proposals to improve the quality of federal statistics. The proposals were the FY 1992 initiative (Boskin Initiatives). Attached are copies of the testimony by Boskin, Darby, Norwood, Fleming, and Hawkes. Martin Fleming also presented a report of the NABE Statistics Committee, *Improving the Quality of Economic Statistics*, dated March 1, 1991.

- U.S. Congress. Joint Economic Committee. Hearings. March 1, 1991.

The following speech discusses efforts to improve economic statistics.

- U.S. Department of Commerce. Bureau of the Census. *Improving the Quality of Federal Economic Statistics*, 1991 Annual Research Conference, March 17-20, 1991. Remarks by Michael Boskin.

The following article discusses the state of federal statistics, particularly the Boskin Initiatives and the FY 1992 proposals for improvements.

- Stanfield, Rochelle L. "Statistics Gap," *National Journal*, April 13, 1991, pp. 844-849.

Pages 30-34 of the *Minutes and Report of Committee Recommendations* deal with the FY 1992 Census budget request for improving its current economic statistics program as part of the Boskin Initiatives.

---

- U.S. Department of Commerce. Bureau of the Census. *Minutes and Report of Committee Recommendations.* Census Advisory Committees of the American Statistical Association, on Population Statistics, of the American Marketing Association, and of the American Economic Association, April 25-26, 1991.

Pages 316-319 from *Mid-Session Review: The President's Budget and Economic Growth Agenda* concern improvements to federal statistics. Listed are the 1991 accomplishments for economic statistics and the objectives for 1992 and 1993 for improving economic data.

- Executive Office of the President. Office of Management and Budget. *Mid-Session Review: The President's Budget and Economic Growth Agenda.* Washington, D.C., U.S. Government Printing Office, July 24, 1992.

Sections in the following reports on "Economic Statistics" contain information on the proposals in the President's budget for improving economic statistics (the Boskin Initiatives).

- U.S. Executive Office of the President. Office of Management and Budget. *Statistical Programs of the United States Government, Fiscal Year 1990.* Washington, D.C., U.S. Government Printing Office, 1990. 45 pages.

- U.S. Executive Office of the President. Office of Management and Budget. *Statistical Programs of the United States Government, Fiscal Year 1991.* Washington, D.C., U.S. Government Printing Office, 1990. 39 pages.

- U.S. Executive Office of the President. Office of Management and Budget. *Statistical Programs of the United States Government, Fiscal Year 1992.* Washington, D.C., U.S. Government Printing Office, 1991. 41 pages.

- U.S. Executive Office of the President. Office of Management and Budget. *Statistical Programs of the United States Government, Fiscal Year 1993.* Washington, D.C., U.S. Government Printing Office, 1992. 45 pages.

Pages 134-135 from *Budget Baselines, Historical Data, and Alternatives for the Future* concern federal statistics, in particular, economic statistics.

- U.S. Executive Office of the President. Office of Management and Budget. *Budget Baselines, Historical Data, and Alternatives for the Future.* Washington, D.C., U.S. Government Printing Office, January 1993.

In November 1984, the House Committee on Government Operations submitted a report ( *The Federal Statistical System 1980 to 1985*).

- Criticizing OMB for not monitoring changes in source data (p. 23);

- Listing changes in source data (pp. 127-137); and

- Listing proposed improvements in the source data (pp. 138-147).

Excerpts from this document are provided in this appendix.

- U.S. Congress. House of Representatives. Committee on Government Operations. *The Federal Statistical System 1980 to 1985.* A Report Prepared by Baseline Data Corporation for the Congressional Research Service of the Library of Congress. Washington, D.C., U.S. Government Printing Office, November 1984. 284 pages.

For additional information about the GNP data, see also the material list cited previously about the quality of economic statistics.


## Income Data

The following two reports identify the limitations of the March supplement to the CPS as follows: "Incomplete reporting of income amounts, particularly from property and welfare; income and employment data that represent annual totals with no information available on intrayear fluctuations in economic circumstances that could make some families eligible for government programs for part of the year; scanty and suspect information on the numbers and characteristics of program participants, and especially on persons and families receiving benefits from more than one program; data on family composition and characteristics that were reported, not for the prior income year, but for March (the interview month); and the absence of information on asset holdings and taxes, which are needed to determine program eligibility and also fully characterize the economic status of the household sector."

As a result of the Income Survey Development Program (ISDP), the Census Bureau expanded the data collected in the March CPS income supplement on both cash and in-kind income. The Survey of Income and Program Participation (SIPP) has the goal to improve further the current estimates of income and income change, including annual and sub-annual estimates by source of income. SIPP collects income data by month from samples of households followed over time. While SIPP has achieved major improvements in the reporting of many sources of income, and data are available for sub-annual periods, SIPP data on asset holdings and income for high income individuals has not improved and these data are not useful for tax modeling. As a result, SIPP has tended to focus on the population economically at risk.

The Committee on National Statistics recently completed a review of SIPP covering the survey's goals, design, data collection and processing, data products, methodological research, and the survey's management. Included here is that portion of the report listing the recommendations for improvement.

- National Research Council. Commission on Behavioral and Social Sciences and Education. Committee on National Statistics. *The Survey of Income and Program Participation: An Interim Assessment.* Washington, D.C., National Academy Press, 1989.

- National Research Council. Commission on Behavioral and Social Sciences and Education. Committee on National Statistics. Panel to Evaluate the Survey of Income and Program Participation. *The Future of the Survey of Income and Program Participation.* Constance F. Citro and Graham Kalton, Eds. Washington, D.C., National Academy Press, 1992. 284 pages.

An excerpt from the following report is provided detailing the data quality problems with the March income supplement to the CPS.

- National Research Council. Commission on Behavioral and Social Sciences and Education. Committee on National Statistics. Panel to Evaluate Microsimulation Models for Social Welfare Programs. *Improving Information for Social Policy Decisions: The Uses of Microsimulation Modeling. Volume I: Review and Recommendations.* Constance F. Citro and Eric A. Hanushek, Eds. Washington, D.C., National Academy Press, 1991.

The portion of the report (Minutes and Report of Committee Recommendations) provided in this appendix discusses the Census Bureau's plans to improve and integrate SIPP and CPS income statistics.

- U.S. Department of Commerce. Bureau of the Census. Minutes and Report of Committee Recommendations. Census Advisory Committees of the American Statistical Association, on Population Statistics, of the American Marketing Association, and of the American Economic Association, April 25-26, 1991.

**Labor Force Data**

The complete article below by Sar A. Levitan and Frank Gallo (*Workforce Statistics...*) discusses problems with labor force data (pp. 25-29 in particular) and makes recommendations for improvements (pp. 31-35).

- Levitan, Sar A. and Frank Gallo. *Workforce Statistics: Do We Know What We Think We Know—and What Should We Know?* December 26, 1989. 43 pages.

**M3 Data**

Improvement of the quality of data from the Manufacturers' Shipments, Inventories and Orders Survey (M3) was also addressed by associations previously cited, meeting October 31-November 1, 1991 (Minutes and Report of Committee Recommendations). The excerpt provided here (pp. 31-35) concerns the Census Bureau's plans in 1992 to improve coverage of M3 data.

- U.S. Department of Commerce. Bureau of the Census. Minutes and Report of Committee Recommendations. Census Advisory Committees of the American Statistical Association, on Population Statistics, of the American Marketing Association, and of the American Economic Association. October 31-November 1, 1991.

**Policy-Relevant Data**

An excerpt from the following report commenting on policy-relevant data is provided.

- National Research Council. Commission on Behavioral and Social Sciences and Education. Committee on National Statistics. Panel to Evaluate Microsimulation Models for Social Welfare Programs. *Improving Information for Social Policy Decisions: The Uses of*

*Microsimulation Modeling. Volume I: Review and Recommendations.* Constance F. Citro and Eric A. Hanushek, Editors. Washington, D.C., National Academy Press, 1991.

A lecture by Janet L. Norwood on "Data Quality for Public Policy," included here below, discusses the importance of maintaining and improving the quality of government statistical data which are used in making and implementing public policy, as well as in private sector decision making. Ms. Norwood also discusses the importance of the conceptual frameworks for data series.

- Norwood, Janet L. "The 1989 Distinguished Lecture on Economics in Government: Data Quality for Public Policy," *Journal of Economic Perspective*, Vol. 4, No. 2, Spring 1990.

**Poverty Data**

In 1988 a workshop was held which reviewed the conceptual and measurement problems in the collection of income and poverty statistics. A complete report is provided.

- National Research Council. Commission on Behavioral and Social Sciences and Education. Committee on National Statistics. *Income and Poverty Statistics: Problems of Concept and Measurement. Report of a Workshop.* Daniel B. Levine and Linda Ingram, Eds. Washington, D.C., National Academy Press, 1988. 23 pages.

On September 3, 1992, hearings were held in conjunction with the release of the annual poverty estimates; witnesses gave their views on the adequacy of the poverty measures and suggestions for improving this measure.

- U.S. Congress. Joint Economic Committee. Hearings. September 3, 1992.

**Services Sector Data**

The House Committee on Government Operations in 1984 addressed the federal data collections' need to expand coverage of the services sector.

- U.S. Congress. House of Representatives. Committee on Government Operations. *The Federal Statistical System 1980 to 1985. A Report Prepared by Baseline Data Corporation for the Congressional Research Service of the Library of Congress.* Washington, D.C., U.S. Government Printing Office, November 1984. 284 pages.

The following report (an excerpt) discusses expanding service industry coverage in the 1992 Economic Censuses.

- U.S. Department of Commerce. Bureau of the Census. Minutes and Report of Committee Recommendations. Census Advisory Committee of the American Statistical Association, on Population Statistics, of the American Marketing Association, and of the American Economic Association, April 9-10, 1992.

For further information, see material listed under "Economic Statistics."

## Standard Industrial Classification

The following Census Bureau staff materials point out the criticisms of the SIC. The conference cited below contains a discussion of the shortcomings of the present Standard Industrial Classification (SIC) system and the kind of system that should be developed to measure the U.S economy in the 21st century.

- U.S. Department of Commerce. Bureau of the Census. 1991 International Conference on the Classification of Economic Activity, November 6-8, 1991, *Proceedings*. Washington, D.C., U.S. Government Printing Office, 1992. 587 pages.

Minutes from the following meeting are excerpted and contain a discussion of the Fall 1991 International Conference on the Classification of Economic Activity.

- U.S. Department of Commerce. Bureau of the Census. Minutes and Report of Committee Recommendations. Census Advisory Committee of the American Statistical Association, on Population Statistics, of the American Marketing Association, and of the American Economic Association, April 9-10, 1992.

## Statistical Policy

A hearing on June 3, 1982, was held following OMB's abolishing the Statistical Policy Branch and examined the status of the Federal government's statistics and OMB's implementation of the statistical policy provisions of the Paperwork Reduction Act of 1980.

- U.S. Congress. House of Representatives. Committee on Government Operations. *Federal Government Statistics and Statistical Policy*. Hearing June 3, 1982. Washington, D.C., U.S.

Government Printing Office. 405 pages.

Listed below is a chapter from a report dealing with OMB's statistical policy oversight responsibilities.

- U.S. Senate. Committee on Governmental Affairs. *Office of Management and Budget: Evolving Roles and Future Issues.* Senate Report 99-134 prepared by the Congressional Research Service of the Library of Congress. February 1986.

Testimony in the following transcript discusses proposals for the organizational arrangements of the statistical policy function.

- Slater, Courtenay. Statement to the Legislation and National Security Subcommittee, Committee on Government Operations, U.S. House of Representatives, August 1, 1989.

The report below reviews OMB's efforts to coordinate the federal statistical system and discusses some of the barriers to a more coordinated system.

- U.S. Congress. Library of Congress. Congressional Research Service. *Federal Economic Statistics: Would Closer Coordination Make for Better Numbers?* November 4, 1992. 30 pages.

Note: The above references reflect a concern by Congress as to how OMB was carrying out its statistical policy responsibilities under the Paperwork Reduction Act of 1980.


## Environment

### Environmental Data

In 1989, GAO issued a report illustrating that the National Air Monitoring Network is inadequate. The EPA, in order to focus its efforts and determine the effect of its cleanup and control programs, needs sound air monitoring data to determine where pollution problems are. Accurate air monitoring is essential to EPA in determining whether current regulations are achieving their intended objectives and in determining the viability of the states' control strategies. Without accurate, timely, comparable, and reliable data, EPA cannot effectively determine the level of pollutants in the air, assess whether its past policies have been effective, and therefore provide sufficient scientific data for use in future policy decisions (p. 10).

In response to the Clean Air Act Amendments of 1977, EPA established and oversees the operation of a nationwide air monitoring network of approximately 4,700 monitors. These monitors are used to determine compliance with EPA's national air quality standards. Although EPA regulations required EPA to have a national air monitoring network in place no later than July 1982, the network was still incomplete as of the following GAO 1989 report. Additional funds are needed to complete the monitoring network and will continue to be needed to purchase additional monitors and replace outdated equipment, or upgrade equipment (pp. 2-3).

EPA quality control measures, such as biannual reviews of state and local monitoring programs, have not met their objective of assuring that national, state, and local air monitoring networks provide accurate and reliable data. In some cases, quality controls do not meet EPA criteria for frequency or thoroughness. For example, EPA regions are not reviewing some state monitoring programs every two years as required, and site visits by EPA have not always identified monitors that have been placed at sites which are of maximum usefulness. Furthermore, EPA's testing of the accuracy of state and local air monitors is questionable since the agencies are allowed to select specific monitors to be tested (p. 3).

The 1989 GAO report made a number of recommendations to EPA for improving its air monitoring program (p. 5):

- EPA should develop a national strategy for completing the national monitoring network and replacing older monitors;

- EPA should work with state and local agencies to identify opportunities through existing Clean Air Act authorization or alternative sources to generate additional funds to purchase needed monitors;

- Specific attention should be given to either reducing the minimum population requirements for National Air Monitoring Stations (NAMS) monitors, or establishing criteria requiring monitors in cities with populations too small to require NAMS monitors; these cities would be either experiencing or have the potential for significant pollution problems; and

- EPA should perform its quality control measures as frequently and comprehensively as required by established guidelines; it should clarify the guidance for state and local quality control measures to ensure results are used properly to validate air monitoring data.

- U.S. General Accounting Office. *Air Pollution. National Air Monitoring Network is Inadequate.* GAO/RCED-90-15. November 1989. (50 pages).

GAO did a comprehensive evaluation of EPA data systems that produce hazardous waste data. This included the Resource Conservation and Recovery Act of 1976 (RCRA) biannual reporting system which serves as the principal data base for the states' capacity assurance plans required by the Superfund Amendments and Reauthorization Act of 1986 (SARA). GAO has three conclusions:

- EPA's system and the data it produces are severely flawed;

- Many of these flaws could have been avoided; and

- Some appropriate methodological revisions in the underlying system design could greatly improve our ability in the future to rely on the data produced by SARA capacity assessments (p. 2).

GAO determined the total information requirements for SARA capacity assurance assessments along with other assessments. It then compared those data requirements with the data encompassed by EPA's data collection systems. The result was an absence of data collection on such important items as:

- The total quantities and types of waste present at CERCLA (Comprehensive Environmental Response, Compensation and Liability Act of 1980) and corrective action sites (these will ultimately require treatment and secure disposal at RCRA-regulated facilities); and

- The management capacity of potential disposal technologies such as salt domes and other geological formations.

As a result, the SARA capacity assurance assessments will necessarily contain significant omissions. The 1985 and the 1987 RCRA reporting cycles contain major data gaps. The 1985 cycle has extensive omissions in the areas of waste and waste characteristics, management data, waste sources, and waste minimalization required for SARA capacity assessments. The 1987 cycle, although an improvement over the 1985 version, still has critical data gaps, principally in the areas of waste characteristics and management data (pp. 11-16).

GAO also looked at measurement problems that would likely produce significant errors in determining the volume of each type of waste generated, the type of treatment technologies used, the total capacity of management technologies (such as some types of incineration), and the degree of waste minimalization. GAO found the RCRA waste codes, which are used on all data collection instruments, will produce inaccurate counts of the volumes of regulated waste streams because of misclassification; this is a result of their ambiguous meaning. Although EPA developed new, improved measures on the types of management technologies between the 1985 and 1987 reporting cycles, misclassification again remains likely if clarification and the reclassification is not established. The development of a valid general waste classification system with mutually exclusive, exhaustive, and hierarchical categories would fully correct these problems (p.16).

GAO found that the measures for the extent of waste minimalization developed by EPA will not produce valid data on changes in waste generation per unit of production. The measures do not account for the production of different products from one year to the next which may generate unequal amounts of hazardous waste (p. 17).

The GAO review of the data collection methods indicated in the RCRA reporting system have made three problems likely:

- An inaccurate identification of the regulated population;

- The development of inconsistent information; and

- Failures of quality control (p. 20).

GAO testimony recommended that EPA should:

- Close existing data gaps by collecting data in areas including:

  1. volumes of wastes located at CERCLA and corrective action sites which will ultimately require management capacity; and

  2. the potential capacity of salt domes and other geological formations that are capable of preventing migration of wastes;

- Assure the use of the most appropriate measures of relevant attributes of hazardous waste generation and management. Specifically, quantitative measures should be used to measure waste characteristics (such as those needed for assessing management capacity or waste minimalization) and, in addition, a valid general classification system be developed for treatment technologies;

- Ensure state data collection and quality control efforts receive full adequate support and include specific indicators related to data collection and verification in the agency's mechanism for monitoring state performance;

- Use probability sampling rather than a census of waste handlers whenever feasible for routine data collection and quality control; this would ensure EPA obtains the information necessary to develop regulations efficiently and without unnecessary data collection burden; and

- Amend federal recordkeeping and reporting regulations so that states are required to collect and provide standard data elements in the disaggregated form, and hazardous waste handlers are required to provide sufficiently detailed data (pp. 29-30).

The above information is cited from:

- U.S. General Accounting Office. *SARA Capacity Assurance: Data Problems Underlying the 1989 State Assessments.* Statement of Eleanor Chelimsky, Assistant Comptroller General, Program Evaluation and Methodology Division, before the Subcommittee on Environment, Energy, and Natural Resources, Committee on Government Operations, House Representatives, May 2, 1991. (31 pages).

In the next report summarized, it is noted that since 1986 EPA has worked toward redesigning the hazardous waste information system. The principal components of the information system design are new and revised data collection mechanisms, such as sample surveys and censuses. In February 1990, GAO published an evaluation of the information system design and its components, including its assessment of progress on waste minimization. GAO identified measurement and data collection problems that were likely to impair data reliability, validity, and accuracy. The August 1991 GAO report presents initial findings regarding the quality of the actual waste generating and minimization data that have proceeded from the system. The GAO analysis is based upon data collected from EPA's National Survey of Hazardous Waste Generators (p. 2).

All the data quality problems identified in the February 1990 GAO report as likely to occur did occur. These problems included the system's inability to integrate data, uncertain data validity based on inappropriate measurement, and uncertain data reliability based on inadequate data collection methods. Some of these problems were of such severity that EPA had to abandon all of the central analyses of waste minimalization progress the agency had originally planned to prepare for the Congress.

Problems such as the extent of missing data were of special importance, negatively affecting the assessment of progress on hazardous waste minimalization. These findings suggested that the information EPA planned to present to the Congress would not be useful for understanding the extent and determinants of waste minimalization or for determining whether mandatory or other requirements may need to be included in the reauthorization of the Resource Conservation and Recovery Act (RCRA) (p.2).

The 1991 GAO report recommends that EPA:

- Amend federal record keeping to ensure the information EPA requests about hazardous waste minimalization will be methodologically sound and readily accessible;

- Devise waste minimalization measures that account for the mix of production processes and for nonproduction activity, which generates hazardous waste; and

- Investigate industry's perception of EPA efforts at measuring waste minimalization, initiating changes as appropriate.

This summary is cited from:

- U.S. General Accounting Office. *Waste Minimalization: EPA Data Are Severely Flawed.* GAO/PEMD-91-21. August 1991. 9 pages.

The GAO report, *Disinfectants: Concerns Over the Integrity of EPA's Data Bases,* identifies several problems concerning the integrity of data in the Pesticide Product Information System (PPIS), the Pesticide Document Management System (PDMS), and the Federal Insecticide, Fungicide, and Rodenticide Act and Toxic Substances Control Act Enforcement System (FATES). The problems may limit the extent to which data can support EPA's disinfectant program and its managers. Specifically, the systems contained inaccurate and/or incomplete data or were missing information on disinfectants. For example, although PPIS is intended to include essential regulatory data on disinfectant product claims, as much as 60% of the data in the system may be inaccurate or incomplete. Furthermore, although intended to capture relevant information, the systems could not be used to identify all types of disinfectants and their product performance claims (p. 1). There are inconsistencies in some data that both PPIS and FATES are supposed to contain. Since EPA officials use the data in these three systems for registration and enforcement purposes, problems with the integrity of the data could impair, among other things, EPA's ability to identify all labels which generate disinfectant efficacy studies for inspection (p. 3).

Specific problems identified included:

- PPIS contained inaccurate data on the number of disinfectants registered to kill tuberculosis bacteria;

- PDMS was missing some data on the disinfectant efficacy studies which registrants had submitted to EPA between January 1, 1985, and June 26, 1989;

- An analysis that EPA conducted—matching disinfectant registrations from PPIS and production data in FATES—indicated that FATES does not contain production data for some disinfectants; and

- Although some of the data elements in the systems were intended to contain the same data, there are strong indications that they do not (pp. 3-4).

The GAO report recommended EPA establish procedures to ensure data are accurately, completely, and consistently entered into automated systems and that the data are kept up to date (p. 8).

- General Accounting Office. *Disinfectants: Concerns Over the Integrity of EPA's Data Bases.* GAO/RCED-90-232, September 1990. 10 pages.

In *Pesticides: Food Consumption Data of Little Value to Estimate Some Exposures* the EPA estimates to establish safe levels of pesticide residues in or on food dietary exposure to pesticide residues uses data from the USDA's Nationwide Food Consumption Survey, conducted every ten years. For budgetary reasons, the sample size of the most recent survey (1987-88) was about one third the sample size of the 1977-78 survey. Because of this reduced sample size, as well as the survey's low response rate, data were obtained from about one third as many individuals—10,172 individuals, as opposed to 30,770. Furthermore, the survey's low response rate (below 34%) could result in exposure estimates that are not representative of the U.S. population (p. 1).

The GAO report concluded it is unlikely that the data obtained from the reduced sample size used in USDA's 1987-88 food consumption survey are adequate for EPA's use in calculating reliable exposure estimates for such subpopulations as nursing infants, pregnant women, and other groups in which only a small number of people were surveyed. Although the data may be adequate for the large subpopulations analyzed by EPA, the limitations of USDA's food consumption survey discussed above raise questions about its usefulness for even the large subpopulations (p. 2).

Because information on food consumption patterns serves as a basis for predicting the safety level of pesticide residues, EPA needs to increase its effort to make its data needs in this area understood (e.g., improved coverage of subpopulations) and communicate them to appropriate USDA officials (p. 8).

- U.S. General Accounting Office. *Pesticides: Food Consumption Data of Little Value to Estimate Some Exposures.* GAO/RCED-91-125, May 1991. 20 pages.

## Health

### Disability Statistics

*Disability Statistics: An Assessment* explores concepts, definitional, and measurement problems, data needs and gaps, problems of coordination and communication within and between producer and user groups, data dissemination, the usefulness of current national data sources, and the integration of various types of data.

- National Research Council. Commission on Behavioral and Social Sciences and Education. Committee on National Statistics. *Disability Statistics: An Assessment.* Report of a Workshop. Daniel B. Levine, Meyer Zitter, and Linda Ingram, Eds. Washington, D.C., National Academy Press, 1990. 71 pages.

In *AIDS Forecasting: Undercount of Cases and Lack of Key Data Weaken Existing Estimates,* the GAO identifies thirteen national forecasts of the cumulative number of AIDS cases through the end of 1991. It found that these forecasts understate the extent of the epidemic primarily because of biases in the underlying data obtained. Definitional problems and lack of key studies contributed to an underrepresentation of the epidemic in the national AIDS surveillance data and in most forecasts. Taking account of whether the existing forecasts have been adjusted to compensate for data biases, GAO estimates that a realistic range of forecasts would be 300,000 to

480,000 cumulative cases. This compares with a range of most likely called "best" estimates from the thirteen models of 120,000 to 400,000 cases through the end of 1991 (p. 2).

GAO found some problems with the comprehensiveness, empirical basis, or assumptions of each forecasting model. The absence of data on key components of the epidemic has led all thirteen forecasts to rely on the national AIDS surveillance data. These data represent cases that have been diagnosed and reported by the medical community to the Centers for Disease Control Prevention(CDC). Although not developed for use in forecasting, these data were used for this purpose both by CDC and other forecasters (p. 3).

GAO estimates the net effect of these problems may be that only about two thirds of all cases of AIDS and other fatal HIV-related illnesses were captured in the data underlying existing national forecasts. This implies that to capture all such illnesses, AIDS surveillance data should be increased by an estimated 50%. CDC's most recent forecast adjusted the data by only 19%, taking into account fewer problems than were recognized by GAO (p. 3).

This report recommended that the CDC:

- Conduct rigorous national studies of the net effect of biases in the national AIDS surveillance data in order to improve national estimates of the current and projected size of the epidemic;

- Assess whether CDC's Surveillance Branch for tracking cases of AIDS and HIV-related diseases has sufficient resources to plan, fund, monitor, review, and disseminate such studies; and

- Incorporate additional information on risk group membership into the CDC public use data (p. 5).

- U.S. General Accounting Office. *AIDS Forecasting: Undercount of Cases and Lack of Key Data Weaken Existing Estimates.* GAO/PEMD-89-13, June 1989. 102 pages.

## International Trade

### Foreign Investment Data
During the course of the following review, the GAO identified twenty government entities that collect data on foreign investment in the U.S.

There is no central repository to track and store all information necessary to analyze foreign investment in the U.S. There appears to be some duplication of data collected (pp. 1-2).

- U.S. General Accounting Office. *Foreign Investment: Federal Data Collection on Foreign Investment in the United States.* GAO/NSIAD-90-25BR, October 1989. 18 pages.

**Trade Data**

In *Trade and Economic Data: Many Federal Agencies Collect and Disseminate Information* the GAO identifies seventeen federal agencies that collect, maintain, and disseminate foreign trade and economic data held by the Federal government. Seven agencies collect the greatest amount of this information: the Departments of Commerce, State, Labor, Energy, and Agriculture; the Federal Reserve System; and the U.S. International Trade Commission (p.1).

One notable effort at setting up a centralized dissemination point has been the National Trade Data Bank (NTDB). The Commerce Department established the NTDB in August 1990 as a one-stop source of information on foreign economies and trade as intended by the Omnibus Trade and Competitiveness Act of 1988 (p. 2).

The GAO study identified additional federal data bases not currently included in the NTDB that could make it more useful and recommended that the Commerce Department add them. See pages 14-16 of the GAO report for a list of these data bases.

- U.S. General Accounting Office. *Trade and Economic Data: Many Federal Agencies Collect and Disseminate Information.* GAO/NSIAD-91-173. May 1991. 17 pages.

In a report to the Chairman, Panel on Foreign Trade Statistics, Committee on National Statistics, National Academy of Sciences in April 1989, the GAO reviewed the committee's major concerns with trade data (summarizing them on p. 12 and giving more details on pp. 18-40); initiatives taken by the U.S. Customs Service and Census to make improvements in problem areas are identified (p. 42), as well as additional areas that warrant consideration for improvement (pp. 46-52).

- U.S. General Accounting Office. *Federal Statistics—Merchandise Trade Statistics: Some Observations.* Briefing Report to the Chairman, Panel on Foreign Trade Statistics, Committee on

National Statistics, National Academy of Sciences. GAO/OCE-89-1BR. April 1989. 53 pages.

A Census Bureau staff paper by Bruce C. Walter discusses issues related to the quality of trade data and offers proposals for making improvements. This paper was written before the CNSTAT Panel study was started.

- Walter, Bruce C. "Quality Issues Affecting the Compilation of the U.S. Merchandise Trade Statistics." 18 pages.

A report edited by Anne Y. Kester of the Panel on Foreign Trade Statistics established by the National Academy of Science's Committee on National Statistics makes a summary of the panel's recommendations for improving foreign trade statistics. The summary was prepared by the chair of the panel, Robert E. Baldwin, for *NABE News;* both the report and its summary are included in this appendix.

- National Academy of Sciences. National Research Council. *Behind the Numbers: U.S. Trade in the World Economy.* Anne Y. Kester, Ed., Washington, D.C., National Academy Press, 1992.

Until recently, the Commerce Department had no comprehensive data on firms engaged in exporting merchandise. The 1987 Exporter Data Base paper prepared by Michael G. Farrell discusses the development of the 1987 Exporter Data Base and the Problem of establishing an ongoing program.

- Farrell, Michael G. *The 1987 Exporter Data Base.* Paper prepared for the Census Advisory Committees of the American Economic Association and the American Marketing Association, at the Joint Advisory Committee Meeting, October 22-23, 1992.

## Social and Demographic Data

### Aging Data
In Recent Changes in the Availability of Federal Data on the Aged reductions are identified in data collection activities relevant to the U.S. aged population that were a result of budget cuts and staff reductions in the early 1980s.

- Storey, James R. *Recent Changes in the Availability of Federal Data on the Aged.* A Report of the Gerontological Society of America, February 11, 1985. 64 pages.

Recommendations for improving the availability and the quality of data on the aging population are contained in selected pages from the following report in this appendix:

- National Research Council. Commission on Behavioral and Social Sciences and Education. Committee on National Statistics. Panel on Statistics for an Aging Population. *The Aging Population in the Twenty-First Century: Statistics for Health Policy.* Dorothy M. Gilford, Ed., Washington, D.C., National Academy Press, 1988.

## Census Data

In Census Reform Needs Attention Now, planning efforts must focus on fundamental reform rather than incremental refinements; three issues should be studied:

- A streamlined questionnaire;

- The use of sampling; and

- The increased use of administrative records, such as Social Security records (pp. 3-7).

Census reform must address the issue of how to get quality and timely data decision makers need, so any reform effort must include representatives from a wide range of organizations and interests (pp. 7-9). The Census Bureau must be willing to invest sufficient funds early in the decade to achieve cost savings and census improvements in the year 2000 (pp. 9-11).

- U.S. General Accounting Office. *Census Reform Needs Attention Now.* Statement of L. Nye Stevens, Director, Government Business Operations Issues, General Government Division, before the Subcommittee on Census and Population, Committee on Post Office and Civil Service, House of Representatives, March 12, 1991. 13 pages.

As a result of its investigation, GAO estimates the 1990 census contained a minimum of 14.1 million gross errors and perhaps as many as 25.7 million errors, depending on how broadly census error is defined. In either case, these are substantially more errors than those indicated by the Bureau's widely reported 1990 census net undercount of about 5.3 million persons. A focus on the net undercount obscures the true magnitude of the error in the census because while millions of persons were missed by the census, millions of other persons were improperly counted. Examining the amount of gross error, therefore, provides a more complete picture of the quality of the census (p. 1).

- U.S. General Accounting Office. *1990 Census. Reported Net Undercount Obscured Magnitude of Error.* GAO/GGD-91-113. August 1991. 10 pages.

In an article for *The New York Times Magazine* James Glick argues that the current methods for enumerating the population are outmoded.

- Glick, James. "The Census: Why We Can't Count," *The New York Times Magazine,* July 15, 1990, pp. 22-26, 54.

**Current Population Survey**
The minutes of a meeting held October 31-November 1, 1991 by three associations cited below address a planned modernization process for the Current Population Survey (CPS); the pages addressing this issue are 53- 57.

- U.S. Department of Commerce. Bureau of the Census. Minutes and Report of Committee Recommendations. Census Advisory Committees of the American Statistical Association, on Population Statistics, of the American Marketing Association, and of the American Economic Association. October 31-November 1, 1991.

**Education Data**
The following *Guide* offers a data improvement itinerary for overcoming significant limitations in the ability of the present data system in addressing important policy concerns. Improvements are recommended in the following areas:

- Student and community background statistics;

- Education resource statistics;

- School process statistics; and

- Student outcome statistics.

The Guide of the Executive Summary contains thirty-six recommendations in these areas.

- U.S. Department of Education. Office of Educational Research and Improvement. National Center for Education Statistics. *A*

*Guide to Improving the National Education Data System: Executive Summary.* March 1991, 28 pages.

*Education Counts: An Indicator System to Monitor the Nation's Educational Health* contains recommendations for improvements in federal data collection and reporting.

- U.S. Department of Education. Office of Educational Research and Improvement. National Center for Education Statistics. *Education Counts: An Indicator System to Monitor the Nation's Educational Health.* Report of the Special Study Panel on Education Indicators to the Acting Commissioner of Education Statistics. Washington, D.C., U.S. Government Printing Office, September 1991. 123 pages.

*Creating a Center for Education Statistics: A Time for Action* evaluates the National Center for Education Statistics and its data and products. Recommendations by the Panel to Evaluate the National Center for Education Statistics are included in this excerpt.

- National Research Council. Commission on Behavioral and Social Science and Education. Committee on National Statistics. Panel to Evaluate the National Center for Education Statistics. *Creating a Center for Education Statistics: A Time for Action.* Daniel B. Levine, Ed. Washington, D.C., National Academy Press, 1986.

The GAO review, *Education Information: Changes in Funds and Priorities Have Affected Production and Quality,* covered the years 1973-1986. It concluded that production of federally sponsored research, statistical, and evaluative information on education has declined notably. New data collection efforts that were undertaken during the period of this review became increasingly more narrowly focused and the scope of investigation was also restricted by increased use of contracts awarded to institutions rather than field-initiated grants. While some high quality statistical information was being produced, the quality was variable. In the Common Core of Data, data quality problems have persisted for several decades. The major influence on information production was severe reduction in funding levels; funding for statistics and evaluation also declined more in these areas than for the government in general (pp. 2-4).

Statistical surveys, planned or conducted, fell 31% between 1980 and 1983 from 55 to 38. The intervals between data collection increased and technical support to the states for data collection was sharply reduced (pp. 3, 20-24).

With regard to the quality of statistical programs, the GAO review of relevance, timeliness, technical adequacy, and impact showed that quality varied. The National Assessment of Educational Progress received generally high marks; the Fast Response Survey System received relatively high marks on relevance and medium ratings on technical adequacy and timeliness. The Common Core of Data, adequate in some respects, was generally poor in its quality of information (p. 4, 39-66).

Chapter 3 of the GAO report contains details of its findings on the quality of information from the National Assessment of Educational Progress, the Common Core of Data for elementary and secondary education, and the Fast Response Survey System. Although the quality of information was presented in detail, the GAO did not follow with any recommendations in this particular study.

- U.S. General Accounting Office. *Education Information: Changes in Funds and Priorities Have Affected Production and Quality.* GAO/PEMD-88-4. November 1987, 121 pages.


## Energy

The GAO review *Energy Emergency Information Needs—Adequacy of Data Dissemination: State, Industry, and Government Views* found that states believe Energy Information Administration (EIA) data are reliable and of high quality. GAO uses the data in developing baseline data (on petroleum supply and consumption patterns) to analyze policy alternatives and to develop energy emergency contingency plans. According to state officials, the data base provides an historical reference, and, when and if an oil shortage occurs, the data base will be used to assess significant changes occurring in the supply and consumption of crude oil and petroleum products. Although states believe that EIA data meet their non-emergency planning and analysis needs, if an oil shortage occurs, they would also like a provision for reducing lag time in making the data available.

An important aspect of EIA data is their uniformity and comparability from state to state. This allows comparison of similar data from one state to another and provides a common base from which to assess the effects of an oil disruption; without the historical baseline data that EIA provides, it would be difficult to make rational decisions during an energy emergency (p. 17).

- U.S. General Accounting Office. *Energy Emergency Information Needs — Adequacy of Data Dissemination: State, Industry, and Government Views.* GAO/RCED-86-58 BR, December 1985, 39 pages.

# Errors in GDP Estimates

## Introduction

The struggle between timeliness and accuracy is illustrated in the quarterly estimates for Gross Domestic Product. The first estimate is published approximately 25 days after the end of the quarter, even though for many components the data available only covers the first or second month of the quarter. The preliminary estimate is then released after 55 days and a "so-called" final estimate is published approximately 85 days after the end of the quarter. Further refinements of the estimates are published in the July revisions after the year is over. Subsequent July revisions are also introduced in later years with the five-year rebenchmarking (based upon the five-year cycle of the quinquennial censuses of business) when more detailed data is available.

These revisions have long been a subject of controversy. Many observers who do not understand statistical programs think that someone is "manipulating" the numbers, yet every analysis of the process reveals that these revisions are the final result of professional judgment based upon a deep understanding of available information. The classic study of the revisions was conducted by Rosanne Cole.[9A] A more recent study was conducted by Stephen K. McNees of the Boston Federal Reserve.[10A] Currently, Martin Fleming, Chairman of the Statistics Committee of the National Association of Business Economists, has completed a more recent review.[11A]

As part of the study for the present report, data were developed by the Bureau of Economic Analysis for Haver Analytics of New York. That data base was used by Martin Fleming for his study. The data were also analyzed by George Feeney of Haver Analytics as an input to this book. The Feeney

---

9A. Rosanne Cole, "Data Errors and Forecasting Accuracy," Chapter 2 in *Economic Forecasts and Expectations: Analyses of Forecasting Behavior and Performance* (Jacob Mincer, Ed.). New York: National Bureau of Economic Research, 1969.

10A. Stephen K. McNees, "Estimating GNP; The Trade-off between Timeliness and Accuracy," *New England Economic Review*, January/February 1986, pp. 3-10.

11A. His report to the 1993 NABE Annual Meeting in Chicago is entitled "Measurement Error in the National Income and Product Accounts-Its Nature and Impact on Forecasts, 1993." He includes an up-to-date discussion of the points summarized in this brief appendix. A copy of his paper is available from the authors of this book.

study used the third year revision as an estimate of truth for the individual GDP components, while Fleming used the second year revision as the benchmark for the "true" estimate. In the Feeney study the early quarterly estimates (estimates 1, 2, and 3) and the 1st and 2nd July revisions were compared with the 3rd July revision (assumed truth) to see the pattern of variance. The results are presented in Figure 1A.

A table from Fleming's study is shown as Figure 2A; a graphic representation is shown in Figure 3A. The conclusions are similar to those statistically shown in Figure 1A. The estimates 1, 2, and 3 were below the final number in 1986, 1987 and 1988 and were higher than the final number in 1989 and early 1990. Most significantly, the error terms in Feeney's analysis are similar for estimates 1, 2, and 3 with the July revisions getting closer to the truth.

*These two studies lead to our recommendation in Chapter 9 that the 1st estimate be retained since it is as good as estimates 2 and 3, and that published revisions be limited to the July revisions. This would not reduce our understanding of the economy and it would reduce confusion.*

## Analysis of Variance of Quarterly Growth Rate Estimates
### (Assuming Third July Revision Equals Correct Final Estimate)

| | 25 | 55 | 85 | First July Revision | Second July Revision | Third July Revision |
|---|---|---|---|---|---|---|
| **TOTAL GDP** | | | | | | |
| No. of qtrs. | 44 | 44 | 44 | 44 | 40 | 0 |
| xbar | -0.42 | -0.26 | -0.20 | -0.05 | 0.03 | 0.00 |
| sigma | 1.75 | 1.59 | 1.68 | 1.10 | 0.69 | 0.00 |
| **CONSUMPTION (67%)*** | | | | | | |
| xbar | -0.15 | -0.09 | -0.11 | -0.20 | 0.10 | 0.00 |
| sigma | 1.62 | 1.58 | 1.66 | 1.24 | 0.76 | 0.00 |
| Durables (9%) | | | | | | |
| xbar | -0.91 | -0.64 | -0.42 | -0.46 | -0.19 | 0.00 |
| sigma | 4.95 | 4.95 | 5.43 | 4.08 | 2.35 | 0.00 |
| Nondurables (22%) | | | | | | |
| xbar | -0.23 | -0.21 | -0.18 | -0.28 | 0.14 | 0.00 |
| sigma | 2.39 | 1.99 | 1.94 | 1.60 | 1.14 | 0.00 |
| Services (37%) | | | | | | |
| xbar | 0.11 | 0.17 | 0.03 | -0.08 | 0.11 | 0.00 |
| sigma | 1.45 | 1.42 | 1.52 | 1.07 | 0.90 | 0.00 |
| **INVESTMENT (14%)** | | | | | | |
| xbar | -0.54 | -0.22 | 0.89 | 0.92 | -0.11 | 0.00 |
| sigma | 12.09 | 11.13 | 11.13 | 8.40 | 5.56 | 0.00 |
| Fixed Investment (15%) | | | | | | |
| xbar | -0.61 | 0.51 | 1.00 | 0.82 | 0.30 | 0.00 |
| sigma | 5.46 | 4.73 | 4.47 | 3.60 | 2.89 | 0.00 |
| Nonresidential (11%) | | | | | | |
| xbar | -0.86 | 0.66 | 1.45 | 10.5 | 0.53 | 0.00 |
| sigma | 6.09 | 5.16 | 4.86 | 4.63 | 3.98 | 0.00 |
| Structures (4%) | | | | | | |
| xbar | 0.68 | 1.14 | 1.24 | 1.19 | 0.10 | 0.00 |
| sigma | 9.52 | 8.04 | 7.94 | 7.11 | 7.41 | 0.00 |
| PDE (8%) | | | | | | |
| xbar | -1.78 | 0.30 | 1.36 | 0.78 | 0.55 | 0.00 |
| sigma | 6.78 | 5.93 | 5.30 | 5.71 | 4.48 | 0.00 |
| Residential (4%) | | | | | | |
| xbar | 0.50 | 0.94 | 0.58 | 0.75 | 0.49 | 0.00 |
| sigma | 9.49 | 9.03 | 7.98 | 5.55 | 5.15 | 0.00 |
| Exports (11%) | | | | | | |
| xbar | -2.88 | -2.06 | -1.75 | -1.03 | -1.52 | 0.00 |
| sigma | 8.04 | 7.24 | 7.90 | 6.84 | 5.53 | 0.00 |
| Imports (11%) | | | | | | |
| xbar | 0.93 | 0.98 | 1.44 | 0.83 | -0.34 | 0.00 |
| sigma | 14.67 | 16.19 | 16.20 | 12.70 | 5.53 | 0.00 |
| **GOVERNMENT (19%)** | | | | | | |
| xbar | -0.52 | -0.34 | -0.61 | -0.26 | -0.08 | 0.00 |
| sigma | 4.07 | 4.35 | 4.04 | 2.93 | 1.90 | 0.00 |
| Federal (8%) | | | | | | |
| xbar | 0.02 | 0.54 | -0.12 | 0.54 | 0.20 | 0.00 |
| sigma | 9.08 | 9.78 | 9.19 | 7.05 | 4.59 | 0.00 |
| State and Local (11%) | | | | | | |
| xbar | -0.75 | -0.84 | -0.79 | -0.71 | -0.30 | 0.00 |
| sigma | 1.55 | 1.76 | 1.76 | 1.38 | 0.90 | 0.00 |

*Average percent of GDP

Source: Haver Analytics, Inc., New York.

## Average Revision in Year-to-year Change without Regard to Sign
**Annual Revisions Published from 1988 to 1991**

(billions of dollars)

|  | Most Recent Year | 2nd Most Recent Year | 3rd Most Recent Year |
|---|---|---|---|
| GDP | 16.9 | 5.5 | 6.5 |
| PCE | 18.9 | 6.4 | 6.4 |
| Goods | 7.9 | 4.9 | 3.0 |
| Services | 11.5 | 2.4 | 6.3 |
| Fixed investment | 4.5 | 3.9 | 2.1 |
| Nonresidential structures | 3.4 | 2.8 | 1.2 |
| PDE | 2.1 | 3.8 | 1.0 |
| Residential structures | 3.7 | 0.7 | 0.3 |
| Change in bus. inventories | 5.0 | 6.6 | 4.3 |
| Net exports | 2.9 | 1.1 | 2.6 |
| Government | 2.3 | 3.3 | 3.1 |
| Federal | 1.3 | 1.9 | 1.0 |
| S & L | 1.8 | 2.5 | 3.3 |

Source: Martin Fleming, "Measurement Error in the National Income and Product Accounts; Its Nature and Impact on Forecasts," Statistics Committee, National Association of Business Economists, June 1, 1993.

## Figure 3A

## GDP - Estimated Errors*

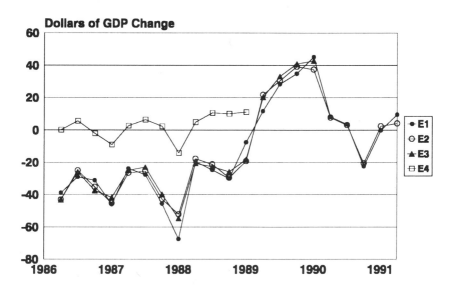

*Note: Acutual value is assumed to be the 2nd July revision

E1 - 25 day estimate less 2nd July revision.
E2 - 55 day estimate less 2nd July revision.
E3 - 85 day estimate less 2nd July revision.
E4 - 1st July revision less 2nd July revision.

Source: Martin Fleming, "Measurement Error in the National Income and Product Accounts; Its Nature and Impact on Forecasts," Statistics Committee, National Association of Business Economists, June 1, 1993.

# Statistical Budgets

Figure 4A shows the budgets in current dollars (excluding decennial census funds) for the main statistical agencies for the period 1977 to 1993. The agencies are:

- Economic Reporting Service - U. S. Department of Agriculture (ERS)

- National Agricultural Statistics Service - U. S. Department of Agriculture (NASS)

- Bureau of Economic Analysis - U. S. Department of Commerce (BEA)

- Bureau of the Census - U. S. Department of Commerce (Census)

- Energy Information Administration - U. S. Department of Energy (EIA)

- National Center for Education Statistics - U.S. Department of Education (NCES)

- National Center for Health Statistics - U.S. Department of Health and Human Services (NCHS)

- Bureau of Justice Statistics - U. S. Department of Justice (BJS)

- Bureau of Labor Statistics - U. S. Department of Labor (BLS)

These numbers are taken from the annual reports prepared by the Office of Management and Budget as part of its responsibility for reporting on budgets for statistical activities. The latest report covers 1993.[12A] While the budgets for these statistical agencies are less than 50% of the total funding available for statistical activities as is shown in Figure 5A, these major agencies are responsible for producing some of the more important data that are used to measure the performance of the economy, to describe the country's social situation, and to determine what Federal Government polices and

---

12A. Executive Office of the President. Office of Management and Budget. *Statistical Programs of the United States Government, Fiscal Year 1993.* 1992.

programs are appropriate.

Given the impact of the statistics produced by these agencies on the government decision making and budgetary processes, it is no wonder that there is concern among users of these data when the level of agency funding is reduced (or does not grow in response to new demands) especially since statistical funding levels affect the amount and quality of data available.

This report is not an analysis of the adequacy of funding levels, nor is it a critique of statistical agency priorities. But it is clear, as noted in previous reports of the National Association of Business Economists and others that during the past two decades the statistical system has been faced with increasing demands and with reduced budgets in real terms.

One important initiative discussed on page 16 is the Boskin Initiative. Progress on budget enhancements is shown in Figure 6A.

## Nine Agency Budgets as a Percentage of the Total Statistical Budget*

| | All Statistical Agencies | Main Statistical Agencies** | | |
|---|---|---|---|---|
| | Total Statistical Budget (current dollars) | Nine Agency Budgets (current dollars) | Deflators (1990) | Constant 1990 Dollars (millions) |
| 1994 | 2637 | 1048 | 127.03 | 825 |
| 1993 | 2451 | 977 | 123.36 | 792 |
| 1992 | 2491 | 1003 | 117.57 | 853 |
| 1991 | 2005 | 787 | 117.57 | 669 |
| 1990 | 1824 | 719 | 100.00 | 719 |
| 1989 | 1635 | 700 | 95.88 | 730 |
| 1988 | 1527 | 692 | 91.61 | 755 |
| 1987 | 1363 | 637 | 88.90 | 717 |
| 1986 | 1459 | 594 | 86.46 | 687 |
| 1985 | 1510 | 573 | 84.73 | 676 |
| 1984 | 1418 | 530 | 81.75 | 648 |
| 1983 | 1285 | 487 | 78.79 | 618 |
| 1982 | 1245 | 458 | 75.40 | 607 |
| 1981 | 1128 | 456 | 71.06 | 642 |
| 1980 | 1073 | 449 | 63.00 | 713 |
| 1979 | 791 | 429 | 58.01 | 740 |
| 1978 | 755 | 402 | 53.98 | 745 |
| 1977 | 637 | 340 | 50.44 | 674 |

* Excluding decennial census funds.
**See Figure 5A for agency details.

Source: Various U.S. Government budget appendices for the time period covered.

# Budgets for Main Statistical Agencies

(millions of dollars)

| | ERS | NASS | BEA | Census* | EIA | NCEs | NCHS | BJS | BLS | Total |
|---|---|---|---|---|---|---|---|---|---|---|
| 1994 | 51.5 | 62.3 | 44.3 | 352.6 | 80.4 | 136 | 88.4 | 24.2 | 200.4 | 1040.1 |
| 1993 | 58.9 | 81 | 41.5 | 243.8 | 84.3 | 87.5 | 80.4 | 24.1 | 275.1 | 976.6 |
| 1992 | 58.9 | 82.6 | 34.8 | 310.1 | 74.7 | 86.6 | 79.1 | 24.5 | 251.4 | 1002.7 |
| 1991 | 54.4 | 76.5 | 30.5 | 184.7 | 69.1 | 73.3 | 70.4 | 24.4 | 203.7 | 787 |
| 1990 | 50.6 | 66.8 | 25.6 | 181.9 | 64.1 | 48.7 | 66.1 | 22.7 | 192.6 | 719.1 |
| 1989 | 49.4 | 63.5 | 24.6 | 190.3 | 62.4 | 39.6 | 60.7 | 21.8 | 187.7 | 700 |
| 1988 | 48.1 | 61.2 | 23.6 | 216.6 | 61.4 | 29.2 | 54.4 | 21.8 | 175.3 | 691.6 |
| 1987 | 44.8 | 57.6 | 23 | 189.6 | 60.3 | 20.1 | 52.1 | 22.1 | 167.1 | 636.7 |
| 1986 | 44.6 | 56.1 | 21.2 | 146 | 57.7 | 17.3 | 44.4 | 19.9 | 186.6 | 593.8 |
| 1985 | 46.4 | 58.1 | 21.8 | 138.9 | 60.9 | 14.1 | 42.8 | 19.7 | 170.6 | 573.3 |
| 1984 | 43.7 | 54.4 | 21 | 139.8 | 55.6 | 14.1 | 46 | 18.6 | 136.3 | 529.5 |
| 1983 | 38.8 | 51.7 | 19.1 | 131.4 | 58.1 | 8.6 | 40.8 | 17.1 | 121.3 | 486.9 |
| 1982 | 39.3 | 51.2 | 18 | 96.5 | 77.8 | 8.5 | 37.7 | 17.7 | 111.6 | 458.3 |
| 1981 | | 93 | 17.1 | 92.2 | 89.8 | 8.4 | 33.7 | 12.3 | 109.9 | 456.4 |
| 1980 | | 90.2 | 15.8 | 81.3 | 88.2 | 9.9 | 43.3 | 17.8 | 102.9 | 449.4 |
| 1979 | | 78.9 | 14.6 | 95.4 | 65.6 | 13 | 38.9 | 28.1 | 94.9 | 429.4 |
| 1978 | | 77.1 | 14 | 95.5 | 50.7 | 13.9 | 37.3 | 29.4 | 83.8 | 401.7 |
| 1977 | | 69 | 12.8 | 76 | 29.9 | 13.1 | 29.3 | 25.4 | 84.3 | 339.8 |

* Excludes decennial census funds
1974-1992 figures are actual
1993 figures are estimates
1994 figures are from the President's budget request and, therefore, do not reflect congressional appropriation actions.

**Current Status of FY 1992 Economic Statistics Initiative\***

| Initiative | 1991 Enacted | 1992 President's Budget | 1992 Enacted | 1993 President's Budget | 1993 Enacted | 1994 President's Budget |
|---|---|---|---|---|---|---|
| **Bureau of the Census (S&E)** | 111,249 | 132,484 | 125,290 | 138,406 | 123,955 | 140,798 |
| Improve service sector data coverage & detail | 900 | 1,400 | 1,400 | 3,122 | 0 | 1,363 |
| Improve construction statistics | 0 | 1,300 | 0 | 1,300 | 0 | 1,300 |
| SIC Research/monitor emerging industries | 0 | 400 | 0 | 300 | 0 | 0 |
| Improve corporate financial data | 200 | 800 | 0 | 1,626 | 0 | 808 |
| Develop model to measure underpricing of exports | 0 | 400 | 0 | 500 | 0 | 0 |
| Census Bureau totals | 1,100 | 4,300 | 1,400 | 6,848 | 0 | 3,471 |
| **Economic and statistical analysis** | 36,360 | 43,494 | 40,380 | 56,427 | 46,953 | 49,802 |
| **Bureau of Economic Analysis (BEA)** | 30,865 | 37,807 | 34,699 | 50,534 | 41,473 | 44,232 |
| Maintain GDP estimates | 1,200 | 1,300 | 1,300 | 2,691 | 0 | 600 |
| Adopt UN System of National Accounts transition | 1,300 | 1,700 | 500 | 2,010 | 0 | 1,200 |
| Improve quality balance of payments data | 700 | 1,500 | 500 | 1,952 | 0 | 400 |
| Improve quality international investment and services data | 2,100 | 800 | 2,300 | 897 | 0 | 800 |
| BEA totals | 5,300 | 5,300 | 2,300 | 7,550 | 0 | 3,000 |
| **Bureau of Labor Statistics (BLS)** S&E | 203,669 | 258,504 | 251,343 | 282,315 | 274,992 | 280,448 |
| Trust Fund | 51,488 | 50,399 | 49,799 | 51,539 | 48,907 | 50,227 |
| Total BLS | 255,157 | 308,903 | 301,142 | 333,854 | 323,899 | 330,675 |
| Improve accuracy of labor force data | 0 | 3,900 | 4,234 | 4,969 | 4,969 | 4,863 |
| Improve coverage of service sector employment detail and service industry output measures | 1,578 | 7,910 | 6,009 | 6,845 | 4,691 | 4,336 |
| Separate quality & inflation changes in price data | 0 | 1,340 | 946 | 1,108 | 857 | 857 |
| Improve quality of service sector establishment list | 0 | 1,400 | 543 | 576 | 76 | 76 |
| Develop automated data collection techniques | 0 | 3,000 | 2,171 | 1,237 | 1,237 | 1,237 |
| BLS totals | 1,578 | 17,550 | 13,903 | 14,735 | 11,830 | 11,369 |
| **National Agricultural Statistics Service (NASS)** | 76,465 | 86,866 | 82,601 | 87,087 | 81,004 | 82,479 |
| Improve farm sampling frames | 1,200 | 2,400 | 1,195 | 1,425 | 0 | 0 |
| NASS totals | 1,200 | 2,400 | 1,195 | 1,425 | 0 | 0 |
| **National Science Foundation** | | | | | | |
| Improve quality of federal statistics workforce | 0 | 400 | 400 | 700 | 700 | 1,000 |
| NSF totals | 0 | 400 | 400 | 700 | 700 | 1,000 |
| **Totals** | 9,178 | 29,950 | 19,198 | 31,258 | 12,530 | 18,840 |

\*This table describes statistical program recommendations developed under the leadership of Michael Boskin, Chairman of the Council of Economic Advisors of the Bush Administration.

Source: The above categories are estimates of program levels as described in various budget documents and other reports. This table illustrates the difference between budget requests and congressionally authorized spending levels.

# Services and Invisibles Methodology Problems

## Travel and Tourism

Data are compiled from a voluntary survey conducted by the U.S. Travel and Tourism Administration (USTTA). This survey is not necessarily a representative sample of travel abroad and may be subject to considerable inaccuracy. Missing data are supplemented by information from the Immigration and Naturalization Service (INS).

**Tourism Definition:** The tourism account covers purchases of goods and services by U.S. travelers abroad, and by foreigners in the U.S. Expenditures include: food, lodging, recreation, gifts and incidental items. A traveler is defined as a person who stays for less than one year in a country of which he is not a resident.

Estimations for receipts and expenditures are made on the basis of the following procedures.

A. *Total, except Canada and Mexico*

Receipts and payments are derived from surveys taken by the USTTA. The survey is conducted aboard a random sample of scheduled flights departing the U.S. It covers about 70% of U.S. carriers and 35% of foreign carriers. Travelers are asked about their expenditures for airfare, travel, hotels, meals, and miscellaneous expenses.

Since the results of the USTTA survey become available only after a considerable lag, the most recent quarters are estimated in the following manner:

1. The number of visitors is obtained from INS, from which the year to year change is calculated;

2. Price changes are approximated by the year on year in the CPI; and

3. Both these changes are applied to travel receipts and expenditures of the same quarter of the previous year.

There are a number of problems with this existing data collection methodology. These problems include:

1. The USTTA survey is strictly voluntary. Many surveys are not turned in while others are incomplete. The missing data items are treated as if the reply matched the average for completed cards;

2. Sampling techniques may lead to biases. There may be misrepresentation of particular destinations;

3. The sample size is small, about 1/10 of 1%;

4. U.S. residents travelling abroad take the survey before they reach their destination. They must estimate their expenditures;

5. Other complications arise when U.S. residents travel to several destinations. The BEA uses the information about how many nights the traveler expects to spend at each destination to prorate total expenditures for each destination;

6. The sample from the USTTA is then expanded using the number of people departing the U.S. obtained from the Immigration and Naturalization Service (INS);

7. Results of the USTTA survey are available only with a lag; and

8. Surveys such as these can be grossly inaccurate—some people want to overestimate their expenditures while others want to "forget" or possibly downplay some of their expenditures.

### B. Canada

For Canada, the procedures are different. In order to estimate U.S. receipts, estimates are derived from questionnaires distributed to Canadians returning from the U.S. Estimates of expenditures by U.S. citizens in Canada are derived from monthly data on the number of U.S. residents visiting Canada, which are supplied by Statistics Canada by port of entry. The data are combined with average expenditure figures developed from BEA sample data in the BE 536.

### C. Mexico

Since two-way traffic across the border between Mexico and the U.S. is enormous, the border area and the interior are treated separately.

For border data, U.S. estimates of receipts are derived from Bank of Mexico surveys of Mexicans returning from the U.S. For estimates of U.S. expenditures, the number of U.S. visits to the border area are compiled by the Immigration and Naturalization Service (INS). The number of border crossings is combined with average expenditures developed from BE 575 data.

For data on interior tourism, the number of Mexicans visiting the U.S. is based on monthly INS data. It is estimated that all Mexican air travelers and 60% of land and sea travelers visit the interior. Average expenditures are estimated by adjusting the average expenditure figure for the same quarter of the previous year by the change in the U.S. CPI. This is multiplied by the number of Mexican visitors. For estimating U.S. expenditures in the interior, the number of U.S. travelers is obtained from the Bank of Mexico, based on counts by Mexican immigration officials of alien arrivals by air and land. (80% of all visitors are U.S. residents.)

Estimates of travel costs for transportation vary by mode of transportation, and the methods vary by data sources in some countries. Fare paid by residents of one country to carriers of other countries are important in the balance of payments. Travel expenditures of passengers using their own country's carriers are not included in the balance of payments.

Since 1975, nearly all U.S. ocean passenger liners have been taken out of service. For air travel, the number of foreign visitors to the U.S. is tabulated from the INS entry documents, but these data are not available by flag of carrier. The proportion of foreign visitors arriving on U.S. carriers is estimated from the USTTA surveys. Cost of travel is obtained from USTTA surveys. Fare receipts of U. S. citizens traveling to foreign points are estimated based on BEA data obtained from the quarterly BE 37 survey, "U.S. Airline Operators' Foreign Revenues and Expenses."

## Transportation

Collection of data on freight and shipping is one of the oldest categories in the services area. For ocean shipping on the payments side, the convention is to consider that all payments are paid by the importer. Determining the total freight bill is relatively simple since imports are compiled on both cost-insurance-freight (c.i.f) and free-on-board (f.o.b.) The difference is the freight and insurance. It is assumed that insurance comprises 1% of the total c.i.f. and freight is 99%.

**Transportation Cost Definition:** This category includes all freight charges when shipping services are performed by residents of one country for residents of another country. It also includes operating expenses that transportation companies incur in foreign ports and payments for vessel charters and aircraft and car rentals. The residency of the *operator* must be determined because it may differ from the country of registry of the vessel.

Receipts are estimated with differing procedures in the alternate modes of transportation.

For ocean shipments the earnings of U.S. vessels carrying U.S. merchandise exports to foreign ports are calculated as follows:

1. Data on waterborne export tonnage carried by U.S. flag vessels are obtained from U.S. Waterborne Exports, Domestic and Foreign SM 704;

2. This figure is increased by an estimate of the share of export tonnage carried by U.S. operators of foreign-flag vessels;

3. The resulting total tonnage carried by U.S. operated vessels is multiplied by an average freight rate per ton (quarterly BEA survey of U.S. carriers (BE-30); and

4. Receipts are adjusted to include subsidies paid by the U.S government to U.S. vessel operators on grain shipments under foreign aid programs and negotiated rates on grain shipments to Eastern Europe (data compiled by USDA).

The number of U.S. ocean carriers is relatively small—fewer than 50. It is believed that the coverage of U.S. carriers is comprehensive but there are several problems. The SM 704 does not give residency of the operator. The share of foreign-flag shipping for U.S. exports is assumed to be the same as that for U.S. imports tabulated in U.S. Waterborne Imports SM 304.

For air carriers it is important to estimate the earnings of U.S. air carriers transporting U.S. exports and earnings for transporting freight between foreign points. Data come from the U.S. Airline Operators' Foreign Revenues and Expenses (BEA survey BE 37). Reported earnings are increased 5% to compensate for small carriers that are exempt from reporting. The expansion factor is derived by comparing export freight tonnage as reported in BE 37 with tonnage data in the Census Bureau AM 754, U.S. Exports by Air.

Pipeline transportation requires estimates of the earnings of U.S. affiliates of Canadian pipeline companies for transporting oil and gas unloaded from tankers at Portland, Maine to Canada. Transportation of oil through pipelines in the Northeast U.S. that eventually is headed to Canada is also included. Data are obtained quarterly from the four U.S. affiliates of Canadian companies.

For railroads, earnings are derived from:

1. U.S. rail carriers transporting Canadian exports to and imports

from third countries through the U.S.;

2. U.S. exports from the U.S. customs frontier to other rail connections in Canada; and

3. Goods within Canada transported on U.S. rail carriers' leased trackage in Canada.

Four U.S. rail carriers operate in Canada. They submit revenue data to the BEA annually. Quarterly estimates are made for Balance of Payments purposes.

For the Great Lakes region, earnings of U.S. ship operators transporting goods between U.S. and Canadian Great Lakes ports are derived in the following way: Tonnage is obtained from SM 704; total receipts are derived by multiplying export tonnage by estimates of average freight rates BE 30.

Transportation earnings include port service receipts. A large portion of gross shipping revenue is spent in the ports of the importing countries. BEA collects this information on form BE 29 which is sent to U.S. agents of foreign shippers. They are asked to complete the form for ten ports of call during the year. Data requested include the amount spent by the operators of the vessels and the shipping weight of the cargo. Since the total shipping weight of all imports is known, the figures derived from the sample in BE 29 are blown up accordingly.

Some problems with this method are:

1. agents' responses may not be reliable;

2. data for shipping weight are often missing; and

3. data for one of the most important elements, bunker fuel, is often incomplete.

Despite these problems of estimation, over the 1980 to 1988 period port expenditure receipts averaged 74% of the ocean freight payments, and there were no large year-to-year variations. Recent evidence suggests that port receipts are increasing. The ratio of port receipts to ocean freight payments from 1989 to 1991 was 81%, 76% and 83%, respectively.

On the payments side, the following procedures are currently used. By convention, for ocean shipments it is assumed that all freight payments are paid by the importer. Data on earnings of foreign ship operators carrying U.S. imports are derived from Census Bureau SM 304. This form gives data on import charges, shipping weights by flag of vessel. To determine residency of the operator, the BEA uses Customs Forms 1400, Records of Vessels

Engaged in Foreign Trade and Entered or Arrived Under Permit to Proceed. BEA takes a sample from SM 304 and redistributes import charges from a flag of vessel to residency of the operator basis.

Earnings of foreign air carriers for transporting U.S. imports from foreign countries to the U.S. are estimated on the basis of special surveys. The annual BE 36 survey is the source of the data. Annual estimates are increased by 5% to account for earnings by small carriers that are exempt from reporting. Quarterly estimates are made by distributing the annual estimate according to the shipping weight of imports as reported in Census Bureau AM 354.

Earnings of Canadian rail carriers transporting U.S. imports in transit through Canada, and U.S. goods through Canada from one U.S. point to another, are important in the area of rail transportation. Quarterly estimates are obtained from Statistics Canada.

Also on the expenditures side, data are collected on the earnings of Canadian carriers transporting goods from Canada to U.S. Great Lakes' ports; expenditures of U.S. ship operators in foreign ports; U.S. airline expenditures abroad for fuel, wages, agents' and brokers' fees, repair and maintenance and miscellaneous; expenditures of U.S. rail carriers in Canada for maintenance, repair, fuel, etc.; and several smaller categories of U.S. expenditures to suppliers from other countries.

## Royalties and License Fees

This category involves transactions between U.S. residents and foreign residents involving intangible assets and proprietary rights. Royalties generally refer to payments for the utilization of copyrights or trademarks. License fees generally refer to payments for the use of patents or industrial processes. There is a distinction between affiliated and unaffiliated transactions, each having its own estimation procedures.

**Affiliated Transactions:** These are transactions between U.S. parent companies and their foreign affiliates or U.S. affiliates and their foreign parents. 'Affiliated' is defined as ownership of at least 10%, either directly or indirectly. Affiliated transactions, for the past several years, averaged 75% of the total royalties and licenses.

Data for receipts and payments are obtained from a series of BEA benchmark studies and sample surveys of U.S. direct investors and U.S. based affiliates of foreign direct investors. Receipts are proceeds from royalties and license fees, received or accrued, by U.S. parents from their foreign affiliates. Net receipts are calculated by subtracting payments by U.S. parents to their foreign affiliates from receipts by U.S. parents from their foreign affiliates, after deducting U.S. and foreign withholding tax.

On the payments side are net payments of royalties and license fees by U.S. affiliates to their foreign parents and other members of the foreign parent group. Net payments are calculated by subtracting receipts of U.S. affiliates from the foreign parent group from payments by U.S. affiliates to the foreign parent group, after deducting U.S. and foreign withholding tax.

**Unaffiliated Transactions:** Data are obtained from the Annual Survey of Royalties, License Fees, and Other Receipts and Payments for Intangible Rights Between U.S. and Unaffiliated Foreign Persons, BE 93. Completion of the survey is mandatory. The list was developed from industry directories and includes persons who reported transactions with unaffiliated foreigners in previous surveys. Quarterly estimates are interpolations of the annual estimates. Amounts are reported net of taxes.

There have been serious problems involving international copyright infringement and non-payments for licenses and royalties. U.S. receipts are likely to be understated, possibly to a considerable extent.

## Other Private Services

This category includes services not specifically covered in travel, passenger fares, other transportation, or royalties and license fees accounts. There are different data collection procedures for affiliated and unaffiliated transactions as well as for the different categories.

**Affiliated Transactions:** Data for accounts covered in this category are obtained from a series of BEA benchmark and sample surveys of U.S. direct investors abroad and U.S. based affiliates of foreign investors.

On the receipt side it is necessary to estimate net receipts of U.S. parents from their foreign affiliates for service charges, fees for the use of tangible property, and film and television tape rentals. The data are based on the books of the U.S. parents and are reported as of the date the funds are either received from, or paid to, foreign affiliates, or entered into intercompany accounts with foreign affiliates, whichever occurs first. In 1991, affiliated transactions comprised 31% of total other services and this share has been relatively stable over the past five years.

The payment side includes net payments by U.S. affiliates to their foreign parents and other members of the foreign parent group for service charges, fees for the use of tangible property and film and tape rentals. Affiliated transactions accounted for 38% of the total in 1991 and the share has been relatively steady over the past five years.

**Unaffiliated Transactions:** These are transactions between U.S. residents and unaffiliated foreigners for services including education, financial, insurance, business, professional and technical services. Data are derived from various sources including four annual mandatory BEA surveys, data provided directly to BEA, private organizations, foreign governments and international organizations. This category is extremely broad covering a vast array of different services. The complexity of this category makes data collection difficult and often unreliable. Since 1986, when a new mandatory reporting system was put in place (first BE 20 and subsequently BE 22) data collection has improved considerably, though there are still many gaps. Reports are mandatory for individual transactions over $250,000.

There are also three other surveys:

1. BE 93 covers receipts and payments of royalties and license fees. The number of respondents is over 400;

2. BE 48 covers premiums earned and paid for insurance. The number of respondents is about 300; and

3. BE 47 covers services related to construction and engineering operations. Although the number of respondents is fewer than 100, this is considered rather complete since there are a small number of firms operating in this area.

These miscellaneous categories contain many areas that are difficult to estimate.[13A] Categories include:

1. Education. Expenditures of foreign students enrolled in institutions of higher education in the U.S.;

2. Financial Services. This category includes commissions and fees transactions associated with the stock and commodity transactions, and non-interest income of U.S. and foreign banks paid and received;

3. Insurance. This consists of net premiums received, less losses paid

---

13A. The authors have compiled a report on methods used for these categories. It is available upon request.

to the ceding companies or individuals abroad, less cancellations and commissions charged by the ceding company abroad;

4. Telecommunications. Receipts for telephone, private leased channel service, telex, telegram, electronic mail, and fax. It also includes repair and the launching of communications satellites;

5. Business, Professional and Technical Services. Includes a broad range of services including: accounting, auditing, bookkeeping, advertising, agriculture, computer and data processing, legal, engineering and construction, public relations, etc.; and

6. Other. Consists of expenditures associated with diplomatic activities, expenditures of agents of foreign governments, and expenditures for the construction of embassy building and related facilities.

Abramson, Bruce; Finizza, Anthony. 1991. "Using Belief Networks to Forecast Oil Prices." *International Journal of Forecasting* 7(3):299-315.

Ambler, Carole A.; Mesenbourg, Thomas L. "November 1992. EDI [Electronic Data Interchange] - Reporting Standards for the Future." In Proceedings of the 1992 Annual Research Conference; 1992 March 22-25; Arlington, VA. Washington, D.C.: U.S. Bureau of the Census: 289-310.

Andrews, Stephen H.; Abbott, Thomas A. July 1988. "An Examination of the Standard Industrial Classification of Manufacturing Activity Using the Longitudinal Research Data Base." In Proceedings of the Fourth Annual Research Conference; 1988 March 20-23; Arlington, VA. Washington, D.C.: U.S. Bureau of the Census: 467-488.

Armington, Catherine; Odle, Marjorie. 1982. "Associating Establishments into Enterprises for a Microdata File of the U.S. Business Population." In Proceedings of the American Statistical Association Section on Survey Research Methods 1981 Annual Meeting; 1981 August 10-13; Detroit, MI. Washington, D.C.: American Statistical Association: 541-546.

Ashbury, Penny L.; Barsky, Carl. 1989. "The Industry Wage Survey Program: An Evaluation of the Quality of Program Estimates." In Proceedings of the American Statistical Association Business and Economic Statistics Section 1988 Annual Meeting; 1988 August 22-25; New Orleans, LA. Alexandria, VA: American Statistical Association: 361-365.

Bailar, Barbara A.; Rothwell, Naomi D. 1984. "Measuring Employment and Unemployment." Charles F. Turner and Elizabeth Martin, eds., *Surveying Subjective Phenomena. Vol. 2.* New York: Russell Sage Foundation: 129-142.

Baumgartner, Thomas; Midttun, Atle, eds. 1987. *The Politics of Energy Forecasting: A Comparative Study of Energy Forecasting in Western Europe and North America.* New York: Oxford University Press. 314 p.

Beaver, Ronald D.; Huntington, Hillard G. 1992. "A Comparison of Aggregate Energy Demand Models for Global Warming Policy Analyses." In Proceedings of the American Statistical Association Business and Economic Statistics Section 1991 Annual Meeting; 1991 August 18-22; Atlanta, GA. Alexandria, VA: American Statistical Association: 11-18.

Beck, M. B. 1987. "Water Quality Modelling: A Review of the Analysis of Uncertainty." *Water Resources Research.* 23(8):1393-1442.

Bell, Daniel. 1969. "The Idea of a Social Report." *The Public Interest.* 15(Spring):72-84.

Bell, William. 1983. "Historical Overview and Comments on Issues in Seasonal Adjustment." In Proceedings of the American Statistical Association Business and Economic Statistics Section 1982 Annual Meeting; 1982 August 16-19; Cincinnati, OH. Washington, D.C.: American Statistical Association: 400-402.

Berndt, Ernst R.; Triplett, Jack E., eds. 1990. "Fifty Years of Economic Measurement: The Jubilee of the Conference on Research in Income and Wealth." National Bureau of Economic Research Conference on Research in Income and Wealth, 50th Anniversary Conference; 1988 May 12-14; Washington, D.C. *Studies in Income and Wealth,* Vol. 54. Chicago, IL: The University of Chicago Press. 454 p.

Bishop, Yvonne M.; Werbos, Paul J. 1983. "An Interagency Review of Time-Series Revision Policies." In Proceedings of the American Statistical Association Section on Survey Research Methods 1982 Annual Meeting; 1982 August 16-19;

Cincinnati, OH. Washington, D.C.: American Statistical Association: 180-184.

Bonnen, James T.; Clemence, Theodore G.; Fellegi, Ivan P.; Jabine, Thomas B.; Kutscher, Ronald E.; Roberson, Larry K.; Waite, Charles A. May 1980. "Improving the Federal Statistical System: Report of the President's Reorganization Project for the Federal Statistical System." *Statistical Reporter.* 80-2:197-212. Also reprinted in *American Statistician,* November 1981, 35(4):183-209.

Boskin, Michael J.; Robinson, Marc S.; Huber, Alan M. 1989. *Government Saving, Capital Formation, and Wealth in the United States, 1947-85.* See reference: Robert E. Lipsey and Helen Stone Tice, eds. 287-353.

Boskin, Michael J. September 1991. "Improving the Quality of Federal Economic Statistics." In Proceedings of the 1991 Annual Research Conference; 1991 March 17-20; Arlington, VA. Washington, D.C.: U.S. Bureau of the Census: 247-251.

Bradburn, Norman M.; Frankel, Martin; Hunt, Edwin; Ingels, Julie; Wojcik, Mark; Schousa-Glusberg, Alicia; Pergamit, Michael. September 1991. "A Comparison of Computer-Assisted Personal Interviews (CAPI) with Personal Interview in the National Longitudinal Survey of Labor Behavior-Youth Cohort." In Proceedings of the 1991 Annual Research Conference; 1991 March 17-20; Arlington, VA. Washington, D.C.: U.S. Bureau of the Census: 389-403.

Bryant, Barbara E.; Miskura, Susan M.; Dinwiddie, James L. August 1992. "Strategic Issues for 2000 Census Design." For Presentation at the Joint Statistical Meetings, Boston, Massachusetts, August 1992. Washington, D.C.: U.S. Bureau of the Census. 21 p.

Butz, William P.; Plewes, Thomas J. August 1989. "A Current Population Survey for the 21st Century." In Proceedings of the Fifth Annual Research Conference; 1989 March 19-22; Arlington, VA. Washington, D.C.: U.S. Bureau of the Census: 3-13.

Campbell, Angus; Converse, Philip E.; Rodgers, Willard L. 1976. *The Quality of American Life: Perceptions, Evaluation and Satisfactions.* New York: Russell Sage Foundation. 583 p.

Cohen, Morris. 1983. *The GNP Data Improvement Project (The Creamer Report): Overview and Business Cycle Perspective.* See reference: Murray F. Foss, ed. 383-397.

Cohen, Steven B.; Burt, Vicki L. 1985. "Data Collection Frequency Effect in the National Medical Care Expenditure Survey." In Proceedings of the American Statistical Association Section on Survey Research Methods 1984 Annual Meeting; 1984 August 13-16; Philadelphia, PA. Washington, D.C.: American Statistical Association: 646-651.

Cormack, R. M. 1988. "Statistical Challenges in the Environmental Sciences: A Personal View." *Journal of the Royal Statistical Society, Series A (Statistics in Society).* 151(Pt. 1):201-210.

Cox, Brenda G.; Cohen, Steven B. 1985. *Methodological Issues for Health Care Surveys.* New York, NY: Marcel Dekker, Inc. 446 p.

Dagum, Estela Bee; Morry, Marietta. 1984. "Seasonal Adjustment of Labour Force Series During Recession and Non-Recession Periods." In Proceedings of the American Statistical Association Business and Economic Statistics Section 1983 Annual Meeting; 1983 August 15-18; Toronto, Canada. Washington, D.C.: American Statistical Association: 644-649.

David, Martin H.; Fitzgerald, John. August 1987. "Measuring Poverty and Crises: Insights into SIPP [Survey of Income and Program Participation] Data Quality." In Proceedings of the Third Annual Research Conference; 1987 March 29-April 1; Baltimore, MD. Washington, D.C.: U.S. Bureau of the Census: 662-670.

Denison, Edward F. 1961. "Measurement of Labor Input: Some Questions of Definition and the Adequacy of Data." In National Bureau of Economic Research Conference on Research in Income and Wealth. *Output, Input, and Productivity Measurement. Studies in Income and Wealth*, Vol. 25. Princeton, NJ: Princeton University Press: 347-372.

Denison, Edward F. 1971. "Welfare Measurement and the GNP." *Survey of Current Business.* 5(1):13-16, 39.

Doyle, Pat; Dalrymple, Robert. August 1987. "The Impact of Imputation Procedures on Distributional Characteristics of the Low Income Population." In Proceedings of the Third Annual Research Conference; 1987 March 29-April 1; Baltimore, MD. Washington, D.C.: U.S. Bureau of the Census: 483-508.

Duncan, Joseph W.; Shelton, William C. 1978. "Revolution in United States Government Statistics, 1926-1976." Washington, D.C.: U.S. Government Printing Office. 257 p. SUDOC: C 1.2:St2/10/926-76.

Duncan, Joseph W. May 1, 1989. "The History and Future of Social Indicators." Paper presented at: Symposium on Social Indicators, Washington, D.C.

Duncan, Otis Dudley. 1975. "Developing Social Indicators." In Proceedings of the National Academy of Sciences; 1974 December; Washington, D.C. Washington, D.C.: National Academy of Sciences: 5096-5102.

Faruqui, Ahmad. 1987. "On the Search for Accuracy in Electric Utility Forecasting: Preface." *Journal of Forecasting.* 6(2):93-95.

Ferrari, Pamela W. 1984. "Preliminary Results from the Evaluation of the CATI [Computer-Assisted Telephone Interviewing] Test for the 1982 National Survey of Natural Scientists and Engineers." Washington, D.C.: U.S. Bureau of the Census.

Fienberg, S. E. 1978. "Victimization and the National Crime Survey: Problems of Design and Analysis." In *Nambodiri, N. D. Survey Sampling and Measurement.* New York, NY: Academic Press: 89-106.

Fienberg, Stephen. June 1986. "Adjusting the Census: Statistical Methodology for Going Beyond the Count." In Proceedings of the Second Annual Research Conference; 1986 March 23-26; Reston, VA. Washington, D.C.: U.S. Bureau of the Census: 570-577.

Foss, Murray F., ed. 1983. "The U.S. National Income and Product Accounts: Selected Topics." National Bureau of Economic Research Conference on Research in Income and Wealth, Conference on National Income and Product Accounts of the United States; 1979 May 3-4; Washington, D.C. *Studies in Income and Wealth*, Vol. 47. Chicago, IL: University of Chicago Press. 438 p.

Frumkin, Norman. 1992. *Tracking America's Economy.* 2nd ed. Armonk, NY: M. E. Sharpe. 340 p.

Garnick, Daniel H.; Gonzales, Maria Elena. 1980. "Statistical Uses of Administrative Records: Where Do We Go From Here?" In Proceedings of the American Statistical Association Section on Survey Research Methods 1979 Annual Meeting; 1979 August 13-16; Washington, D.C. Washington, D.C.: American Statistical Association: 89-94.

Greenspan, Alan. 1985. "Assessing the Usefulness of Current Economic Statistics."

In Proceedings of the First Annual Research Conference; 1985 March 20-23; Reston, VA. Washington, D.C.: U.S. Bureau of the Census: 147-150.

Griliches, Zvi. 1990. "Hedonic Price Indexes and the Measurement of Capital and Productivity: Some Historical Reflections." See reference: Ernst R. Berndt and Jack E. Triplett, eds. 185-202.

Gross, Bertram M., ed. 1969. *Social Intelligence for America's Future: Explorations in Societal Problems.* Boston, MA: Allyn and Bacon. 541 vol.

Gunel, Ipek. 1987. "Forecasting System Energy Demand." *Journal of Forecasting.* 6(2):137-156.

Hawkes, William J., Jr. 1980. "What Marketing Research Needs from the Mid-Decade Census." In Proceedings of the American Statistical Association Business and Economic Statistics Section 1979 Annual Meeting; 1979 August 13-16; Washington, D.C. Washington, D.C.: American Statistical Association: 46-48.

Hellerstein, Judith. 1990. "The Effects of Sample Size on Variances of the Producer Price Index." In Proceedings of the American Statistical Association Section on Survey Research Methods 1989 Annual Meeting; 1989 August 6-10; Washington, D.C. Alexandria, VA: American Statistical Association: 170-175.

Herriot, Roger A.; Bateman, David V.; McCarthy, William F. 1990. "The Decade Census Program - A New Approach for Meeting the Nation's Needs for Sub-National Data." In Proceedings of the American Statistical Association Social Statistics Section 1989 Annual Meeting; 1989 August 6-10; Washington, D.C. Alexandria, VA: American Statistical Association: 351-355.

Hidiroglou, Michael A.; Drew, J. Douglas; Gray, Gerald B. November 1992. "Dealing with Nonresponse to Sample Surveys at Statistics Canada." In Proceedings of the 1992 Annual Research Conference; 1992 March 22-25; Arlington, VA. Washington, D.C.: U.S. Bureau of the Census: 207-224.

Hostetter, Susan C. 1984. "The Verification Method as a Solution to an Industry Coding Problem." In Proceedings of the American Statistical Association Section on Survey Research Methods 1983 Annual Meeting; 1983 August 15-18; Toronto, Canada. Washington, D.C.: American Statistical Association: 499-503.

Jabine, Thomas B.; Scheuren, Frederick (Fritz) J. 1985. "Goals for Statistical Uses of Administrative Records: The Next Ten Years." In Proceedings of the American Statistical Association Section on Survey Research Methods 1984 Annual Meeting; 1984 August 13-16; Philadelphia, PA. Washington, D.C.: American Statistical Association: 66-75.

Johnson, Bruce; Herriot, Roger; Rowland, Sandra. 1990. "Directions for the Future of the U.S. Decennial Census in the 21st Century." In Proceedings of the American Statistical Association Social Statistics Section 1989 Annual Meeting; 1989 August 6-10; Washington, D.C. Alexandria, VA: American Statistical Association: 339-344.

Juster, F. Thomas; Land, Kenneth C., eds. 1981. *Social Accounting Systems: Essays on the State of the Art.* New York, NY: Academic Press. 479 p.

Kirkendall, Nancy; Miller, Renee. June 1986. "Survey Evaluation and Data Quality Activities in the Energy Information Administration." In Proceedings of the Second Annual Research Conference; 1986 March 23-26; Reston, VA. Washington, D.C.: U.S. Bureau of the Census: 54-72.

Kovar, Mary Grace. 1991. "Functional Ability and the Need for Care: Issues for Measurement Research." In Manning Feinleib, ed., Proceedings of 1988

International Symposium on Data on Aging Washington, D.C.: U.S. Government Printing Office: 97-103. SUDOC: HE 20.6209:5/6.

Leontief, Wassily. June 1986. "The Next Step in Expanding the Input-Output Data Base." In Proceedings of the Second Annual Research Conference; 1986 March 23-26; Reston, VA. Washington, D.C.: U.S. Bureau of the Census: 527-530.

Lessler, Judith T.; Holt, Mimi. 1988. "Using Response Protocols to Identify Problems in the U.S. Census Long Form." In Proceedings of the American Statistical Association Section on Survey Research Methods 1987 Annual Meeting; 1987 August 17-20; San Francisco, CA. Alexandria, VA: American Statistical Association: 262-266.

Lipscomb, Emanuel A.; Walter, Bruce C. 1979. "Impacts of Reporting Burden Reduction on the Quality of Export Statistics." In Proceedings of the American Statistical Association Business and Economic Statistics Section 1978 Annual Meeting; 1978 August 14-17; San Diego, CA. Washington, D.C.: American Statistical Association: 500-503.

Lipsey, Robert E.; Tice, Helen Stone, eds. 1989. "The Measurement of Saving, Investment, and Wealth." National Bureau of Economic Research Conference on The Measurement of Saving, Investment, and Wealth; 1987 March 27-28; Baltimore, MD. *Studies in Income and Wealth*, Vol. 52. Chicago, IL: The University of Chicago Press. 861 p.

Mark, Jerome A. 1981. "Measuring Productivity in Government." *Public Productivity Review*. 41:21-44.

Marx, Robert W.; Saalfeld, Alan J. July 1988. "Programs for Assuring Map Quality at the Bureau of the Census." In Proceedings of the Fourth Annual Research Conference; 1988 March 20-23; Arlington, VA. Washington, D.C.: U.S. Bureau of the Census: 239-259.

Mascon, Charles C.; Duncan, Robin J.; Butler, Clifford B. 1988. "Consumer Price Index Revision: Improvements to Expenditure Weights." In Proceedings of the American Statistical Association Business and Economic Statistics Section 1987 Annual Meeting; 1987 August 17-20; San Francisco, CA. Alexandria, VA: American Statistical Association: 541-546.

McLeod, A. Ian; Hipel, Keith W.; Bodo, Byron A. 1991. "Trend Analysis Methodology for Water Quality Time Series." *Environmetrics*. 2(2, June):169-200.

Meyers, Dowell. 1988. "Building Knowledge about Quality of Life for Urban Planning." *Journal of the American Planning Association*. 54(3):347-358.

Miskura, Susan M. June 1992. "Forward from 1990: Designing the 2000 Census." Washington, D.C.: U.S. Bureau of the Census. 29 p.

Moriyama, I. M. 1989. "Problems in Measurement of Accuracy of Cause-of-Death Statistics." *American Journal of Public Health*. 79:1349-1350.

Morton, Herbert C. 1981. "The Environmental Data Dilemma." *Resources for the Future*. 66(Spring):22-23.

Moynihan, Daniel P. 1967. "Urban Conditions: General." *The Annals of the American Academy of Political and Social Science*. 371(May):159-177. Special issue, *Social Goals and Indicators for American Society*, Vol. 1.

National Association of Business Economists. September 1989. "Report of the Statistics Committee." Washington, D.C.: National Association of Business Economists. 40 p.

National Bureau of Economic Research. National Accounts Review Committee; U.S. Congress. Joint Economic Committee; U.S. Bureau of the Budget. Office of Statistical Standards. 1958. "National Economic Accounts of the United States: Review, Appraisal and Recommendations." The National Economic Accounts of the United States, General Series. Washington, D.C.: U.S. Government Printing Office. 202 p.

National Occupational Information Coordinating Committee (NOICC). 1979. "Feasibility Study for a Project on Improvement of Occupational Information. Final Report." Washington, D.C.: National Academy of Sciences.

National Research Council. Committee on National Statistics; Institute of Medicine. Division of Health Care Services. 1992. Gooloo S. Wunderlich, ed., *Toward a National Health Care Survey: A Data System for the 21st Century*. Washington, D.C.: National Academy Press. 190 p.

National Research Council. Committee on National Statistics. 1988. Dorothy M. Gilford, ed., *The Aging Population in the Twenty-First Century: Statistics for Health Policy*. Washington, D.C.: National Academy Press. 323 p.

National Research Council. Committee on National Statistics. 1985. Constance F. Citro and Michael L. Cohen, eds., *The Bicentennial Census: New Directions for Methodology in 1990*. Washington, D.C.: National Academy Press. 404 p.

National Research Council. Committee on National Statistics. 1985. Daniel B. Levine, Kenneth Hill and Robert Warren, eds., *Immigration Statistics: A Story of Neglect*. Washington, D.C.: National Academy Press. 328 p.

National Research Council. Committee on National Statistics. 1988. *Income and Poverty Statistics: Problems of Concept and Measurement*. Washington, D.C.: National Academy Press. 23 p.

National Research Council. Committee on National Statistics. 1979. *Measurement and Interpretation of Productivity [Rees Report]*. Washington, D.C.: National Academy of Sciences. 449 p.

National Research Council. Committee on National Statistics. 1985. *Natural Gas Data Needs in a Changing Regulatory Environment*. Washington, D.C.: National Academy Press. 161 p.

National Research Council. Committee on National Statistics. 1982. *A Review of the Statistical Program of the Bureau of Mines*. Washington, D.C.: National Academy Press. 210 p.

National Research Council. Committee on National Statistics. Panel on Foreign Trade Statistics. 1992. "An Alternative Seasonal Adjustment Procedure for Merchandise Trade Data [Appendix E]." In *Behind the Numbers: U.S. Trade in the World Economy*. Washington, D.C.: National Academy of Sciences: 237-244.

National Research Council. Committee on National Statistics. Panel on Foreign Trade Statistics. 1992. Anne Y. Kester, ed., *Behind the Numbers: U.S. Trade in the World Economy*. Washington, D.C.: National Academy Press. 297 p.

National Research Council. Committee on Occupational Classification and Analysis. 1980. Ann R. Miller, ed., *Work, Jobs, and Occupations: A Critical Review of the Dictionary of Occupational Titles*. Washington, D.C.: National Academy Press.

Natrella, Vito; Popkin, Joel. 1987. "International Comparability of Industry Classification Systems." In Proceedings of the American Statistical Association Business and Economic Statistics Section 1986 Annual Meeting; 1986 August 18-21; Chicago, IL. Washington, D.C.: American Statistical Association: 13-16.

Norwood, Janet L. 1990. "Distinguished Lecture on Economics in Government: Data Quality and Public Policy." *Journal of Economic Perspectives.* 4(2):3-12.

Norwood, Janet L. 1985. "What the Labor Market Data Tell Us Today About the Data Needs for the Future." In Proceedings of the First Annual Research Conference; 1985 March 20-23; Reston, VA. Washington, D.C.: U.S. Bureau of the Census: 153-156.

Organisation for Economic Co-operation and Development. 1991. "Environmental Indicators: A Preliminary Set." Paris: OECD. 77 p.

Orshansky, Mollie. 1965. "Counting the Poor: Another Look at the Poverty Profile." *Social Security Bulletin.* 28(1):3:29.

Parke, Robert; Seidman, David. 1978. "Social Indicators and Social Reporting." *The Annals of the American Academy of Political and Social Science.* 435(January):1-22. Special issue *America in the Seventies: Some Social Indicators.*

Parker, Robert. 1985. "The Underground Economy and the National Income and Product Accounts." In Proceedings of the First Annual Research Conference; 1985 March 20-23; Reston, VA. Washington, D.C.: U.S. Bureau of the Census: 399-412.

Parker, Robert P. 1983. "The GNP Data Improvement Project (The Creamer Report): A Bureau of Economic Analysis Perspective." See reference: Murray F. Foss, ed. 424-427.

Plewes, Thomas J. 1989. "Focusing on Quality in Establishment Surveys." In Proceedings of the American Statistical Association Section on Survey Research Methods 1988 Annual Meeting; 1988 August 22-25; New Orleans, LA. Alexandria, VA: American Statistical Association: 71-74.

Rice, Dorothy P. 1977. "The National Center for Health Statistics and the Data Needed for National Health Insurance." *Bulletin of the New York Academy of Medicine.* 53(10):893-900.

Richardson, Elliot L. August 1990. "Social Choices and the Democratic Process: The Need to Stretch the Limits of Statistial Capacity." In Proceedings of the 1990 Annual Research Conference; 1990 March 18-21; Arlington, VA. Washington, D.C.: U.S. Bureau of the Census: 275-378.

Rosenberg, Harry M.; Burnham, Drusilla. 1980. "Occupation and Industry Information from the Death Certificate: Assessment of the Completeness of Reporting." In Proceedings of the American Statistical Association Section on Survey Research Methods 1979 Annual Meeting; 1979 August 13-16; Washington, D.C. Washington, D.C.: American Statistical Association: 286-292.

Ruggles, Richard. 1980. "The United States National Income Accounts, 1947-1977: Their Conceptual Basis and Evolution." See reference: Murray F. Foss, ed. 15-96.

Russell, Clifford S.; Smith, V. Kerry. 1990. "Demands for Data and Analysis Induced by Environmental Policy." See reference: Ernst R. Berndt and Jack E. Triplett, eds. 299-336.

Rymes, Thomas K. 1989. "The Theory and Measurement of the Nominal Output of Banks, Sectoral Rates of Savings, and Wealth in the National Accounts." See reference: Robert E. Lipsey and Helen Stone Tice, eds. 357-390.

Sanders, Larry D.; Walsh, Richard G.; McKean, John R. 1991. "Comparable Estimates of the Recreational Value of Rivers." *Water Resources Research.* 27(7):1387-1394.

Scarr, Harry A.; Groves, Robert M.; Darby, Michael R. March 1991. "Terms of Reference: Task Force for Designing the Year 2000 Census and Census-Related Activities for 2000-2009." Washington, D.C.: U.S. Bureau of the Census. 7 p.

Scheuren, Frederick (Fritz) J.; Oh, H. Lock. 1978. "Some Unresolved Issues in Raking Ratio Estimation." In *Imputation and Editing of Faulty or Missing Survey Data.* Washington, D.C.: U.S. Social Security Administration: 128-135.

Scheuren, Frederick (Fritz) J.; Schwartz, Otto; Kilss, Beth. 1984. "Statistics from Individual Income Tax Returns: Quality Issues and Budget Cut Impact." *Review of Public Data Use.* 12:55-67.

Schirm, Allen L.; Preston, Samuel H. 1987. "Census Undercount Adjustment and the Quality of Geographic Population Distributions." *Journal of the American Statistical Association.* 82(400):965-978.

Schwartz, Anna J. 1989. Comment [on "The Theory and Measurement of the Nominal Output of Banks, Sectoral Rates of Savings, and Wealth in the National Accounts" by Rymes, Thomas K.]. See reference: Robert E. Lipsey and Helen Stone Tice, eds. 390-393.

Shapiro, Gary M.; Bettin, Paul J. October 1992. "Coverage in Household Surveys. Presented to the Census Advisory Committee of the American Statistical Association and the Census Advisory Committee on Population Statistics at the Joint Advisory Committee Meeting," October 22-23, Suitland, MD. Washington, D.C.: U.S. Bureau of the Census. 23 p.

Sheldon, Eleanor Bernert; Moore, Wilbert E., eds. 1968. "Indicators of Social Change: Concepts and Measurements." New York, NY: Russell Sage Foundation. 822 p.

Shipp, Kenneth. 1991. "Cooperation of Federal/State Agencies in the Current Employment Survey: A Case History of Automation." In Proceedings of the American Statistical Association Business and Economic Statistics Section 1990 Annual Meeting; 1990 August 6-9; Anaheim, CA. Alexandria, VA: American Statistical Association: 152-156.

Silberstein, Adriana R. 1988. "Respondent Characteristics and Recall Bias in the Consumer Expenditure Interview Survey." In Proceedings of the American Statistical Association Section on Survey Research Methods 1987 Annual Meeting; 1987 August 17-20; San Francisco, CA. Alexandria, VA: American Statistical Association: 227-232.

Sims, C. A. 1986. "Are Forecasting Models Usable for Policy Analysis?" *Federal Reserve Bank of Minneapolis Quarterly Review.* 10:2-16.

Smeeding, Timothy. April 1982. "Alternative Methods for Valuing Selected In-Kind Transfers and Measuring Their Effect on Poverty." *U.S. Bureau of the Census Technical Paper No. 50.* Washington, D.C.: U.S. Government Printing Office. 162 p. SUDOC: C 3.212:50.

Smith, R.E.; Vanski, J.E. 1979. "Gross Changes Data: The Neglected Data Base." *U.S. National Commission on Employment and Unemployment. Counting the Labor Force, Appendix II: Data Collection, Processing and Presentation: National and Local.* Washington, D.C.: U.S. Government Printing Office: 132-150.

Spencer, Bruce. 1981. "Issues of Accuracy and Equity in Adjusting for Census Undercount." In Proceedings of the American Statistical Association Social Statistics Section 1980 Annual Meeting; August 11-14, 1980; Houston, TX. Washington, D.C.: American Statistical Association: 127-129.

Spencer, Bruce D. 1982. "Feasibility of Benefit-Cost Analysis of Public Data." In

Proceedings of the American Statistical Association Social Statistics Section 1981 Annual Meeting; August 10-13, 1981; Detroit, MI. Washington, D.C.: American Statistical Association: 318-320.

Stone, Richard. 1971. *Demographic Accounting and Model Building.* Paris, France: Organization for Economic Cooperation and Development. 125 p.

Stone, Richard. 1981. "The Relationship of Demographic Accounts to National Income and Product Accounts." In Juster, F. Thomas; Land, Kenneth C. *Social Accounting Systems: Essays on the State of the Art.* New York, NY: Academic Press: 307-376.

Stone, Richard. 1975. "Transition and Admission Models in Social Indicators Analysis." Land, Kenneth D.; Spilerman, Seymour. *Social Indicator Models.* New York, NY: Russell Sage Foundation: 253-300.

Tanur, Judith M. August 1990. "Reporting Job Search Activity Among Youths: Preliminary Evidence from Reinterviews." In Proceedings of the 1990 Annual Research Conference; 1990 March 18-21; Arlington, VA. Washington, D.C.: U.S. Bureau of the Census: 746-776.

Taylor, Stephen. 1989. "World Payments Imbalances and U.S. Statistics." See reference: Robert E. Lipsey and Helen Stone Tice, eds. 401-428.

Terleckyi, Nestor E. 1973. "National Goals Accounting: A Framework for Evaluating Opportunities for the Achievement of National Goals." Washington, D.C.: National Planning Association.

Trelogan, Harry C. 1976. "Toward More Accurate Farming Data." *Agricultural Economics Research.* 28(2):79-81.

Triplett, Jack E. 1991. "The Federal Statistical System's Response to Emerging Data Needs." *Journal of Economic and Social Measurement.* 17:155-177.

Triplett, Jack E. 1975. "The Measurement of Inflation: A Survey of Research on the Accuracy of Price Indexes." Earl, Paul H., ed. *Analysis of Inflation.* Lexington, MA: Lexington Books: 19-82.

Triplett, Jack E., ed. 1983. "The Measurement of Labor Cost." National Bureau of Economic Research Conference on The Measurement of Labor Cost; 1981 December 3-4; Williamsburg, VA. Studies in Income and Wealth, Vol. 48. Chicago, IL: University of Chicago Press. 540 p.

Triplett, Jack E. August 1990. "The Theory of Industrial and Occupational Classifications and Related Phenomena." In Proceedings of the 1990 Annual Research Conference; 1990 March 18-21; Arlington, VA. Washington, D.C.: U.S. Bureau of the Census: 9-25.

U.S. Bureau of Economic Analysis. 1991. "Improving the Quality of Economic Statistics: The 1992 Economic Statistics Initiative." *Survey of Current Business.* 71(3):4-5.

U.S. Bureau of the Census. August 1990. In Proceedings of the 1990 Annual Research Conference. Papers Presented at the Sixth Annual Research Conference; 1990 March 18-21; Arlington, VA. Washington, D.C.: U.S. Bureau of the Census: 893 p.

U.S. Bureau of the Census. September 1992. Updates. "Census 2000 Research and Development." Washington, D.C.: U.S. Bureau of the Census. 6 p.

U.S. Department of Health and Human Services. Public Health Service. 1991. "Healthy People 2000: National Health Promotion and Disease Prevention Objectives." Full Report. Washington, D.C.: U.S. Government Printing Office. 692 p. SUDOC: HE 20.2:D 63/8/report. DHHS Pub. No. (PHS)91-50212.

U.S. Economic Policy Council. Working Group on the Quality of Economic Statistics. April 1987. "Report of the Working Group on the Quality of Economic Statistics to the Economic Policy Council." Final Report. Washington, D.C.: U.S. Economic Policy Council.

Vatter, Robert H. 1986. "The Numbers Game: A Business Economist's Point of View." In Proceedings of the Annual Meeting of the American Statistical Association Social Statistics Section; 1985 August 5-8; Las Vegas, NV. Washington, D.C.: American Statistical Association: 88-91.

Verma, Ravi B.P.; Basavarappa, K.G.; Bender, Rosemary K. 1985. "Estimation of Local Area Population: An International Comparison." In Proceedings of the American Statistical Association Social Statistics Section 1984 Annual Meeting; 1984 August 13-16; Philadelphia, PA. Washington, D.C.: American Statistical Association: 324-329.

Waite, Charles A. 1987. "Census Bureau Economic Statistics—Data Quality, Budget Austerity, and Other Dimensions of Change." In Proceedings of the American Statistical Association Business and Economic Statistics Section 1986 Annual Meeting; 1986 August 18-21; Chicago, IL. Washington, D.C.: American Statistical Association: 3-6.

Waksberg, Joseph. 1985. "Integration of the Sample Design for the National Survey of Family Growth with the National Health Interview Survey." In Proceedings of the American Statistical Association Section on Survey Research Methods 1984 Annual Meeting; 1984 August 13-16; Philadelphia, PA. Washington, D.C.: American Statistical Association: 22-32.

Westman, W. E. 1978. "Measuring the Inertia and Resilience of Ecosystems." BioScience. 28:705-710.

Wilk, Martin B. August 1987. "The Concept of Error in Statistical and Scientific Work." In Proceedings of the Third Annual Research Conference; 1987 March 29-April 1; Baltimore, MD. Washington, D.C.: U.S. Bureau of the Census: 223-228.

World Commission on Environment and Development. 1987. Our Common Future. Oxford: Oxford University Press. 1 vol.

Yeh, Stephen H. K. 1976. "The Use of Social Indicators in Development Planning." In The Use of Socio-Economic Indicators in Development Planning. Paris, France: UNESCO: 61-86.

Ziegler, Martin. [1978]. "Linking CPS [Current Population Survey] Unemployment Estimates with Administrative Records on Unemployment." In Interrelationships Among Estimates, Surveys and Forecasts Produced by Federal Agencies. Paper presented at the Conference on Small Area Statistics, Chicago, Illinois Series GE-41(4). Washington, D.C.: American Statistical Association: 34-42.